22.50

The Villas of Le Corbusier
1920–1930

Tim Benton

THE VILLAS OF LE CORBUSIER
1920–1930

with photographs in the Lucien Hervé collection

Yale University Press
New Haven and London
1987

My first debt of gratitude is to the Fondation Le Corbusier and to the many people who have responded generously with their time and expertise over more than a decade of research. I am well aware that errors in transcription and attribution will inevitably have crept into this work, but hope that the book will in some degree compensate for these, in providing researchers with some guide to the very rich documentation in the Foundation.

I would like to thank Brigitte Hermann for her very valuable help in researching some of the projects with which I was less familiar, notably the ateliers Ozenfant and Lipchitz-Miestchaninoff and the apartment de Beistegui. Her criticisms, and those of Philippe Sers, have been essential for the resolution of the text.

Sue Staig helped type the manuscript, despite an unduly heavy workload at the Open University. Travel and research expenses were contributed by the Arts Faculty of the Open University, and I am grateful for these and to the allowance of study leave which made the preparation of the book possible.

I would like to thank my wife and son who have patiently endured the disruption to family life and holidays this book brought about. I hope it was worth it.

Tim Benton

The publisher would like to thank the students of the school of architecture, U.P.A.6, Paris, under the direction of their professor Fernando Montès, whose drawings are reproduced on pages 54, 55, 90, 178, 179, 198, 199 and 214: Aleluïa, L. D'Alencon, E. Badoche, M. Bensaïd, P. Biro, T. Carbonet, P. Chatelain, P. Chavanes, F. Chochon, M. Chodya Razavi, F. Cortes, D. Courant, Ph. Delmas, Drouet, M. Ferrier, F. Fricker, J.F. Gallienne, M. Gambier, T. Hartmann, E.M. and H. Jamin, M. Jaouënne, O. Karras, J.B. Lacoudre, J.P. Mallet, Ch. H. Ouriel, Ch. Pailherey, D. Papalexopoulos, V. Pignot, F. Pirasteh, J. Poupard, D. Quantinet, P. Quintard-Hofstein, D. Renault, Steinebach.

The Figures on page 194 were produced by the Open University, Milton Keynes.

Abbreviations

FLC number: Drawing reference numbers in the Fondation Le Corbusier.

LC number: Numbers stencilled onto some drawings by the Le Corbusier atelier, and listed in a black log book in the Fondation Le Corbusier, giving dates and, after 1928, authorship.

References to the documents in the Fondation Le Corbusier archive have mostly been removed, because these are in the process of revision.

References to FLC drawings have been limited to those illustrated in this book. For a comprehensive listing, see the catalogue on pp. 221–4.

Frontispiece: Villa Savoye 1928–31, roof garden.

CONTENTS

INTRODUCTION

It is often said of architects of the Modern Movement as a criticism that they preached social building but practised private domestic architecture for the rich. After all the contingencies have been accounted for – the political context, the need to earn a living, the need to seduce the cultivated bourgeoisie with *form* as a means of convincing it of the power of the *content* – the problem still remains. Many of the fundamental dogmas of modern architecture grew out of various flavours of social utopianism and reform, and the historian must ask himself how many of these doctrines were fundamentally compromised by architects who depended on a fashionable and wealthy clientele for their commissions.

In the case of Le Corbusier and Pierre Jeanneret, these debates are not trivial. Although there were some 'social' projects during the 1920s, including a number of housing projects of which Pessac was by far the most important, the prime source of actual income was from fees for domestic architecture, much of it in the Paris area (see pp. 218–19). By the end of the decade, the 'era of the *grands travaux*' was beginning, with the commissions for Centrosoyus, the Salvation Army Hostel, the Swiss Pavilion, the Maison Clarté in Geneva and the flats at rue Nungesser et Coli, Paris. It was this work, as well as Le Corbusier's world-wide reputation, which allowed him the freedom to withdraw from the regular practice of domestic architecture and concentrate on the protracted and frustrating studies of urbanism for cities all over the world, from Algiers to Rio de Janeiro, from Stockholm to Paris. A second important source of income, of course, during the 1920s, was publication – not only the six major books, several editions of *L'Architecture Vivante*, the first volume of *L'Oeuvre Complète*, but also innumerable articles and pamphlets. Even the involvement with *L'Esprit Nouveau*, of which Le Corbusier was the major shareholder, produced some income, despite its rocky finances.

The question of the relationship between domestic architecture and publication is itself instructive. The books can be divided between those which are primarily theoretical (*Vers Une Architecture, Urbanisme, Précisions*) and those whose central role was to publicise and explain his own work (*Une Maison Un Palais, Zwei Wohnhäuser*, the *L'Architecture Vivante* issues and *L'Oeuvre Complète*). What counts, in the latter type of publication, to make an impression on architectural circles, is the ability to demonstrate built work, well illustrated with photographs and drawings. Here, the domestic work was essential, at a time when it was extremely difficult to obtain commissions for other kinds of work. The case of Gropius' *Internationale Architektur*, 1925 (based on photographs collected for the Bauhaus exhibition of 1923) is instructive: Le Corbusier's Ozenfant atelier and Besnus house at Vaucresson were among the relatively few modern buildings, as opposed to projects, to be illustrated, and helped to reserve a place for him in the canon of international modernists. Houses were also a way of making contacts and influencing people in positions of power. The designs for Mongermon, one of the directors of Voisin car and aeroplane industries, helped him to secure financial and moral support for the Esprit Nouveau Pavilion and the Plan Voisin de Paris in 1925. Three years later, the project for a house for Mme Ocampo helped to prepare the way for his Argentinian lecture tour of 1929.

The question of the symbolic relationship between the standard housing prototypes (Dom-Ino, Citrohan I and II, Immeuble-Villas (Esprit Nouveau Pavilion), the maisons Loucheur) and the private houses undermines, furthermore, any easy distinction between the two. Most of the houses of the 1920s can be classified by type according to their derivation from one or other of these 'standard cells', and that applies as much to luxury projects for Mme Meyer, Stein-de Monzie and Savoye as to the small houses. Almost all the features of the private houses can be tied into Le Corbusier's general theory of urbanism, new materials, the spirit of the age, standardisation and the Fordian revolution, and so forth. If you ask, for example, why the exposed *pilotis* should play such an important role in these houses, precise functional or practical answers will be unenlightening. The *piloti* was rooted in a general theory of the need to raise the built fabric of cities off the ground, to allow free circulation for automobiles underneath, as in the Project for the City for Three Million Inhabitants (1922). But it can also be referred to dogmas about the necessity to use the 'correct' material for the twentieth century – reinforced concrete – using arguments of structural rationalism depending on Choisy or Viollet-le-Duc.

A poignant example of interchangeability of values

1. Villa La Roche-Jeanneret, Auteuil, Paris. Corner of gallery showing terrace and accacia.

between mass housing and private houses is provided by the exhibition buildings. The Esprit Nouveau Pavilion was intended to represent a standard cell in a block of flats – the Immeuble-Villa – itself a standard unit extendable into the urban scale in the Plan Voisin de Paris. But Le Corbusier also used the publicity derived from the exhibition to advertise a house based closely on the Pavilion as a model for speculative builders and private clients. And it was the Esprit Nouveau Pavilion, with its partially enclosed hanging garden which formed the prototype for the later projects for Mme Meyer, for the Stein-de Monzie house and the Villa Savoye.

To select one 'genre' in Le Corbusier's work, therefore, is not to split off artificially an arbitrary and merely contingent form of architectural practice, but to focus on a central strand in his cultural politics of the 1920s. As we shall see, however, the 'problem' of the luxury house, especially in the latter half of the decade, was a real one, and Sigfried Giedion was one of the first to draw attention to it. One area in which the bourgeois house posed acute problems for an architect of Le Corbusier's idealist mentality was its success or failure in satisfying clients at the minimum level of acceptance. It will be seen, from the case studies which follow, that a typical commission involved delays in prepared plans, a frequently high-handed approach to the client's stated requirements, building costs typically above estimate by a factor of two or three, chaotic accounting procedures and a catalogue of disastrous technical failings requiring urgent and expensive repairs and anguished correspondence running late into the 1930s. Close personal friendships were strained to the limit and sometimes broken off irrevocably. Few of the houses were lived in for long by the original clients or escaped alteration or demolition. Of course, there were many factors behind all this, not least penurious clients or eccentrics. Le Corbusier's sister-in-law, for example, Lotti Raaf, had an obsession about the high levels of arsenic in French paint, and insisted on having samples tested in Sweden with the result that the whole house had to be repainted on her return. And most of the clients must have known something of what they were letting themselves in for, since many of them knew each other and presumably had the opportunity to listen to horror stories before committing themselves. The American clients, for example, William Cook, Michael Stein, Henry Church, all knew each other.

It was indeed an essential part of Le Corbusier's strategy to ensure that a regular flow of potentially interested people visited his houses. Several clients referred to features of other Corbusian houses which they wanted incorporated into their own. Le Corbusier clearly expected satisfied customers to take pride in the notoriety of their houses. Thus, on the inauguration of the Villa Savoye, after innumerable difficulties and disputes with the long-suffering Mme Savoye, he wrote:

> You should place on the table of the downstairs hall a book (pompously designated 'Golden Book'), and in it each of your visitors should inscribe their name and place of origin. You'll see what fine signatures you'll collect.[1]

But Henry Church was probably not alone in resenting the intrusion:

> Be so kind as to refrain from sending people to visit my property. You don't visit houses any more, and my staff have strict instructions on this matter.[2]

Few clients seem to have had the loyal enthusiasm of Raoul La Roche and the realism to accept that what they were living in was best appreciated as architecture rather than in the conventional terms of a 'house'. He wrote a New Year's letter to Le Corbusier commenting on an album of photographs taken by the well known photographer Boissonas:

> I have to confess to you that, despite the art of Mr Boissonas, the Villa La Rocca is more beautiful in reality than in 'painting'. Why is this? Certainly because the best of reproductions can produce only imperfectly the emotion felt in direct contact with their symphony of prisms. Oh, those prisms! You and Pierre must have the secret of them, since I have searched in vain for them elsewhere. You have demonstrated their beauty and taught their meaning and, thanks to you, we now know what Architecture is. We have understood both its theory and practice. Let your buildings arise during the years ahead – many of them large and small, whose authorship will be immediately apparent, not because your names will be inscribed on them (like those of the *Société des Architectes Diplômés du Gouvernement*) but because the spectator, moved, will cry out spontaneously 'That is architecture'.[3]

This was what Le Corbusier wanted to hear. And yet, Le Corbusier did have a model of an acceptable life-style in the modern spirit which he advocated for his clients and which was based around a notion of

1. Dossier Savoye, Doc. 599, 28 June 1931.
2. Dossier Church, Doc. 174, 22 April 1929.
3. Dossier La Roche, Doc. A5, January 1927.

2. Letter from Le
Corbusier to
M. Savoye, 31 October
1937, placating the
client after the last
round of repairs.

privacy, of freedom, comfort and happiness. He used
later the expression *La coquille de l'escargot*, which
could be set against the more famous slogan of the
machine à habiter as a description of the modern house.
His model house was essentially anthropo-centric,
scaled to human dimensions and constructed around
essentially human incidents. His interiors are full of
'places', points of command, where a man or woman is
meant to stand, or sit, or lie. These places are marked
by balconies, indentations or projections in the concrete shelves or partition walls. Many of the interior
perspectives show the canonic views to be had by the
inhabitant, they reveal how the 'prisms' have been
deployed for consumption, not just for architectural
satisfaction.

But the model demanded sacrifices. His preferences
came out clearly from the finishing and furnishing of
the La Roche house, where his client gave him a free
hand. We shall discuss these in some detail in the case
study because they set the pattern for later interiors.
Bedrooms were generally small and austere, although
the later 'luxury' houses often included more sumptu-
ous bedrooms with generous, rounded forms. Lava-
tories were normally tiny and bathrooms stark, relieved
by splendid French porcelain ware. The later houses
were often given some colour in the bathrooms by the
addition of sunken 'piscine' baths, faced in expensive
ceramic tiles, usually in light blue. Although as much
space as possible was given over to the living rooms,
often with a double-height component at one end, the
real living spaces were often seen as being external, on
roof terraces, verandas, balconies and gardens. Above
all, the essential joys were natural, sun, air, a view of
beautiful scenery if possible, plants and trees conserved
or planted afresh, the sky at night. These attributes of
the elevated life of modern man were listed in the
famous letter to Mme Meyer in October 1925 (p. 143).
And in the description of the Villa Savoye, Le
Corbusier talked about the Virgilian dream; modern
man framed in the products of a mechanised society,
secure in his intellectual superiority, but in face of
beautiful and untouched natural scenery. Like Adolphe

9

Loos, Le Corbusier thought that progress could not be wound back; twentieth century man was too urbane, too civilised, necessarily too intellectual to fantasise in vernacular, Arts and crafts terms. In a world in which the air had been conquered, in which structure had been revolutionised, man belonged in an elevated position, as high above the ground as was necessary to escape the fatal contamination not only of damp and uncontrolled vegetation, but also of the consequences of dense modern urbanism. Le Corbusier's houses frequently rise to a series of 'high points', points of command, not only of external scenery, but of the interior of the house itself. Wherever possible, he constructed *promenades architecturales* (a term first coined to describe the Villa La Roche), which lead you through the spaces of the house in an exemplary way, and which rise, typically, through the levels of human activity to culminate in a library, or in the contemplation of nature. The 'high points' were often deliberately associated with risk, with personal commitment, in the scaling of steep ladders or narrow spiral stairs, in mounting flat roofs to which there are no parapets.

Surfaces were typically austere: small tightly laid tiles (black for the 'public' spaces, white for 'clean' ones), jointless linoleum for bedrooms and reception areas, rubber carpet for ramps. Tribal rugs, typically black and white, and white curtains were allowed. Thonet bentwood chairs and Maples leather armchairs were favoured in the first half of the decade, tubular steel prototypes (also manufactured by Thonet) after the arrival of Charlotte Perriand in 1927. Concrete fireplaces were designed like Purist stoves, free standing and impressive from any angles. Walls were painted in distemper or oil paint, in the range of Purist tones: light greens and blues, burnt umber or black for recessive surfaces, light and dark grey for tonal modelling. Henry Church is on record complaining about the Corbusian colour scheme, but most clients seem to have accepted it.

The clients can be divided into artists (Ozenfant, Lipchitz, Miestchaninoff, Ternisien (a musician), Planeix), amateurs and collectors (La Roche, Stein, Cook) and the rich (Stein again, Church, Savoye). This classification is helpful up to a point – clearly the ateliers can be distinguished from the 'houses' – but a more important distinction emerges from the periodisation of the houses (see p. 220). The Besnus house and the atelier Ozenfant are both concerned, in different ways, with questions of order and symmetry and the ground-work of defining the elements of the Corbusian house: windows, cupboards, doors. From the La Roche house onwards, the theme of the drama-

tic development of picturesque sensations, external and internal, provided one pole in a dialectic with the rigorous analysis of standard forms derived from the housing cells. For this reason, the Casa Fuerte and Mongermon schemes (January–April 1925) and the four Meyer projects (October 1925 to May 1926) are crucial in developing the *promenade architecturale* theme within the rigid constraints of severely limited urban sites. Many of the subsequent projects can be seen to oscillate, often violently, between considerations of order and restraint (and a 'given' form) on the one hand, and a series of explosive eruptions into the picturesque, organic and dynamic. A profoundly romantic impulsion to create impossibly ambitious sensations within a limited site, brief and budget is constantly being re-analysed in order to reassert order. This tension between freedom and restraints manifested itself in a number of specific and practical ways. For example, Le Corbusier's partnership with his cousin Pierre Jeanneret and, as the decade progressed, other personalities within the atelier, often played out these roles of alternating 'fitting together' and 'opening out', with Le Corbusier usually, but not always, playing the latter part. Pierre typically had the task of trying to make the plans work out, in terms of access, the provision of contiguous functions, the relation of plan to elevation, and so forth. Le Corbusier's interventions frequently took the form of adding curving walls, trying to visualise depth in the spaces with heavy shading, adding forms with symbolic or associative resonances (balconies, canopies, alcoves, 'points of command').

In the second place, the dialogue between freedom and constraint was often played out in brutally material terms between architects and client. In many cases, and increasingly as the decade progressed, the first projects were over-ambitious and proved, on securing tenders and calculating estimates, much too expensive for the client's purse. Thus, the need literally to 'compress' projected designs produced many of the notable features of the buildings as constructed. Part, at least, of the interest in complex geometrical grids delimiting the placing of *pilotis* can be illuminated, if not explained, by the labour of trying to compress complex functions within the rigid envelope of a given plan form. This will certainly be part of my argument in the case of the Villa Stein-de Monzie. Another symptom of this labour of compression is what Alan Colquohon has called the 'transference of meaning'. Forms which at one point are introduced in a design for specific purposes and with defined meanings, are transposed later to other parts and different functions of the house as designs progress. This is one of the strongest arguments for the work of research and discovery represented by this book. Uncovering the layers of creation, whose traces remain fossilised in the tangible forms of a building has more than archaeological interest. Le Corbusier himself believed passionately that the *recherche patiente* was itself part of the work of architecture, that the process was embedded in the work, and that the two cannot be separated without fracture. When you enter the great hall of the Villa La Roche and first look around the empty space crossed by a bridge, the first question is why? One answer is that the bridge connects what at quite a late stage of the design was indeed two houses.

Or when you look up at the north-west façade of the Villa Savoye and you see an empty 'window' in the solarium wall, it can be explained in at least two complementary ways. The window was originally the window of the master bedroom, the 'room with a view' and, in one real sense, the heart of the house. When the bedroom was removed from the top floor to make the necessary economies, the window was reused to serve a quite different function, as the point of rest at the end of the *promenade architecturale*, a goal giving a view of sky and nature as you climb the ramp. But both meanings are superimposed and are 'there'.

There is no doubt that these struggles, changes, adaptations, sacrifices, can be partially referred, in Le Corbusier's mind, to an idealistic dialectic between the ideal and the pragmatic. His ideal forms, essentially unrealisable, include the invisibility of structure, the hovering volumes, the untarnished purity of the 'prisms', the opening out of space. But he was also committed to pragmatic discoveries. He was almost obsessively fascinated by detailing. Some of his most

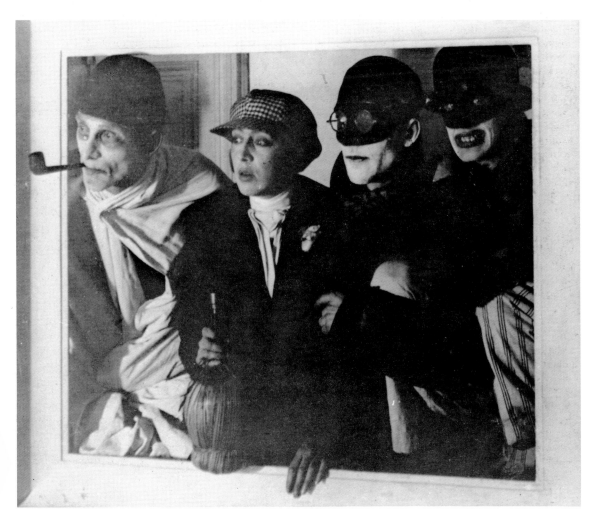

3. Ozenfant, Le Corbusier, Pierre Jeanneret and a woman in fancy dress, c. 1926.

11

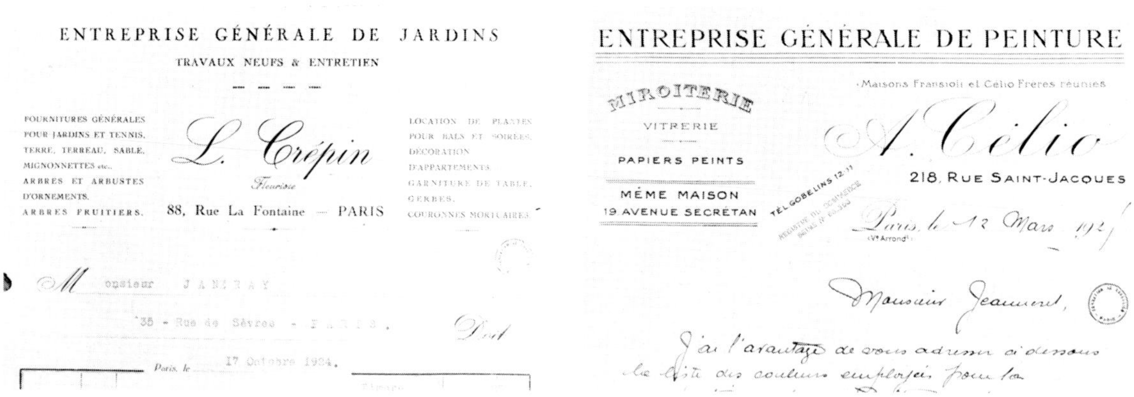

ENTREPRISE GÉNÉRALE DE JARDINS
TRAVAUX NEUFS & ENTRETIEN

FOURNITURES GÉNÉRALES
POUR JARDINS ET TENNIS,
TERRE, TERREAU, SABLE,
MIGNONNETTES etc.
ARBRES ET ARBUSTES
D'ORNEMENTS.
ARBRES FRUITIERS.

L. Crépin
Fleuriste
88, Rue La Fontaine — PARIS

LOCATION DE PLANTES
POUR BALS ET SOIRÉES.
DÉCORATION
D'APPARTEMENTS
GARNITURE DE TABLE,
GERBES,
COURONNES MORTUAIRES

ENTREPRISE GÉNÉRALE DE PEINTURE

MIROITERIE
VITRERIE
PAPIERS PEINTS
MÊME MAISON
19 AVENUE SECRETAN

Maison Franssoli et Celio Frères réunies

J. Celio
218, RUE SAINT-JACQUES

Paris, le 12 Mars 192...

Monsieur Jeanneret,

J'ai l'avantage de vous adresser ci-dessous
le liste des couleurs employées pour la

4. Headed paper of some of the entrepreneurs involved in the La Roche-Jeanneret villas.

impressive drawings are for window mechanisms, gate latches, skylights, lamps and fitments. During the 1920s he made several attempts to patent and have manufactured a standard *fenêtre en longueur*. Patents were taken out in France and Switzerland and approaches made to Ronéo and other industrial firms. But his experience with standardisation was a bitter one, both at Pessac and in the private houses. The Ronéo metal doors supplied for the La Roche-Jeanneret houses and the Lipchitz and Miestchaninoff studios proved endlessly troublesome, requiring extensive repairs and long disputes with Ronéo. Metal windows made industrially for the Villa Savoye were found to be the wrong size when they arrived, due to the usual modifications in the plans, once again causing expensive alterations to the apertures receiving them. Again and again, Le Corbusier designed housings for the Baumann roller blinds to shade large windows (from the Besnus villa onwords). Again and again they caused trouble.

But the story of Le Corbusier's detailing is a poignant one. Most of the houses have a touchingly sincere craftsmanship about the details. The little drainage holes and runnels under the windows to catch condensation and drain it away, the working of latches and door handles, the placing of lights and skylights – these things provide real satisfaction to the visitor, and the correspondence is full of the record of struggle to make these details work.

The pragmatic was not always in conflict with the ideal. The *fenêtre en longueur* was a synthesis of an 'ideal' solution – a general window for all purposes, from the League of Nations to the humble house – a solution which revealed structure, which was 'classical' in avoiding unnecessary incident, which was anthropocentric in avoiding hierarchic internal organisations and which, Le Corbusier believed, was demonstrably

superior to any other form for lighting internal spaces. But it was also the product of an accretion of pragmatic, detailed solutions. The 2.50 metre standard unit which developed during the 1920s was a unit of proportioning, but it was also flexible. Any kind of opening or fixed form could be adopted, whether pivoting on a central point, or side hung or sliding. Minor articulations to accommodate internal partitions need not disrupt the window. Inside, the long window was also a storage solution, invariably finished with a concrete shelf running right along it which could accommodate radiators or cupboards (themselves with side-hung or sliding aluminium doors). Tables could be made out of the concrete shelf, and extensions made to receive fireplaces or other fitments. This is cumulative work, extending from one project to another.

If the design work of detailing is cumulative and coherent through the 1920s, much of the credit must go to the team of craftsmen and builders who built the houses. Little work has yet been done on the Corbusian *équipe*. The closeness of the understanding between architect and entrepreneurs needs some explanation, since each project ended with disputes and more or less acrimonious struggles to extract overdue payment from clients who objected to the very large extras charged for work inadequately specified by the architects. At the heart of the *equipe* were: the mason, Summer; the carpenter and joiner, Louis; the painter and glazier, Celio; the plumber, Pasquier and the electrician, Barth (table on p. 220). A surprising choice for the gardener (in all the projects where records survive) was Crépin, who aroused the hostility of virtually all the clients due to the excessively high prices he charged, but whom Le Corbusier imposed again and again on his clients. A study of the Corbusian garden, and its relationship to *art décoratif* practice in Paris in the

1920s is long overdue. Crépin's work for Le Corbusier, well documented, shows how dependent the architect was on his Arts and Crafts origins and his original love of flowers and plants in the Jura around La Chaux de Fonds.

As the decade progressed, more and more young people, especially foreigners, came to work in the atelier rue de Sèvres. Phrases in German and Spanish crop up on the drawings. Many of them were there to work on the great competition entries, like the League of Nations design. Only Ernst Weissmann and Albert Frey were being paid around 1929. The impact of men of the calibre of José-Luis Sert, Kunio Maekawa, Albert Frey, Alfred Roth has yet to be adequately identified. They brought a certain professionalism into some of the finished drawings, particularly in the handling of 'difficult' techniques such as axonometrics, of which Pierre seems to have been somewhat shy. Only in the case of the later work on the Church estate, the later drawings and details for the Villa Savoye and some of the de Beistegui work can specific draughtsmen be identified with any confidence.

*   *   *

This book represents some of the fruits of over ten years' work in the archives of the Foundation Le Corbusier. When I first inspected the drawings, they were still in rolls in the old apartment of Le Corbusier, rue Nungesser et Coli, and carried no numbers. The first archive documents I saw were similarly unorganised, left in the form in which they had been collected from the atelier. The drawings were a revelation in 1972, being virtually unknown. Since then there have been exhibitions, articles and books.

Le Corbusier's legacy, the Fondation Le Corbusier, was intended to preserve the hidden work of a master

architect. He was convinced that only by pursuing the trails of the archaeologist could a historian uncover the full meaning of his work. Not only were over 32,000 drawings preserved, but also an enormous quantity of documentation, covering in some cases every detail of a building's commissioning, design and construction. It is a fascinating and unique collection, and one difficult to come to terms with. How often have historians dreamt of looking behind the veil, of seeing what really happened? Working at the Fondation, sitting in the salon of Albert Jeanneret and Lotti Raaf, turning the leaves of pages which often have the immediacy of scribbled notes of telephone conversations, the illusion of actuality and of immediacy is sometimes unbearably real. And yet, of course, the most important questions remain unanswered. Why is this form like this, who decided this, what was said over the drawing board, in the cafe, on the site? In the end we are left with the drawings and the buildings.

Some things, however, are irreversibly altered in one's understanding and grasp of the architectural practice of Le Corbusier and Pierre Jeanneret. Many of the conditions of production are known, the pressures, and tensions, the background hubbub of daily crisis and mundane resolution of problems. But if it is essential not to confuse this level of working struggle with the process of design itself, it is also necessary not to separate the two. Some of these designs appear, out of the blue, on paper, in their essentials as built. And we do not have to postulate substantial losses in the preserved corpus of drawings. The Villa Cook and, in a very special sense, the Villa Savoye are cases in point of 'Immaculate Conceptions'. And Le Corbusier himself theorised on this score, referring to his 'hatred of drawings', to his conviction that 'architecture is made in the head'. By far the majority of drawings retained by

the Fondation are not 'working drawings' in the sense that one can discern forms emerging from confusion or in the sense that a set of calculations can be shown to produce a result. Most of the work of drawing is that of detailing, resolving minor difficulties, enriching, purifying, or slimming down. But it is, nevertheless, this work which reveals the way of thinking, the habits and internal discourses by which problems are resolved. And, in many cases, the process of detailing breaks down, usually under pressure from external forces (client, economics, site, materials), and we can trace the modulation from one design to another. These ruptures and interruptions reveal, as in a geological rift, the internal structure of ideas in a design. There is a kind of natural selection, a law of nature at work in the conflict of forces threatening to demolish the integrity of a design. The strong or resilient parts of the design survive, some other parts are proved too brittle to be adapted, and have to be discarded wholesale, while other parts are revealed to be passing fancies, easily shed when the pressure is on.

This is the study I have undertaken.

Bibliographical Note

For an introduction to Le Corbusier's architecture:

Curtis, W.J.R., *Le Corbusier: Ideas and Forms*, Phaidon, 1986
Jencks, C., *Le Corbusier and the Tragic View of Architecture*, Allen Lane, 1987
Moos, S. Von, *Le Corbusier: Elements of a Synthesis*, MIT Press, 1979
The Le Corbusier Archive, ed. H. Allen Brooks, Garland Publishing, New York and London, 1982–84
Le Corbusier: Architect of the Century, The Arts Council of Great Britain, 1987

The sketchbooks have also been published:

Le Corbusier Sketchbooks, vols 1–4, MIT Press and The Architectural History Foundation, New York and London.

5. Le Corbusier in his apartment, rue Nungesser et Coli in the 1950s.

6. Ozenfant studio, square Montsouris, Paris, in 1924.

THE WORLD OF PURISM

The highest delectation of the human spirit is the perception of order and the greatest human satisfaction is the feeling of collaborating or participating in that order... The perception of order is mathematical in kind... The Purist element, derived from the purification of standard forms, is not a copy but a creation whose aim is to materialise the object in all its generality and invariability. Purist elements are therefore comparable to well defined words; the Purist syntax is the application of constructive and modular means; it is the application of the laws which govern pictorial space.
(A. Ozenfant and Ch. E. Jeanneret, 'Le Purisme', *L'Esprit Nouveau*, No 4, p. 386)

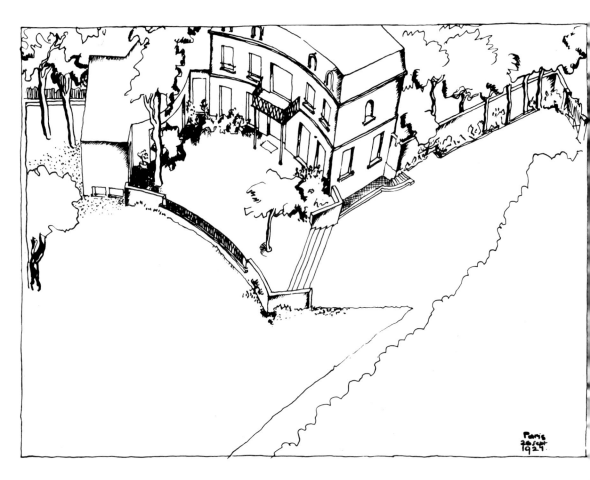

7. Villa Berque,
Auteuil, Bird's eye view
showing the terrace and
the projected salon
25 September 1921
(FLC 9313)

8. Perspective view of
the projected salon
25 September 1921
(FLC 9315)

VILLA BERQUE

A number of drawings exist for alterations to a small villa in classical style situated in the exclusive private estate known as the Villa Montmorency. The drawings can be divided into a set (dated 25 September 1921) illustrating an extension living room, metal balcony and railing and a large curved terrace facing the garden. Other drawings illustrate suggested changes to the rooms of the house, including details of furniture. Another group propose changes to the garden, in a formal French style, and the addition of a pergola at the end reminiscent of Josef Hoffmann's work in Vienna (Primavesi House). A later project (FLC 10332, datable to September 1926), refers to the addition of a garage at the narrow end of the site. There are also some drawings, probably from 1925–26, suggesting a proposed *lotissement* of five houses on the site, requiring the demolition of the old house.

The documentation does not allow for precision in establishing exactly what was carried out of these projects, and according to which drawings. A letter of 18 July 1922 indicates that work totalling 93,500 francs had been nearly completed by that date. More detailed estimates (40, 567 and 60,030 francs on FLC 9338 and 9337) indicate work on the new salon extension and terrace, but not the garden or substantial interior decoration. The increase between these figures and the July 1922 statement of accounts would partly have been due to natural growth in the costs and partly to charges for painting and joinery which could stem from the additional costs of the redecoration of the old house. It has not been possible to secure any certain evidence, however, of the completion of the new salon. The figures given in the letter of July 1922 could be consistent with work in the old building and the construction of the new concrete terrace and iron railing only. And some drawings could support the hypothesis that the new salon was not in fact constructed. A plan (FLC 19334) of the terrace which conforms to the contractors' details for metalwork railings and which shows

two flights of steps down to the basement next to the garden front of the house omits the new salon altogether. Although this might indicate a difference of dates between the different phases of the projected work, two other drawings, (FLC 19337 and 9325), show layouts of the garden without the new salon. The latter, interestingly, also shows a sketch addition of the curved garage at the end of the garden, for which a detailed drawing was prepared in September 1926. It is of course, possible that FLC 19337 was an earlier drawing

9. Villa Berque, Auteuil. Perspective view of the terrace and projected salon (left) and interior (below) 25 September 1921 (FLC 9316)

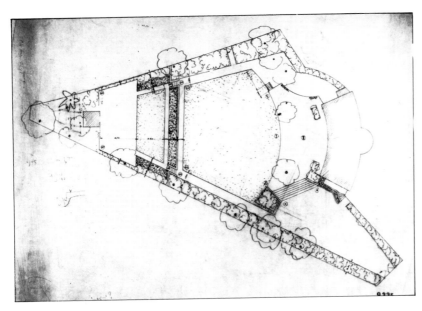

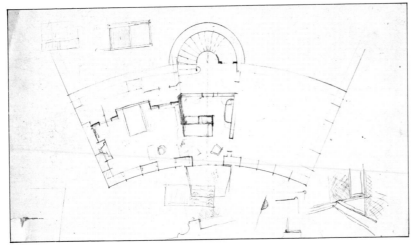

reused in 1926, and that FLC 19337 represents a phase of the design in 1921 before the new salon was planned, or that the new room was simply omitted by error.

A network of lines covering the garden in a site plan is consistent with the planning of the *lotissement* illustrated in five drawings. This extraordinary scheme includes one version in Dom-Ino style, consisting of simple rectangles assembled into a composition. The others correspond more closely to the kind of picturesque massing characteristic of the Immeuble-Villa projects for avenue Versailles or Boulogne around 1925–26. The style of drawing, use of stencilled letters and materials used would support this date.

Considering only the work of 1921–22, we find an interesting bridge between Le Corbusier's own early work in a classical style, influenced by Peter Behrens and his spell in Germany ten years earlier. For example, the Villa Favre Jacot in Le Locle, Switzerland, and his later involvement with an old building in Ville-d'Avray, for Henry Church, form a span of activity in response to classical buildings. The projected extension to the Villa Berque is in sympathy with the building, and his decorative scheme adds colour and a dignified restraint to the interiors. The use of long curtains to filter and control and light, the design of smoothly profiled furniture and built-in cupboards, and the provision of a wide expanse of raised terrace, echoing the curve of the old house, show a clear understanding of that reinterpretation of classical decor which designers like Paul Follot and Jacques-Emile Ruhlmann were exploiting to great effect. The obvious enthusiasm for detailing the cast iron supports of the balcony, the furniture mouldings and interior and exterior mouldings, shows that Le Corbusier had still not left behind his Swiss training and Arts and Crafts legacy.

The raised terrace was an important theme in Le Corbusier's work, forming a controlled mediatory plane between man and nature. A similar, but more

10. Top: Villa Berque, Auteuil. Plan of the property showing a garden layout based on Viennese Sezession principles, c. 1926 (FLC 9325).

11. Above: First floor plan of the existing house, showing proposed redecoration of bedroom and boudoir, 1921–2 (FLC 9333)

12. Right: Coloured sketch of a variant of the boudoir, 1921–2 (FLC 9328)

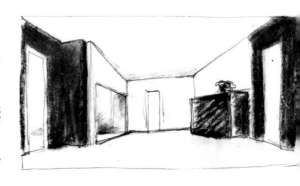

extravagant terrance was proposed for the old house at Ville-d'Avray (1929), and formed the heart of the design of the Villa de Mandrot between 1929 and 1930. The Charles Edouard Jeanneret of 1920 had many friends among the designers and decorators of the Left Bank, for some of whom he designed villas. The Villa Berque decorations form a sharp contrast to the Besnus and Ozenfant houses of a year or so later, but not all of this difference can be attributed to expediency. Le Corbusier always took great interest in the details of furnishing and interior decoration; a part of him was an *artiste-décorateur*.

13. Villa Berque, Auteuil. Coloured sketch of the boudoir, looking towards the balcony and showing the mirror-wall on the right, 1921–2 (FLC 9327)

21

22

VILLA KER-KA-RE

The first known contact between Georges Besnus and Le Corbusier can be dated to December 1922, when the architect was proposing a site for him in the Avenue Reille, at the corner of the newly laid out Square de Montsouris. This was the same site used shortly after for the atelier Ozenfant, and it is noteworthy that Besnus decided to reject the site as too cramped, too lacking in light and too expensive at 400 francs per square metre. In December 1922, Besnus asked him to look for another site for his house, perhaps in Auteuil. This is one of the few pieces of evidence that Le Corbusier had any involvement with sites in Auteuil, apart from the Villa Berque, in 1922 (see Villas La Roche and Jeanneret).

In January 1923, negotiations for one of M. Robert's sites in Vaucresson were in hand. The land was cheap (25 francs per square metre), but the site was small (only 334 square metres) and several efforts were made to add to the area of the plot, either by buying a strip along the side, or an extra piece at the end of the garden. Besnus acquired the site in March, with another small part to add to the garden (39 square metres), in July.

Le Corbusier's designs seem to have begun in January, since a letter from Besnus dated 29 January 1923 carries a rough sketch of the 'L'-shaped version of the house consistent with 'Project A'. In an earlier letter of 25 January, Besnus stated a figure of 70,000 francs (inclusive of the site), as a maximum. In effect, the house appears to have been completed for 82,595 francs (comprising 64,000 for Summer's contract, 4,500 enclosure, 4,795 architects' fees, 8,325 site, 975 extension to the site). At a mere eighteen per cent above the estimate, Besnus must have been a satisfied client, since most of the villas ended up costing between fifty and one hundred per cent more than the original estimate. In the same letter, he gave a brief which included an atelier on the first floor.

By 25 February, Besnus had received some plans and a rough estimate. It is likely that these plans, which pleased Besnus and his wife, have not survived, since the measured drawings for the first scheme (with the staircase at right angles to the house) are dated 4–5 April 1923 (FLC 9241, 9236, 9238). An earlier version of the garden front, with horizontal windows rather than full-height French windows, may correspond to the February scheme. The change to the living room windows from horizontal to full height may be connected to a remark made by Besnus in March:

14. Villa Ker-Ka-Ré, Vaucresson. Garden front in its original state, c. 1924.

23

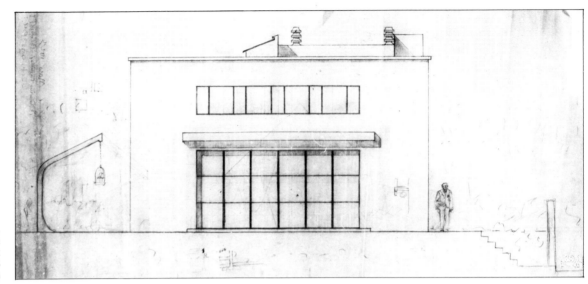

15. Villa Ker-Ka-Ré,
Vaucresson. Garden
elevation, first project
c. 4–5 April 1923
(FLC 9241)

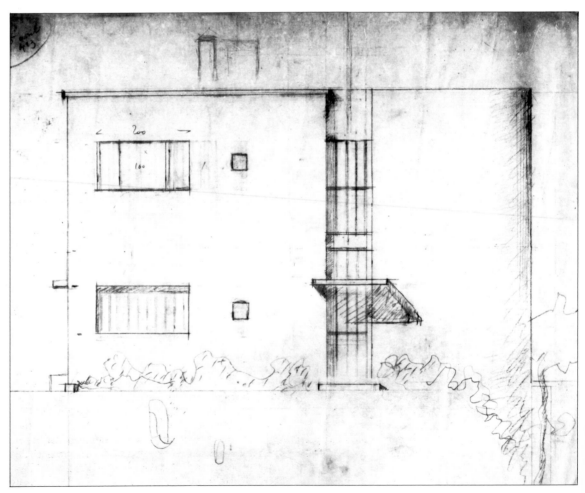

16. Elevation to the rue
Allouard, first project,
5 April 1923 (FLC 9326)

20. Villa Ker-Ka-Ré, Vaucresson. Staircase as built.

21. Ozenfant studio, square Montsouris, Paris. First and second floor plans of an undated project to convert the studio into a family home (FLC 7845)

ATELIER OZENFANT

The precise details of the origins of this project are still unclear, despite the references in Ozenfant's *Mémoires* and the surviving documentation. We know that Georges Besnus had inspected and rejected a site on the avenue Reille in December 1922, and the indications are, from his description, that it was the same site used for the atelier Ozenfant.

By the beginning of February 1923, Ozenfant and Le Corbusier had agreed to proceed with a studio house. On 5 February, Le Corbusier was able to thank his friend for a cheque of 1,000 francs on account for his fees. It is likely therefore that some kind of design had been agreed by that date. Unfortunately, the close working relationship between the two men has led to a great shortage of documentation concerning the early stages of the design. Two elevation drawings (FLC 7821–2), differing in details from the signed set, are all that remains from any earlier stage of design; one of these is dated 'Mars 1923'.

A complete set of plans (FLC 7825), elevations and sections was signed by Ozenfant, presumably to accompany either the contract or the permission to build. Drawings signed in this way were normally used for sending to the mayor's office for permission to build, and we can posit a date between February and April for this. These plans differ from what was built principally in the external staircase, which had a dog-leg form and the absence of the library and mezzanine above the atelier. It is quite possible that the latter were deliberately omitted from the 'official' plans, for reasons of securing planning approval, since even the earliest elevations to the street front show the small library window. A perverse feature of this 'official' scheme was the provision of two free standing flues rising up through the middle of the atelier space.

A more detailed set of drawings, titled and numbered '1–5', and at a scale of '5 cm/m', retain the form of the external staircase but include the library and the mezzanine in the atelier. A further set of interior elevations, lettered 'A–F', correspond with this set and probably formed the group of drawings submitted for tender in April. As well as changes to the external staircase, replaced by a spiral concrete staircase sometime in June, this set differs from what was built only in a few details, such as the placing of the steel ladder-steps to the mezzanine and to the trap door in the roof.

The tender by Pierre Vié is dated 10 April, 1923, two days before his unsuccessful tender for the Besnus property. The date given for completion was 31 August. On 4 June (Doc. 30), Vié still had not received detail plans of the staircase in its revised form. By 3 July, Le Corbusier had still not inspected the contracts with the other tradesmen taken out by Vié, and had not approved their details. Furthermore, although construction was in progress by then, Le Corbusier had still not inspected Vié's construction drawing. The corner *piloti* was recast completely in August. On 25 July, Vié sent his plan of the concrete roof slab, indicating that by then construction was well under way and nearing completion of the carcase.

A mystery surrounds the existences of five drawings providing for a reorganisation of the interior of the house (including FLC 7844–5). The drawings themselves are very sketchy and hard to interpret. The general changes proposed would have been: replacement of the garage and *apartment de concierge* on the ground floor by two bedrooms (*parents*, *enfants*) and a bathroom and a space at the back marked *caves*. The first floor would have been arranged as a living area, with kitchen, dining room and 'reception', although one drawing seems to show bedrooms on this floor, too. A drawing on the back of FLC 7844 suggests that the atelier would have been partially sub-divided. Another drawing suggests the opening out of a double height space at the back (FLC 7842). This whole scheme seems inconsistent with any continuing use of the house by Ozenfant, and might have appeared more plausibly as an early design for another client, perhaps, indeed Besnus, had it not been for the spiral staircase in these drawings, matching the later project for the atelier, and the presence, on some of them, of partially erased fragments of drawings for the Ozenfant atelier. We must assume that this group of drawings represents a proposed change of use and possible sale of the atelier by Ozenfant at some point after its completion.

The Ozenfant studio presents us with one of the most

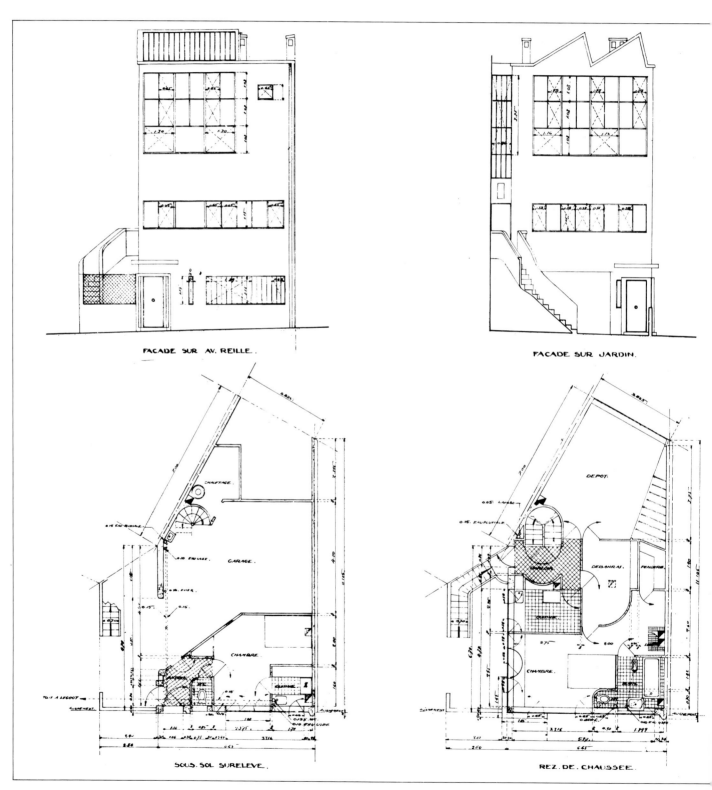

FACADE SUR AV. REILLE.

FACADE SUR JARDIN.

SOUS. SOL SURELEVE.

REZ. DE. CHAUSSEE.

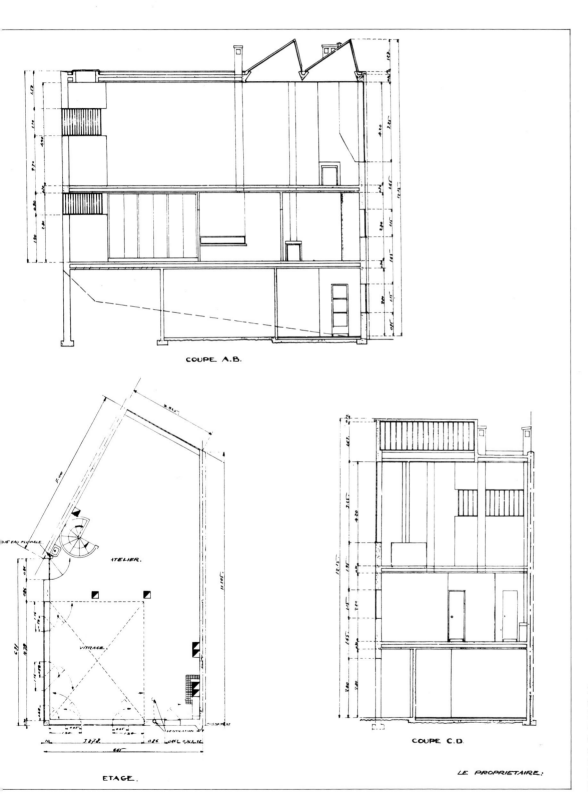

COUPE A.B.

ATELIER.

VITRAGE.

ETAGE.

COUPE C.D.

LE PROPRIETAIRE:

22. Ozenfant studio,
square Montsouris,
Paris. Plans, elevations
and sections of the
contract drawings
signed by Ozenfant
(subsequently modified)
March–April 1923
(FLC 7825)

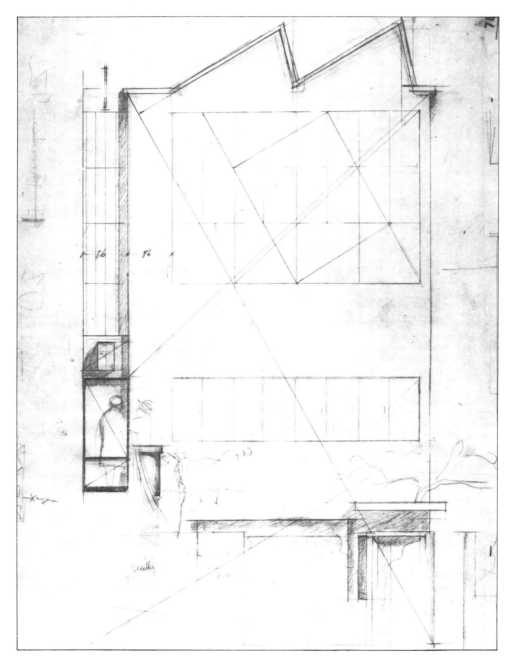

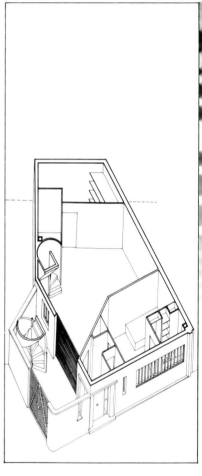

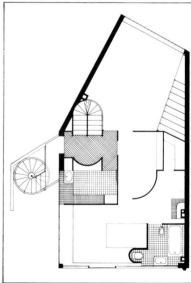

23. Above: Ozenfant studio, square Montsouris, Paris. Elevation to the square Montsouris, a preparatory drawing (with *tracés régulateurs*) for the numbered and titled set, April 1923 (FLC 7849)

24. Facing page, above: Axonometrics based on Le Corbusier's definitive drawings (FLC 31370, etc.)

25. Facing page, below: First, ground, second and third floor plans, redrawn from the definitive set (FLC 7825)

40

29. Villa La Roche-Jeanneret, Auteuil, Paris. Sketches of the first of two projects for four clients (Lotti Raaf, Sigismond Marcel and two others), May 1923 (FLC 15113)

THE ARCHITECTURAL PROMENADE

This second house will be rather like an *architectural promenade*. You enter: the architectural spectacle at once offers itself to the eye. You follow an itinerary and the perspectives develop with great variety, developing a play of light on the walls or making pools of shadow. Large windows open up views of the exterior where the architectural unity is reasserted... Here, reborn for our modern eye, are historic architectural discoveries: the pilotis, the long windows, the roof garden, the glass façade Once again we must learn at the end of the day to appreciate what is available...
(Le Corbusier and Pierre Jeanneret, *Oeuvre Complète*, I, p. 60)

VILLAS LA ROCHE AND JEANNERET

In the unravelling of the early design history for this site, a confusing factor is the date, (1922), given in the *Oeuvre Complète*, I, p. 58, for the first project. In fact, it seems certain that the designs for this rather grand house date from between 30 March and 13 April 1923.

On 29 March 1923, Le Corbusier paid a visit to M. J.M. Esnault, of the Banque Immobilière de Paris. The bank had the rights on a large plot in Auteuil, between the rue du Docteur Blanche to the north-west and rue Henri Heine to the north-east. The site, dotted with pine trees, was being laid out for speculative development. Le Corbusier asked M. Esnault to allow him two weeks to prepare studies for three lots along the private road. By this stage, the first lot, adjoining the rue du Docteur Blanche, had already been sold.

We can be fairly sure of the origins and causes of the 'first' project (including FLC 15135 and 15124), which was to occupy the second plot to the north, along the road. It is certain that the beautifully prepared drawings were intended to impress the bank and probably potential clients, rather than meet any specific brief of a particular client. The bird's-eye view with its flagpole, curved marquee over the entrance, the plan, with three cars in the garage but only twin bedrooms, the interior perspective of the hall, with its uniformed butler and finally the views of the salon with its pseudo-Cubist still life in the foreground, are all calculated to express modern chic. It has been asserted that this 'first project' was intended for Raoul La Roche.[1] Not only does the documentation contradict this assertion, but the pro- gramme, with its twin bedrooms (and double beds), the three cars and absence of La Roche's art collection represented in the interiors, makes this project seem very different from what was required for La Roche. It is quite possible, therefore, that a set of these drawings was taken to the interview with Esnault on 29 May as a 'taster'. This hypothesis is supported by the men- tion of a 'M. Sarmiento', who would according to Le Corbusier, visit the bank 'next Tuesday at 3:30 with a view to a purchase'. We may think of these designs, then, as a preliminary project for a house for M. Sarmiento. No evidence links it with either Albert Jeanneret or Raoul La Roche.

On the other hand, nothing more is heard of M. Sarmiento, and Le Corbusier also refers to designs for three contiguous lots 'beginning with the second over a

30. Villa La Roche-Jeanneret, Auteuil, Paris. Bird's eye view sketch of project for three houses (Lotti Raaf, Mr. Motte, Sigismond Marcel), 7–10 May 1923 (FLC 15111)

1. Russell Walden, *The Open Hand* (MIT, 1977, p. 136, n. 57).

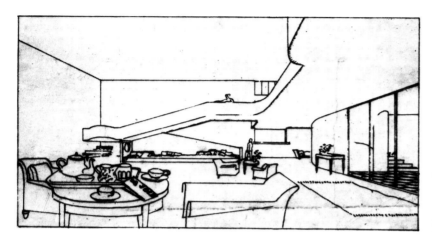

31. Villa La Roche-Jeanneret, Auteuil, Paris. First proposal for a villa at the mouth of the square du Dr. Blanche (for Mr. Sarmiento ?), c. 29 March 1923 (FLC 15135)

distance of approximately 40.50 metres'. He also goes on to say:

> I would be particularly anxious to make a study for you of the whole street, judging that the value of each of these properties would be increased by a judicious architectural scheme, with ingenious plans and elevations providing impeccable unity one with another.[2]

Now designs for these three sites can be pieced together only with difficulty. Significantly, they show houses considerably more humble than the 'Sarmiento' project and can be specifically referred to two clients at least: Lotti Raaf, who was to marry Le Corbusier's brother Albert Jeanneret in June 1923, and Mr Motte, a lawyer.

At the end of the agreed fortnight, on 13 April, Le Corbusier again met Esnault and discussed the arrangements for linking one of the houses to a concierge's lodge. A railing and gate with adjoining lodge had already been shown in the first project, to the south of the 'Sarmiento' house. It can be seen again in a perspective sketch, published in *Oeuvre Complète*, I, p. 60, bottom, and in an outline plan (FLC 15102). On the latter, the houses are identified as 'Mr. M.', 'M.R.' and M. Dup.', reading from the entrance to the private road southwards. Now, in a letter of 14 April, the order of the houses is described differently.

> Mr Motte, a lawyer, will visit you to purchase one of the sites and will make a deposit. This is the second plot after the one which you are reserving for me at Jasmin, from the rue du Docteur Blanche. This first plot, which will include the lodge for the concièrge, is intended for M. Albert Jeanneret, my brother, who will also visit you in the following week.[3]

The conclusion is that a decision was taken to move the Jeanneret-Raaf house further down the private road. The main drawing in FLC 15102 matches a sketch published in *Oeuvre Complète*, I, p. 60 (bottom), but another sketch plan on this drawing shows a plot half way down the private road marked as *retenu* and this conforms to a meeting of 21 April at the bank between Le Corbusier, Lotti Raaf and M. Esnault, in which it was agreed to reserve a plot for Lotti Raaf, who would pay a deposit of 7,000 francs for it. In the event, 7,500 francs was transferred from Lotti's Swedish bank, but

2. Dossier La Roche, Doc. 69, 30 March 1923.
3. Dossier La Roche, Doc. 7, 14 April 1923.

the transfer was not complete by 20 April. It is clear, from the correspondence, that the plot referred to was further down the private road, on the left (northeast).

A page of sketches (FLC 30957) of a small house seems to correspond to the programme of Lotti's house, including the children's bedrooms (for three girls) and a large room on the ground floor for Albert's dance studio. The elevations, too, seem to conform to the disposition of the trees on the site.

Following Esnault's letter of 21 April transmitting Plousey's decision to allow building only at the end of the road and *à gauche* (a mistake, since it was the south west side of the road which was intended) Le Corbusier first tried to brazen it out. In letters to Esnault and Plousey, on 23 April he attempted to enforce the sale of the 10 metre plot to Lotti Raaf on the north east side of the road, while settling with Plousey on the arrangement of plots around the small roundabout at the end of the private road (Plots 'B', 'C', 'D'). Another drawing (FLC 15120) represents an alternative solution from the same moment.

On 24 April, Esnault reported that Plousey would not consent to any house on the north-east side of the private road, but that Lotti Raaf could have a plot on the other side instead, and her deposit was duly accepted as a first instalment on this site, 'adjoining the property of Mlle Stern'.

On 26 April, Le Corbusier came to an agreement with Plousey over the siting of the three houses on the south east and south west side of the roundabout. Between this date and 15 May, the basic scheme for three houses for Albert Jeanneret/Lotti Raaf, M. Motte and Sigismond Marcel, were worked out, in sketch plan and perspective (including FLC 15108, 15100 dated 10 May and 15099 dated 15 May). Most of the key features of the finished project, at least from the exterior, were sketched out in this period. In FLC 15120, the clients are identified as Mme Raaf and M. Motte (the twin houses) and M. Marcel (the larger house at the end).

It is important to reflect on what had transpired. Until 26 April, although Le Corbusier had referred several times to a unified treatment for the various houses, his plans and sketches showed that he was thinking in terms of separate blocks. The presence of numerous trees along the north-east side of the private road had made this inevitable. On the south-west side of the roundabout, however, there was a clear site, and Le Corbusier quickly began to join up two houses to make an imposing frontage (FLC 15108). In effect, he

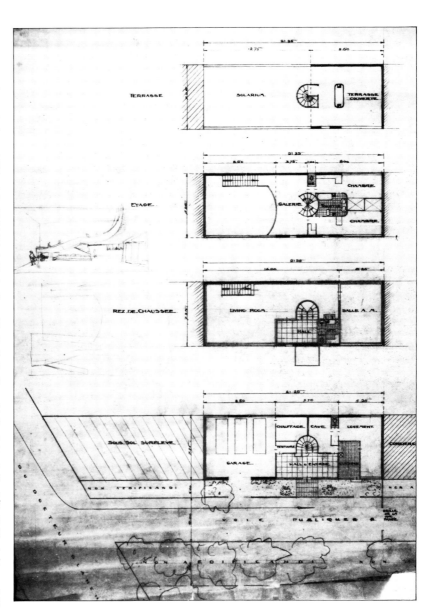

32. Villa La Roche-Jeanneret, Auteuil, Paris. Plans of the proposed villa (for Mr. Sarmiento?), c. 29 March 1923 (FLC 15124)

47

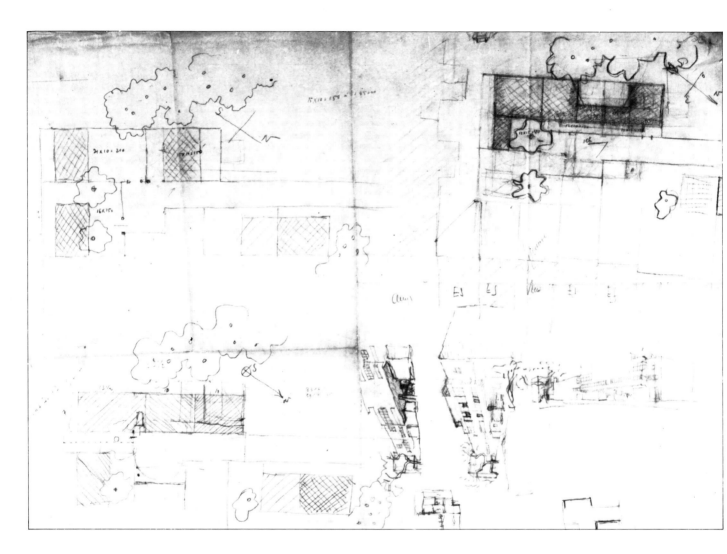

33. Villa La Roche-Jeanneret, Auteuil, Paris. Sketch plans and perspectives showing the development of the end of the square du Dr. Blanche with three houses to the South and one (for Lotti Raaf) to the North, 24–6 April 1923 (FLC 15108)

was simply joining together two small blocks, interspersed with a garage and through passage for each house, tied together by a long window at first floor level, and a roofspace intended to emphasise continuity. The ground floor plans show how the front doors to these houses, opening off little gardens behind the garages, and reveal the detached-house thinking of Le Corbusier particularly clearly. Only after suggestions from the client was direct access from the road carried out in its present form.

For the third house, at the end, designs were complicated by three trees, so that the solution adopted in early May was to place some of the living quarters in line with the twin houses, with a wing at right angles containing two large bedrooms (on the first and third

floors), with a large salon in between (FLC 15099). Thus, the general arrangement – a double house on the right and an attention catching block at the end for a wealthier client – was firmly established in May 1923 (FLC 15111, see p. 44).

An ambiguity concerns the possibility of a fourth house. In most of the plans, a plot at the south east of the roundabout, with a tree almost in the middle, is shown as an extension to the third site, without a specific use being suggested for it. In FLC 15100, this extra plot is incorporated as a garden for Marcel's house, making a site of 327 square metres which, at 325 francs per square metre, would have represented an expensive site. In the studies of the house previously indicated as for M. Motte, (FLC 15282 and 15107), the

1. Villa Berque (FLC 9326)

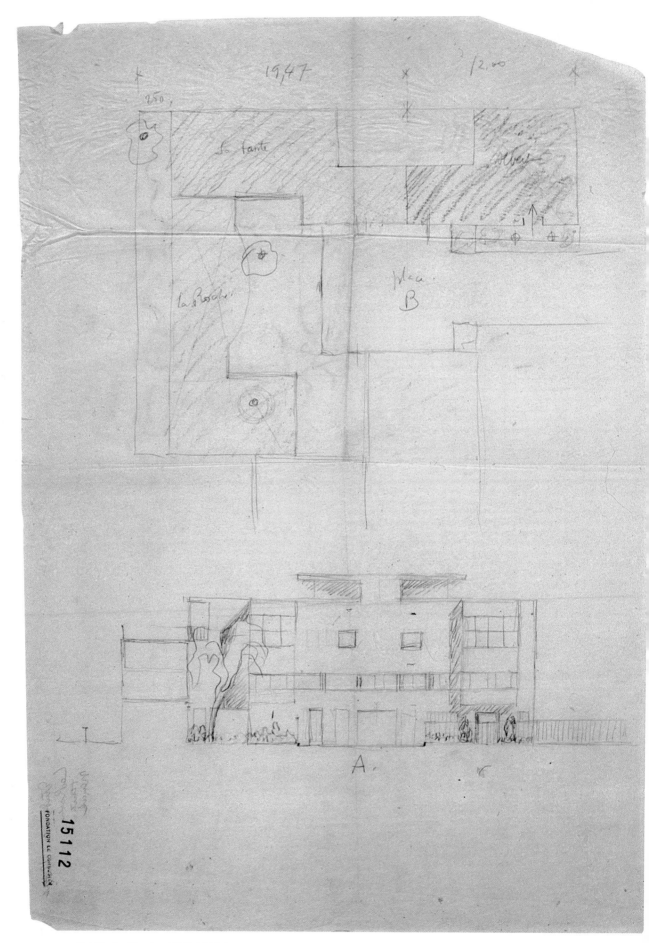

2. Villa La Roche (FLC 15112)

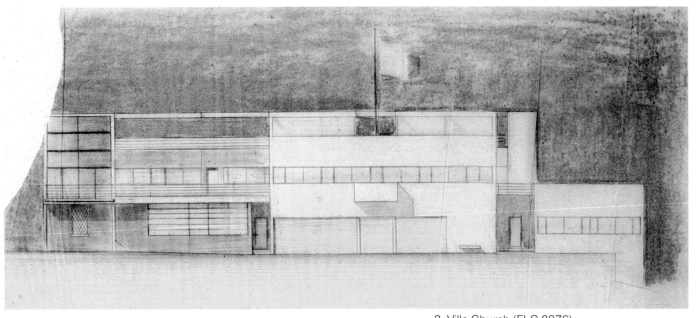

3. Villa Church (FLC 8076)

4. Villa Church (FLC 8075)

5. Villa Church (FLC 8080)

6. Villa Church (FLC 8017)

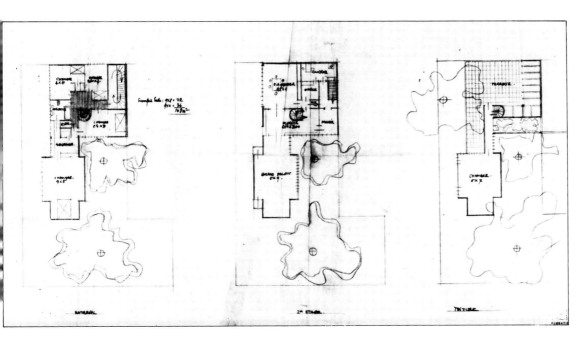

34. Villa La Roche-Jeanneret, Auteuil, Paris. First, second and third floor plans of the house projected for Marcel on the site of the present La Roche house, 15 May 1923 (FLC 15099)

35. Ground floor plan of three houses for Lotti Raaf, Mr. Motte and Sigismond Marcel, 10 May 1923 (FLC 15100)

ground floor shows a *salle de musique* in the place corresponding to Albert's dance studio. If it was intended at this stage for Albert and Lotti to have this other site, the drawing would have to predate the agreement of 26 May, when Lotti went ahead with the purchase of her site in its present position. Whether or not this argument can be sustained, these drawings should almost certainly be dated soon after 15 May, and this would fix the date of the addition of a fourth house on the south-east corner, composed as a 'U' around the tree. Le Corbusier later implied (in a letter of 14 August 1923) that Plousey had approved the four-house scheme in May, when he corrected the arrangement of the roundabout, but there is no actual evidence of this. Significantly, a drawing (FLC 9238 and 30238, already discussed in connection with the Besnus house at Vaucresson) representing the design in this phase, shows the sites of only two of the four houses as sold presumably to Lotti Raaf and Sigismond Marcel, which suggests that M. Motte, who often worked as solicitor for Le Corbusier, had agreed to lend his name to the negotiations until a client could be found. No mention of La Roche, with whom a scrupulously consistent flow of letters begins in the autumn, can be found, either in the documents or in the drawings themselves, until the project which follows this one, probably in July.

Raoul La Roche was a young and successful banker, described as *sous-directeur* of the *Credit Commercial de France*. He lived alone, with a manservant, and none of the plans known to be in accordance with his brief included more than one or two guest rooms. The plans

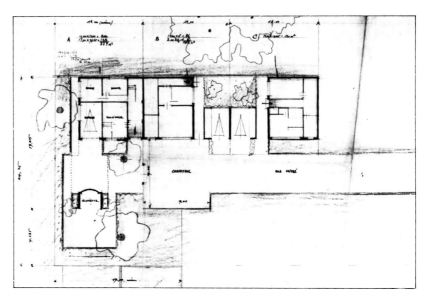

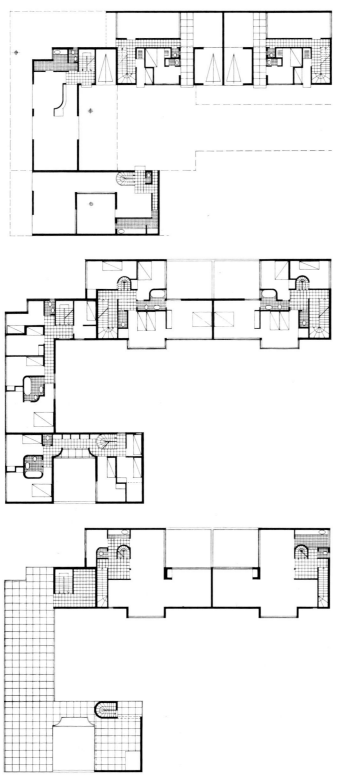

show five bedrooms, of which only one could reasonably be attributed to the use of servants. Furthermore, La Roche had a large and growing collection of Cubist and Purist paintings, in whose acquisition Ozenfant and Le Corbusier had played a leading role. And yet the perspectives of these schemes show paintings and sculptures. We must deduce that both these houses at the end of the private road were designed in the same spirit as the first project near the mouth of the road, in April, as speculative ventures for clients yet to be identified. Sigismond Marcel's role in this is not clarified by the documents. He was a friend of Le Corbusier's, and an industrialist, who lent him a large sum of money in connection with the Auteuil project, probably to put down on one of these sites if a client was not forthcoming in time to settle the deal with the bank.

This role of intermediary and financial supporter did become explicit later, when we know that Marcel's money was used to purchase the small plot next to Lotti Raaf's site, to the north west, on which, as we will see, abortive projects for M. Casa Fuerte and Mongermon were undertaken between January and May 1925.

The moment of La Roche's arrival as a firm client of the site on which his house was built can be fixed by a drawing (FLC 15103), where he is listed, along with Marcel, Albert and 'Boul'. Significantly, the designs for La Roche's house immediately begin to be differentiated radically from the house marked as for Marcel. This drawing marks the origins of the second of the two four house schemes, developed in all probability between July and August 1923. As an indication of the date, a note on FLC 15101 refers to a possible site for a garage adjoining the Marcel site, made necessary by changes in the plans which removed one of the garages from the body of the house. Le Corbusier wrote to Esnault, trying to purchase this small plot for the garage on 17 July, just before his holidays. Esnault's reply of 19 July refused to sell this piece of land, or indeed any land 'to the left' of the private road, until the plots along the rue Henri Heine had been sold.

The plans for the La Roche and Marcel houses of July and August are extremely innovative, within Le Corbusier's work, and prophetic of developments to come. We can see that Marcel's house has been moved to the plot on the left of the little square, with the plan form simply reversed, in terms of the enclosure of the tree, compared to the earlier four-house scheme. Instead of enclosing the tree in a courtyard facing outwards to the rue Henri Heine houses, the tree is actually enclosed on the axis of a spiral staircase. (FLC 15254, see p. 56).

For the first time the La Roche house is given a curved front to the gallery wing. Furthermore, the detailed plans and sketches begin to deploy the voca-

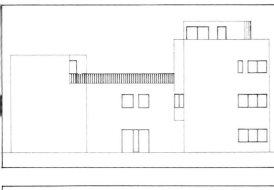
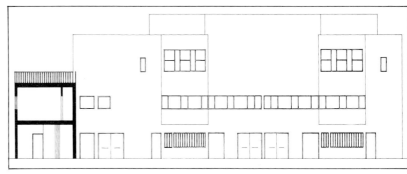
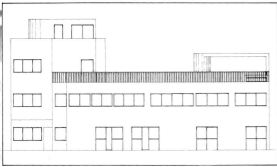
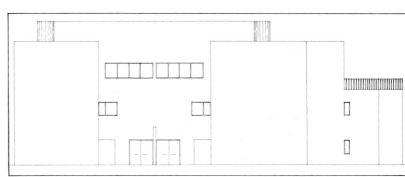

bulary of the *maison de collectionneur*. The entrance now was to be at the south corner, opening into a hall equipped with a ramp rising round three sides of the space and illuminated by a large window. Half-way up the ramp, a landing opens onto a *parloir intermédiare*. The first floor becomes a *piano nobile* providing exclusively ceremonial and reception spaces – a gallery and dining room – and the interior perspectives show the walls libarally supplied with paintings and sculptures. The two bedrooms and dressing room were to have been on the ground floor, with an apartment for the manservant on the right.

On 6 August, Le Corbusier wrote to Esnault:

Having finalised the preparatory studies for the four sites which I have reserved at Jasmin at the end of the private road, I have the honour to request you to prepare the deeds of sale of the three sites not yet purchased, to wit:

a) The site next to that of Madame Raaf, 12 metres wide and approximately 8 metres deep. The adjoining site which forms the end of the cul-de-sac. These two plots for sale to Mr. Raoul La Roche, 25 bis rue de Constantine. The first specified for resale, the second for his personal use (13 metres × 12 metres, approximately).

b) The plot to the left of the small square at the end of the cul-de-sac being 17 metres wide and aproximately 7.50 metres deep. This plot in the name of M. Sigismond Marcel, 3 rue Robert Etienne. Departing on holiday for a few days, I would appreciate it if you would confirm your receipt of this letter. The signatures can be exchanged on my return.[4]

Clearly, Le Corbusier thought that his latest scheme might be accepted, but Plousey informed him that, as he might have expected from the earlier correspondence, the site of the Marcel house was to be reserved until the future owners of the relevant houses on the rue Henri Heine had given their assent. Shortly afterwards, Esnault informed Lotti Raaf that, although he had offered her a site on 28 May 'following on from that of Mlle Stern', a strip of land 5.45 metres wide had been sold, in the interim, to M. Lemasson, the owner of one of the houses on the rue Raffet, on part of the site offered to Lotti Raaf. That this was possible appears to be at least in part the fault of Le Corbusier himself. Before leaving on her honey-moon with Albert, to visit Sweden and Switzerland in July, Lotti had transferred 35,500 francs to Le Corbusier's bank account. This money was intended for the purchase of the site for her house, but it seems that Le Corbusier trusted in the small deposit already paid and he kept the money, conceivably for his own use, but more

36. Villa La Roche-Jeanneret, Auteuil, Paris. Redrawn plans (facing page) and redrawn elevations (above) based on Le Corbusier's original drawings of the first of two projects for four clients, May 1923 (FLC 15113, 15115–7 etc.)

4. Dossier Le Roche, 6 August 1923.

55

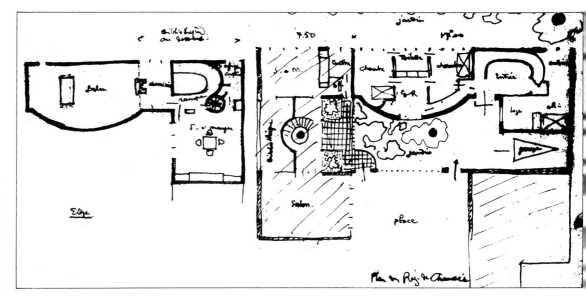

37. Villa La Roche-Jeanneret, Auteuil, Paris. Right and facing page: Sketch plans and perspectives (Dining room, entrance hall) of the house for La Roche in the second four house scheme, July (?) 1923 (FLC 15254)

probably to reserve other sites in anticipation of the arrival of other firm clients. By 20 September, despite the fact that a full set of measured drawings for the Jeanneret-Raaf house had been made, and tenders from builders and the entrepreneurs received, the purchase of the Raaf site had still not been effected although Le Corbusier claimed that the delay had been due to Lotti's absence. He eventually paid 29,272.50 francs for the site, kept 2,000 francs as an advance towards his fees and paid Lotti interest (40.75 francs) on the remainder.

Apparently, Lotti only found out about the sale of part of her plot on her return from holiday in September, but Le Corbusier seems to have discovered the details of the Lemasson sale on a plan sent to him by Esnault on 10 August. Le Corbusier later claimed that the sale had been deliberately engineered by Plousey to foil his plans for the four houses. The consequence of the Lemasson sale was to reduce the length of the site by 5.45 metres. FLC 15112 shows the reduced site and is dated '12 Sept'. Once again, Le Corbusier tried to brazen it out with Plousey, asserting, in a letter of 14 August, that Plousey had specifically agreed to the four house scheme and had indeed insisted on the use of the site to the left of the little square in May.

Le Corbusier's holiday, and the illness of Esnault during September, then introduced a delay. During this time he worked on a number of schemes for the reduced site, trying out a number of alternatives, for three or four houses. As late as 18 September, Le Corbusier tried to persuade Plousey to agree to the use of the site at the left of the square, giving as one reason:

Furthermore, the houses to be built around the small square are to be exhibited in a model at the Salon d'automne where a place has already been reserved for me under the dome.[5]

Plousey seems to have made difficulties even about the purchase of the La Roche site, partly because he was critical of the effect of the house on the neighbouring sites on the rue Jasmin. Le Corbusier sent him a long and dense letter full of assertions about what had been agreed in the correspondence of the last six months. Plousey agreed to the sale on 21 September. On 22 September, Le Corbusier rapidly sketched out a set of plans (including FLC 15291, 15273–7) of the La Roche house which mark the arrival of the penultimate stage in the design. We should look more closely at the crucial stage between 6 August and 22 September because many of the signifying forms of the house originate in decisions taken then.

The loss of the 5.45 metre strip at the north west end of the property left a total length of 19.47, plus the 12 metre extent of the Jeanneret-Raaf house. This left only eight metres between the Jeanneret-Raaf house and the La Roche site, and destroyed the symmetry of the 'double house' which had been a feature of each scheme since late April. A number of responses to this were tried out. One approach, visible in an elevation drawing (FLC 15112), was to create a fictive symmetry in the 'double house', by retaining both bow windows and making the single garage of the Jeanneret house the centre of the composition, thus creating the illusion

5. Dossier La Roche, Doc. 102, 18 September 1923.

that the block was divided evenly between the two
houses. The plan shows that the La Roche house in this
variant would have been moved round to cover part of
the site of Marcel's house, while a new client, referred
to as 'Sa Tante', is given the small site between
Jeanneret-Raaf and La Roche. This is presumably the
client referred to in the letter of 6 August, to whom
La Roche would have resold one of the two plots he
intended to purchase. The primacy of illusory symmetry over an expressive reading of interior functions is
remarkable here, since the 'centre' of the building
would have been in the Jeanneret house.

Another solution would have given La Roche this
'extra' piece of land, while persevering with a house on
the site for Marcel. Calculations on this drawing show
that Le Corbusier was trying to persuade La Roche to

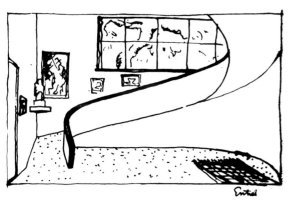

buy two plots (reduced from 256 to 238 square metres
because of the shortened site), but La Roche clearly
wanted to keep the price of the land as low as possible.
Several elevations seem to assume that the La Roche
house would indeed take up the small 8 × 8 metre
plot next to the Jeanneret site. In these elevations
the play with symmetry is modified; a virtual symmetry
is created about the axis of the divide between the
Jeanneret-Raaf and the adjoining property, but the
bow window of the Jeanneret house has to be read as
'extraneous' to this symmetry, or to be read at a
different level as counter-balanced by the big window
in the recessed part of the La Roche house.

I have left the designs from this period incorporating
the 'aunt's house' until last, not because they follow
logically from the designs we have been looking at, but
because the experience of working out this scheme
paved the way for significant features of the final solution. The intention was to create a tiny house out of
the 8 × 8 metre parcel of land separating the Jeanneret
and La Roche houses (FLC 15225). The house was
organised in an 'L' form around a spiral staircase, with
the main living area on the first floor and two bedrooms

above. The effect on the façade, with the front door in
the middle and paired windows on ground and second
floor marking the limits of the house, was to introduce
yet another counter-rhythm on the play of symmetries
and consonances of the elevations. In one drawing the
three-house scheme (La Roche, 'Tante', Jeanneret-
Raaf) is shown without the Marcel house.

On 22 September, with Plousey's agreement on the
sale of the La Roche site, Le Corbusier finally decided
to eliminate the 'aunt's house', but to do so in a way
which preserved intact the key features of its plan. In
doing so, a number of crucial transferences both of
meaning and function took place. In the July–August
scheme (FLC 15254), both the garage and the apartment for La Roche's manservant had been crammed
into the space next to the entrance hall in the top
right corner. This whole arrangement had intrinsic dis-
advantages: poor access to the garage, unsatisfactory
space and lighting for the manservant and a hall too

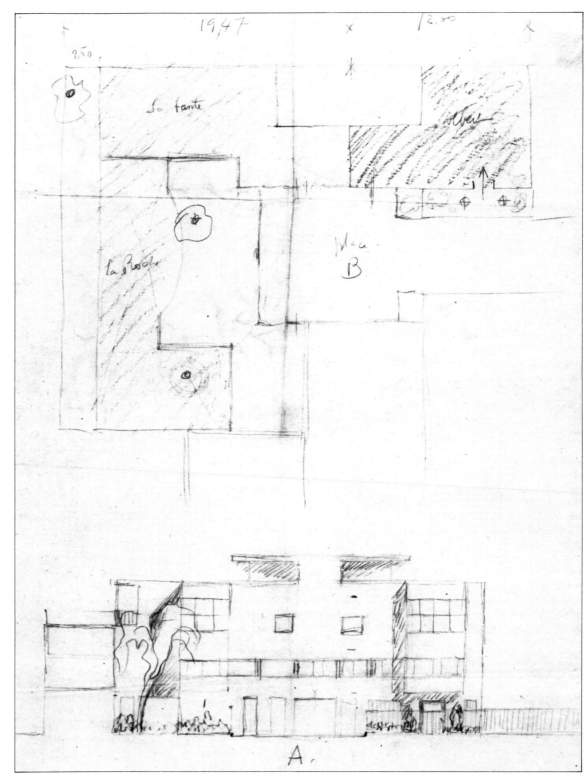

38. Villa La Roche-Jeanneret, Auteuil, Paris. Plan and north-east elevation of the three house project ('La Roche', 'his aunt', 'Albert'), 12 September 1923 (FLC 15112). The La Roche house is shown occupying part of the site to the north east.

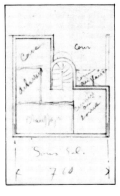 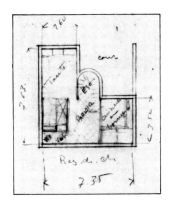 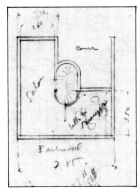 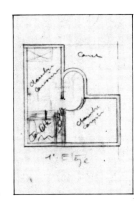 

small to allow the ramp in it to have a reasonable angle of ascent. On the first floor, the dining room, with its prominent window and easy access to the gallery, was a key feature of the July–August design. On 22 September, Le Corbusier literally scooped out the difficult part of the earlier project and allowed the parts to migrate into the 'aunt's house' (FLC 15291, 15273–7). On the ground floor, garage and manservant moved sideways, while the ramp was replaced by a staircase. On the first floor, we find the dining room migrating to its place in the 'aunt's house', and its space in the La Roche house taken up by a vast open space, still lit by the same window which had before signified the important living space of the dining room. To maintain the continuity from dining room to gallery, a bridge spanned the hall. And the ramp, deprived of its function as main access route, turns up in a quite different context in the gallery, as a route of ascent to the library, where views down into the hall mark the end of the *promenade architectural*. Le Corbusier flirted with the idea of a three-sided ramp rising up through the hall but changed his mind in favour of a compact staircase (FLC 15276). The bedroom floor of the 'aunt's house' became a guest suite for La Roche. The elevations show how the essential rhythms of the earlier schemes were reinforced by the mirror-image arrangement of garages and service rooms in both houses, while the bow window and front door of the Jeanneret-Raaf house were answered clearly in the recessed but large hall window and front door of the La Roche house.

In October, a wooden model of this version of the scheme was made, paid for by La Roche, for exhibition in the Salon d'Automne alongside the models of the Vaucresson house and the project for a villa at Rambouillet. The model incorporates a number of changes to the 22 September scheme, of which the most important reflects yet another migratory feature from an earlier phase. Despite several survey plans, intended to fix the dimensions of the properties, no one had bothered to establish with precision the location of a large acacia tree whose roots were in the property of M. Sorel, one of the neighbours on the rue Jasmin, but whose trunk and branches leaned well into the La Roche site. In the September plans, the acacia is shown at the southern corner of the site, necessitating a recess in the angle of the building to accommodate it. Only in FLC 15195 was its true position ascertained, a good four metres in from the edge of the property. Le Corbusier's solution took up the precedent of the Marcel house in the July–August project, creating a large inverted cone, with a concrete cantilevered balcony which encircled its trunk (FLC 15110 and 15205–7). This poetic gesture towards the natural world, which would have filled the upper level of the hall with greenery, could be seen through a long window in the cone. The fact that the consequences on the internal plans had not been fully worked out emerges from a careful study of a set of ink plans and sections which accompanied the model (see pp. 66–7). In FLC 15206, it looks as if the gallery ramp would lead only to a narrow walkway where the library should have been and the inverted cone for the acacia would have created a gigantic work of sculpture in a double height space. Later, this was corrected, to show the library as in the 22 September scheme, abutting the upper part of the inverted cone. But the gallery ramp was also ambiguously defined in this set. Le Corbusier had placed a balcony in the centre of the gallery façade, to form a focus for the drive, and this balcony was flanked by symmetrical windows, past which the ramp was supposed to rise. The obvious impossibility of achieving a rational solution connecting two windows and a balcony to a diagonally sloping ramp behind, led to the solution of treating the ramp as a raised viewing platform, with a short flight of steps at one end, and presumably alterative access to the library. In the earlier drawing, the windows flanking the balcony were removed to prepare the way for the later variant, in which the balcony too was eliminated, to be displaced to the left hand end of the gallery façade. Once again,

39. Villa La Roche-Jeanneret, Auteuil, Paris. Floor plans of the reduced house for 'his aunt', September 1923 (FLC 15225)

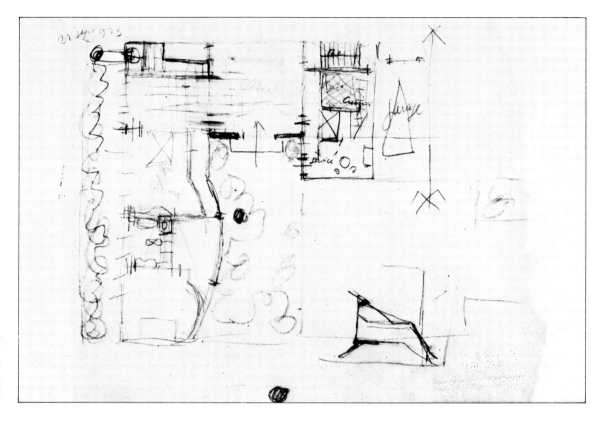

40. Villa La Roche-Jeanneret, Auteuil, Paris. Ground floor plan of La Roche house taking over the site of the aunt's house, 22 September, 1923 (FLC 15291)

the curiously random migration of forms and functions and displacement of concepts seems to have been carried out hurriedly and under the pressure of practical difficulties.

These drawings, prepared during November and December (La Roche had yet to receive them on 13 November), mark another key decision – to remove La Roche's sleeping quarters from the ground floor under the gallery and to put them where the guest suite had been, in the 'aunt's house'. The guest room ended up tucked away in a dead space of the hall. To explain the removal of the ground floor master bedroom suite, we must bear in mind two factors: La Roche's concern about the extra expense of the extra land needed for this scheme, and his corresponding anxiety about the cost of the whole house. He had allowed 250,000 francs for the whole enterprise, to include the purchase of the site and service charges connected with the private road; but he wrote to Le Corbusier, alarmed to discover that he had already spent 107,000 francs on the site, and urged him to economise where he could.

Cutting out the ground floor rooms under the gallery certainly saved some money and significantly reduced the number of rooms to be finished and decorated. By placing La Roche in the 'guest' bedroom, too, Le Corbusier secured from him a commitment to an austerity and modesty of accommodation which makes a poignant contrast with the splendour of the public and ceremonial spaces (gallery, hall, dining room).

But there was another kind of explanation for the removal of the ground floor rooms facing the gardens of the rue Jasmin houses. Plousey had alerted these neighbours to their rights of privacy (so-called *jours de souffrance* and *jours de tolerance*, in French law), and he visited M. Vié and M. Sorel on 21 September. Le Corbusier had planned a series of large French windows all along the south-east front of the La Roche house, facing directly onto the gardens of these neighbours. Any strict reading of the law gave M. Sorel and M. Vié the right to forbid these large windows. A long sequence of wrangles with several of the neighbours on both sides of the Jeanneret and La Roche houses eventually produced agreement over the *jours de souffrance* along the south-west and south-east sides of the two houses, and the net result was to close off all but a few windows, which, unless fulfilling certain specific conditions, were necessarily small, barred and glazed with opalescent glass. Some of these disputes, particularly that with M. Davaray, continued for several months and ended with the threat of legal action. If one effect of this legislation and the strict reading of it imposed by the bank's architect, was to remove the ground floor bedrooms under the gallery, another was to change the naturalistic, 'organic' response to M. Sorel's acacia. Instead of a curved form, in turn sculptural and transparent, which embedded the tree in the space of the library and staircase hall, Le Corbusier designed a rectangular balcony from which windows faced differently according to the floor level. On the first floor, a very large *jour de souffrance* (equipped with the thin vertical glazing strips but not, it seems, with frosted glass) faced directly onto the staircase landing. This treatment can be thought of as analogous to the first approach, filling the interior with the colour and impact of green foliage. On the top floor, however, once the ramp to the library has been mounted, the wall facing the acacia is left blank, while windows are pierced from the side. Bruno Reichlin has argued that this controlled and delimited framing of the natural world reflects both a notion of a heightened intellectual ontology appropriate to the initiation performed by gallery and library, but also the influence of the De Stijl exhibition at the Léonce Rosenberg gallery in October 1923. A more mundane explanation, that the library was essentially a space for cloistered study, for use above all in the evening, does not contradict but supports the others.

The impact of the De Stijl exhibition could also be pursued in other details of the interior space, particularly in the articulation of the double height hall. The treatment of wall surfaces in the finished building was designed to emphasis the planar and elementarist as against the solid and volumetric. Some of the detailed changes which emphasised this illusion, including the lowering of the parapet of the second floor staircase corridor leading to the La Roche's bedroom, (so as to align the top edge of the parapet with the top of the large window), were only added at a later stage, as we shall discover.

Another change from the October–November scheme was in the lighting of the gallery. Instead of a large skylight in the roof, Le Corbusier introduced ribbon windows on both sides, high under the roof slab.

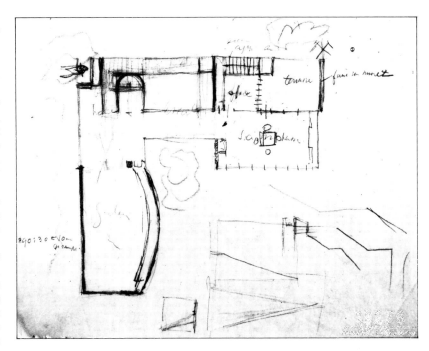

41. Villa La Roche-Jeanneret, Auteuil, Paris. First floor plan of La Roche house, 22 September 1923 (FLC 15276)

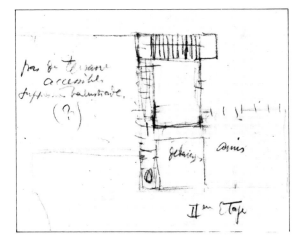

42. Second floor plan, La Roche house, 22 September 1923 (FLC 15277), the guest room, later transformed into the master bedroom

61

From the north west, the result is highly successful, picking up the theme of the long window on the first floor of the side block and transferring it to a higher level. But from the point of view of practical interior lighting, the south-east window allowed shafts of direct sunlight to strike down directly onto the paintings on the end wall of the gallery. La Roche was worried about this:

> Since we may assume that it will not always be raining, we must think about the question of a curtain for my gallery, on the east side. When the sun shines, it strikes fair and square on several of my paintings, and, whatever Le Corbusier may say, I must admit to some anxiety, especially because of the Picassos and Braques which, I fear, were not executed in pigments can stand up to such tests. A white linen curtain, like the others, I think, would have the added advantage of somewhat softening the acoustics of the room which are occasionally disturbing, especially when several people are raising their voices.[6]

Before considering the building history of both houses, we should go back to the initial designs for the Jeaneret-Raaf house, prepared in July (FLC 15148–9). On the basis of these plans, tenders were received (amounting to 104, 740 francs), but incomplete. Summer's first estimate was of the inclusive kind adopted for Vaucresson and the avenue Reille, including all the other trades. The total sum he proposed, 155,580 francs, was marked down by Pierre Jeanneret to 107,580 francs, but it is clear that Summer did not feel himself able to complete the house for this figure, because Summer went on to submit another tender, for the masonry and concrete work alone, totalling 54,500 francs. On the basis of new designs, new tenders were obtained in December 1923 and January 1924. The final estimate was prepared only on 20 March, 1924 and came out at 140,000 francs. The overall cost of the Jeanneret house eventually came to around 180,000 francs, with some sizeable bills for furnishing and decorating.

The main changes to the July scheme for the Jeanneret-Raaf house concerned the entrance, the elimination of a separate steel spiral staircase and the enlargement of garage and music rooms on the ground floor to occupy the space at the back originally given over to a small garden. All these changes were requested by Albert Jeanneret in a letter sent from Bulsjo in Sweden on 13 August, 1923. Albert and Lotti called in several 'experts', including her brother-in-law M. Lilienberg and the engineer-in-chief of Gothenburg, and their wives, 'professionals who have built several garden cities in Sweden and who are actively concerned with housing'. A long list of detailed criticisms, concerning the arrangement of the bedrooms, kitchen and bathrooms, were resolved by removing the secondary staircase and a dense repacking of the small service spaces. Albert concluded:

> All this must be gone into, suggestions of a purely practical order, in order to accommodate to the aesthetic and architectural principles with which I agree as much as you.

And Lotti, fearing a short-tempered response from her brother-in-law added:

> Don't be too cross at this letter, I really do believe that there are some good things among the changes proposed. Take from them those you like.[7]

Although some revised tenders were received through October to December 1923, the definitive plans do not seem to have been prepared until after January 1924, since three drawings of a penultimate scheme are dated 30 January 1924. These include some of the changes specified above, but not the final solution to the kitchen and pantry, and add a curious bevelled edge to the corner of the large bow window, presumably intended to meet objections to the overlooking of the neighbouring Le Masson site, which had been purchased in October by Sigismond Marcel. Once Marcel had bought the 5.45 metre plot, for resale to a future client, the problem of the party wall was effectively resolved. The tenders in January 1924 were clearly based on the penultimate design, since the carpenter included an estimate for the folding screens for the dining rooms eliminated in the finished scheme. The definitive plans, numbered '1' to '7', must have followed shortly afterwards, however, since construction began on the foundations in February. One device to make room for the enlarged dining room in the finished plans was to move one of the water-closets to the landing off the stairs leading up to the roof garden. The box of the water-closet projects down into the space of the kitchen, making a half-length space to the left of the kitchen door. The living area on the second floor was thus made into a large, L-shaped space with an

---

6. Dossier La Roche, Doc. 494, 19 February 1926.

7. Dossier La Roche, Doc. 41, 13 August 1923.

exemplary use of the three Corbusian window types: the bow window, the long window at the back and two square windows on the street front. The roof garden was much appreciated by Lotti and Albert, who were photographed sitting out on it. Lotti seems to have had the intention of sunbathing in the nude on it, and metal screens for greater privacy and wind protection were added in 1926.

The colours, unusually, have been recorded, for the decoration of the house in December 1926, occasioned by Lotti's distrust of the arsenic level in French paint.

Metal screens on the terrace:
  Zinc green, French Vermillion, blue, yellowish with some white.
  Sienna brown, dark grey.

Staircase:
  Lake and vermillion, burnt umber, pure green brown umber.
Dining room:
  Green and pink.
Madame's bedroom:
  Sienna brown, brown umber, blue.[8]

And Lotti has described Albert's bedroom:

The room is small but sufficient for a person who only spends his nights there. A couch with silver grey velvet, two white chairs, a cupboard for clothes, attached to the wall. 'A cell', said a visitor. 'The bedroom of a man with common sense,' said Le

8. Dossier Jeanneret, Doc. 260, 17 December 1926.

43. Villa La Roche-Jeanneret, Auteuil, Paris. South East elevation and North East and North West elevations (folded out) of the La Roche and Jeanneret-Raaf villas in the form of the model exhibited in the Salon d'Automne, October 1923 (FLC 15110)

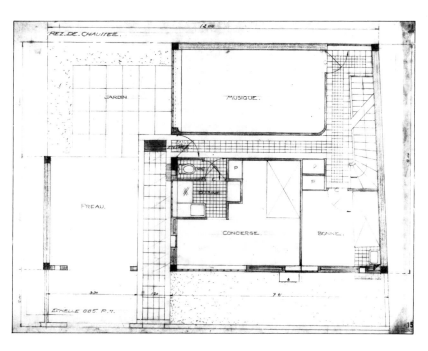

44. Villa La Roche-Jeanneret, Auteuil, Paris. Ground floor plan of the first project for the Jeanneret-Raaf house, as put out to tender in July 1923 (FLC 15148)

Corbusier. Further away is my bedroom, a bit more elaborate than the others. Two walls are white, one is burnt umber. Against this wall is a low, large bed covered with velvet in a leopard pattern with white flounces around the sides. Opposite are cupboards fastened to the wall, stretching from floor to ceiling, painted in light blue, the same as the window sills.[9]

Most of the furniture, including the fitments and tables, was made to Pierre's designs by R. Louis, Le Corbusier's favourite carpenter. A set of tables are among the best documented of Le Corbusier's early tubular steel furniture designs. The description by Louis is worth recording:

The top of poplar, veneered on both sides in tabasco mahogany, framing in the same wood 25mm thick; the total thickness being therefore 50mm French polish. Underneath, the legs of nickelled steel tube. The tube supports 27mm diameter, the horizontals of 35mm tube. The supporting frame of steel section 30mm by 5mm, all according to the sketch.[10]

These tables, somewhat altered in execution, were divided between Lotti and La Roche. Two other tables were made by Henri Dutar in February 1925 in tubular steel while Schmittheissler supplied miscellaneous chairs in February 1925. In addition, Le Corbusier

supplied La Roche with a number of items, in various states of wear and tear, from the Esprit Nouveau Pavilion, as we shall see. We also have a record of the gardener Crépin's bill, detailing the fifty pansies, forty daisies, eight perennials, two dahlias, a rambling rose, a lilac and a laurel bush.

In late 1925, the central heating system of the Jeanneret house was extended. Lotti wrote in May 1926, to complain of damp in one of the girls' rooms and in the staircase and asked for a complete repainting of the interior. She also provided a sketch of a cupboard for Kerstin's room which was made by Selmersheim and Monteil. Otherwise, the Jeanneret-Raaf house seems to have given complete satisfaction and the couple lived there with Lotti's three daughters Ebba, Brita and Kerstin until 1938, when Albert went to live in his parents' house at Vevey.

The finalising of the plans for La Roche is less clear. It is likely that the November set of plans (FLC 15205–7) were reused as the basis of the tenders of January 1924, with corrections supplied by a number of detailed emendations. Summer's dossier of drawings, probably follows soon after the contracts signed by La Roche on 19 February, 1924. Summer's drawings incorporate changes like the rectangular indentation for the acacia, the rounded end of the staircase facing onto the back terrace, and the correct placement of the balcony to the gallery. But further changes were made at a later stage, including the addition of a slit window to the lavatory at the left end of the main façade, and an extension to the cantilever of the main staircase balcony. Summer's concern over the latter alteration necessitated a letter from Pierre (12 April 1924) taking responsibility for carrying it out, although he refused to take responsibility for any accidents to the workmen involved.

The February estimates for the La Roche house amounted to around 200,000 francs which, with the other expenses on land and service charges (107,000 francs), put the total well above the 250,000 francs which La Roche had originally stipulated as the target. In the event, construction costs, including most of the furnishing, came to a further 80,000 francs. Construction began in March 1924 and the house was inaugurated, if not entirely finished, on 13 March, 1925. Permission to build had not actually been obtained from the authorities until 19 July, 1923, although construction was well under way by then. By

9. Walden, *The Open Hand*, MIT, 1975.
10. Dossier La Roche, Doc. 301, 2 April 1925.

September 1924, the interior elevation drawings were still not ready, and the painters had yet to begin work in January 1925. Furnishing and decoration continued until the summer of 1925. One cause of the delay was the decision (11 February 1924) to use Ronéo metal doors for both houses, as for the Lipchitz and Miestchaninof studios in Boulogne. This decision had a knock-on effect. The treatment originally proposed for the interior walls – brick with plaster panels – turned out to be insufficiently rigid to hang the brittle metal doors, so that several walls had to be refaced in concrete. Secondly, the doors, when they arrived, turned out to require repair and adjustment to fit the door jambs.

A second problem concerned the lighting. Most of the electric light fittings were Chalier strip lights, either mounted directly on the wall, or placed in reflectors. Two of these placements of strip lights, in the library and gallery, were composed of four and seven bulbs, respectively, end to end. La Roche had to complain on repeated occasions about the insufficiency of the lighting arrangements:

> The electrician has installed some strip lights in the runnel along the bottom of the gallery windows. This gives quite a pleasant light, but evidently not very bright. Even when all seven lamps are on, you can barely see to read; the loss of light must be considerable, but this system does have the merit of providing a provisional illumination of the room in the expectation of something better.[11]

On 18 October, the situation became worse:

> Lighting: on my return, I find the reinstatement of the *statu quo ante*, with the dining room ceiling full of holes. I had hoped that you were going to carry out the scheme of ceiling lights (provisional system) which we had discussed. I understand perfectly your hesitancy over the way to light my house. But until you find something really good, it is essential at least that I should be able to see clearly in my home. It's six months since I moved in and I am still obliged to use illumination which, particularly in the painting gallery, relies on ad hoc arrangements. What must the many visitors think, and what do you want me to tell them? I come back to the point that a perfectly banal system would be the best solution, at least for the moment... Furthermore it is becoming clear that your various pieces of equipment, however ingenious they might be, do show certain drawbacks and, since they are also very dear, I hesitate to proceed any

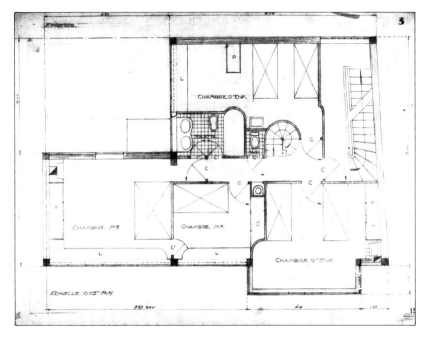

45. Jeanneret-Raaf house, first floor plan, July 1923 (FLC 15148)

further with them... I have seen at Leonce Rosenberg's some fittings which give good light and which are not unpleasant.[12]

This letter might be used as evidence to propose the hypothesis that some of the studies for elaborate lighting schemes for the gallery, normally associated with the redecoration in 1928, may have originated in 1925. The solution to the lighting of the dining room was apparently carried out only in January 1926, and consisted of installing three Argenta 100W reflectors in the ceiling, and seven 100W bulbs suspended from a system of wires strung across the gallery. It met the temporary needs of that room.

The question of lighting the gallery was taken up again in 1928, as were three other features of this space, to which we shall return shortly. One of these features concerned the key question of the storage of paintings. A serious conflict arose between the functions of picture storage and display and the unencumbered role of the wall surfaces as purveyors of architectural values. This was a particularly personal question for Le Corbusier, who had played an important role in buying paintings for La Roche and whose own paintings were

11. Dossier La Roche, Doc. 460, 16 August 1925.
12. Dossier La Roche, Doc. 235, 18 October 1925.

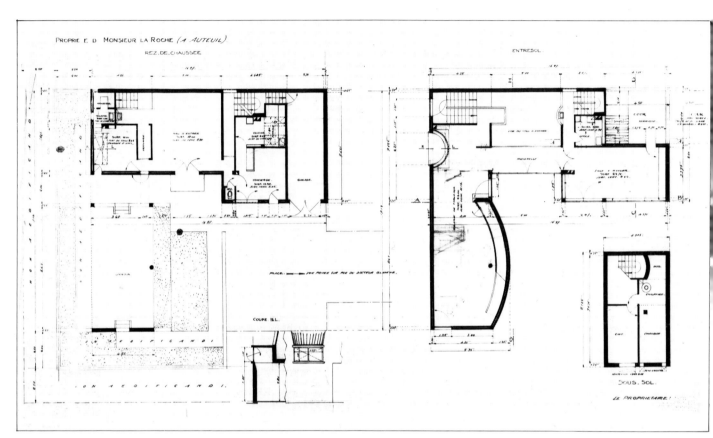

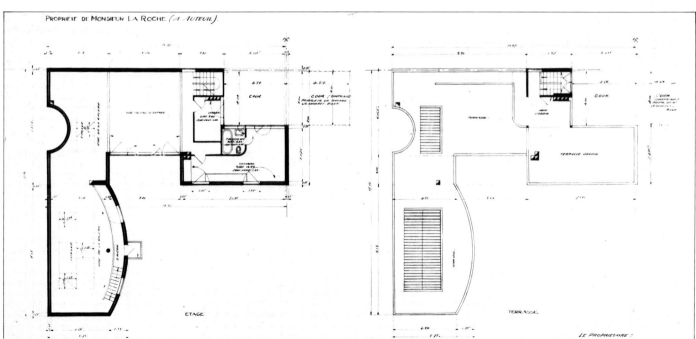

also included, along with Ozenfant's, in the collection. Indeed the photographs of the interior taken in 1925 and 1926 show a hanging policy which must be seen as an extension of the arguments of *La Peinture Moderne* (published as articles in *L'Esprit Nouveau* and as a book in 1925). The objective of these articles was to prove that the Purist canvases (and supporting theory) formed a natural sequel and criticism of Cubism. Le Corbusier wrote to Ozenfant on 16 April 1925:

It's about La Roche's paintings: He had asked me to take care of the hanging of the paintings in such a way that the arrangement should fit in with the architecture. With Pierre, I had carried out a preliminary hanging on La Roche's precise instruction. He had insisted on reserving the gallery exclusively for Purism, having himself removed the Picassos which I had hung there. When I dropped in at La Roche's yesterday on a practical matter, I noted the great transformations which you made. Nothing

could please me more than that you should carry out the hanging, but I would like it done by agreement with me – not with the aim of protecting my own interests (since you will have seen that I kept a good place for you) – but simply with the intention of ensuring that the La Roche house should not take on the look of a house of a (postage-stamp) collector. I insist absolutely that certain parts of the architecture should be entirely free of paintings, so as to create a double effect of pure architecture on the one hand and pure paintings on the other. Since this intention appears to have been modified by the new arrangements which you have made, I appeal to you as a good friend, first to take note of it and secondly to come to an agreement with me over it.[13]

There are two issues here, the relative importance to be given to different Purist paintings and other works and the density of hanging. Photographs taken in 1925,

13. Dossier La Roche, Doc. 506, 16 April 1925.

46. Villa La Roche-Jeanneret, Auteuil, Paris. Facing page: Floor plans of the penultimate project of the La Roche house, October–November 1923 (FLC 15205 and 15206)

47. La Roche house, sections and elevations of penultimate project, October–November 1923 (FLC 15207)

48. Facing page: La Roche's library on the third floor overlooking the hall.

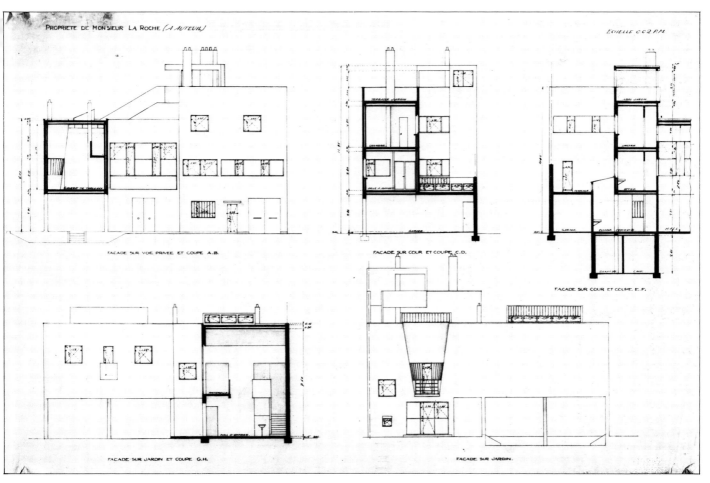

PROPRIETE DE MONSIEUR LA ROCHE (A AUTEUIL)

ECHELLE 0.02 P.M.

FACADE SUR VOIE PRIVEE ET COUPE A.B.

FACADE SUR COUR ET COUPE C.D.

FACADE SUR COUR ET COUPE E.F.

FACADE SUR JARDIN ET COUPE G.H.

FACADE SUR JARDIN.

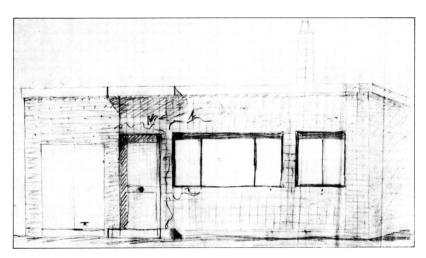

49. Villa La Roche-Jeanneret, Auteuil, Paris. Elevation of the triangular lodge for the concierge, definitive version, autumn–winter 1925 (FLC 15136)

less I did so. How could I have done otherwise? Do I not have certain obligations with regard to my painters, of whom you yourself are one? I commissioned from you a 'frame for my collection'. You provided me with a 'poem of walls'. Which of us two is most to blame?[14]

One practical consequence of this affair was Le Corbusier's experiments with a picture store in the summer of 1925. On one of the plans of 1924, FLC 15205, Le Corbusier at some stage made a rough sketch of a triangular fitment for this purpose. Another drawing, FLC 15243, shows it in greater detail. The date of this drawing is uncertain, although it matches the style of the interior details of March to June 1925. In May 1925, La Roche was still asking for details of this fitment. Three days later, his attitude had hardened against it:

The more I think about it, the more I find it a pity to place it in the middle of the 'painting gallery' (if indeed it still is one!), thus dividing it into two halves and creating yet another antichamber, when I have more than enough of these. If you have already done some plans, please bring me them so that I can study them carefully, but, until further notice, I would rather you kept the space of the room clear.[15]

The furnishing for the La Roche and Jeanneret houses is important as an almost pure example of Le Corbusier's views on equipping the home. La Roche did indeed refuse some items ordered on his behalf, such as an armchair supplied by Abel Motte, but on the whole he agreed with his architect's choice. Curtains were installed by the Grands Magasins du Printemps, mostly in white flannel and cambric. All the curtain rails had to be taken down and replaced, after complaints by La Roche of sloppy workmanship. The tables supplied by Louis had to be repaired:

The legs of these tables look as if they have been in a fire, the nickel being quite spoilt, probably because of welding.[16]

Some of the legs of the Louis tables were quite loose, due to the fact that the supports were simply screwed on, rather than welded. Le Corbusier ordered a large number of Thonet chairs for the two houses, of which La Roche kept three little ones ('18½'), eight of the '1009' desk chairs and three Thonet armchairs

and those taken by Fred Boissonas in 1926 show that Ozenfant had his way on the former debate. In the gallery, key works of analytic and 'crystal' Cubism by Picasso, Braque, Leger, Gris and Lipchitz were confronted with the Ozenfants and Jeannerets. In La Roche's bedroom, austere as a monk's cell, only Purist paintings were allowed. Although Le Corbusier must have approved this layout, with its implied progression, reflecting closely the layout of illustrations in the final chapters of *La Peinture Moderne*, he fell out with Ozenfant over the density of the hanging. This dispute was in part a symptom of and in part a contributing factor in the break-up of the friendship of the two men. It marks the point in Le Corbusier's career when, despite his continuing and indefatigable practice as a painter, he decided to prioritise architecture, and architectural values, over those of painting.

A year later, La Roche tried to take a larger view:

Reading between the lines of your article in the *Cahiers d'Art*, No. 3, I was aware of some criticisms levelled at me. Indeed, you loyally warned me in advance of them. What can I say? No doubt you have reason for complaint if the impact of your walls, of whom I have been one of the chief admirers, is ruined... Do you recall the origin of my undertaking? 'La Roche, when you have a fine collection like yours, you should have a house built worthy of it.' And my response: 'Fine, Jeanneret, make this house for me.' Now, what happened? The house, once built, was so beautiful that on seeing it I cried: 'It's almost a pity to put paintings into it!' Neverthe-

14. Dossier La Roche, Doc. 506 bis, 24 May 1926.
15. Dossier La Roche, Doc. 561, 12 May 1925.
16. Dossier La Roche, Doc. 563, 27 July 1925.

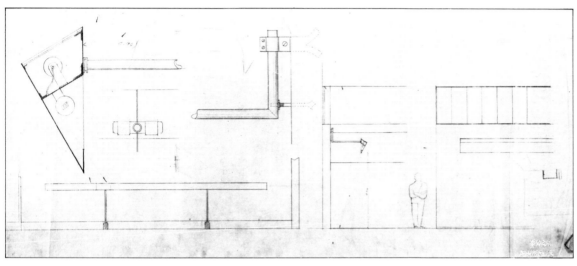

50. Villa La Roche-Jeanneret, Auteuil, Paris. Details of lighting trough added to the La Roche gallery, January–April 1928 (FLC 15284)

('1018'). He also had some metal wire-leg chairs of the Jardin des Tuileries type, not all of which were used outdoors on the roof garden. Le Corbusier also ordered two of the famous Maples leather chairs, a Franklin and Newstead, which were upholstered specially to his requirements.

> These two armchairs should be covered in fawn morocco leather, of the same appearance as those delivered earlier for Mr Levaillant, at La Chaux de Fonds.[17]

These chairs cost 2,225 and 1,975 francs, respectively. A record of the colours used by the painter, Celio, has survived:

Distemper:
    Yellow ochre, red ochre, ivory black, natural Sienna, burnt Sienna.
Oil paint:
    Natural ochre, burnt ochre, English Green, ultramarine blue, 'chasson' blue, chrome yellow.[18]

For the floor surface, small, ten-centimetre tiles were used (black for most of the areas of circulation, white for the bathrooms and service rooms), brown lineoleum for the bedrooms, library and the Jeanneret living room and parquet (*deuxième choix*) for the gallery. The ramp was surfaced in rubber, but La Roche complained that it was so slippery as to be virtually impassable. This again was put right only in 1928.

La Roche was a patient and always courteous patron, with a delightful irony which was expressed even in

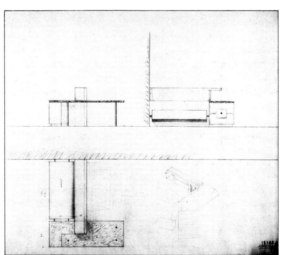

51. Elevations and plan of a proposed fitting intended to incorporate a picture store and divan in the La Roche gallery, c. January 1928 (FLC 15188)

17. Dossier La Roche, Doc. 445, 4 February 1925.
18. Dossier La Roche, Doc. 331, 12 March 1925.

71

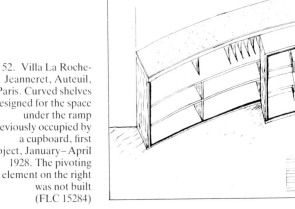

52. Villa La Roche-Jeanneret, Auteuil, Paris. Curved shelves designed for the space under the ramp previously occupied by a cupboard, first project, January–April 1928. The pivoting element on the right was not built (FLC 15284)

conditions of some tension. After a long list of defects and repairs to be carried out, he concluded:

> I apologise for the length of this Rappel à MM les architectes. On reading it, you might be tempted to think that my house is a botched job. Now you know that this is by no means my opinion and that, on the contrary, I take enormous pleasure in it.[19]

Another project which suffered considerable delays and about which there is still some doubt, is the lodge for the concierge of the private road, at the corner of the rue du Docteur Blanche (north west side). Some drawings exist (FLC 15136) and there are clear indications that Summer was paid to build it during 1925. His estimate of 91,650 francs was accepted on 15 June, 1925. In a letter to M. Mongermon of 15 April, 1925, Le Corbusier states that Plousey had prepared an estimate and design which would have cost 35,000 francs, but that his was costed at a mere 18,000 francs. Matters are complicated by references to the *loge de concièrge* on the ground floor of the Jeanneret-Raaf house, and there are, as far as I know, no photographs of the free-standing lodge.

The campaign of redecoration and partial redesign of the La Roche gallery in 1928 is important for a number of reasons. First, it marked the change in attitude from austerity and Purist sobriety evident in the construction of the house, to a more relaxed attitude and eagerness to use the materials and symbols of luxury. Secondly, the campaign coincided with the recent arrival (in the atelier) of Charlotte Perriand, recruited after her successful *Bar sous le toit* installation at the Salon d'Automne in 1927, with its early and successful use of tubular steel chairs. It was at this time that three Corbusier tubular steel chairs were designed, and the

prototype *Grand confort* found a home among the Maples leather chairs of the Purist phase, although La Roche admitted that he had agreed to accept it 'without enthusiasm', given its poor condition and high price.

The stimulus for the redecoration was an event in December 1927, when two radiators in the gallery burst with the cold. One of these was embedded in the brick wall supporting the ramp, and a major operation proved necessary to dig it out and replace it. La Roche considered that this was the moment to face up to the various unfinished features of the gallery, including the lighting system, the provision of bookshelves and storage and the placing of a divan bed near the fireplace (effectively blocking off the French window looking onto the acacia terrace). The central heating could be boosted by simultaneously re-siting the radiators.

The parquet, which a friend of La Roche's had declared *infect* was also removed, to be replaced by pink rubber carpeting supplied by Electro-Cable. The same firm provided a new carpet for the ramp, in grey. A luxurious table, immovably fixed to the floor by a tiled support and 'V' shaped tubular steel brace, was designed, probably by Charlotte Perriand, and supplied with a marble top. The wall and its walk-in cupboard, under the ramp, was removed and a fitment with curving frosted glass sliding doors built in its place. As originally designed, this would have included a large, hinged bookcase running on rollers (FLC 15248). Finally, a lighting trough supported on great tubular steel arms with bulbs reflecting both upwards and downwards, was installed along the right-hand wall. This supplied the gallery with the lighting La Roche had demanded for so long.

This is what was carried out, but the drawings reveal a story of changing intentions and alternative proposals. Several drawings detail a composite divan fitment which would have projected into the space of the gallery (FLC 15188). An estimate of 32,900 francs for all these changes was offered to La Roche in February 1928 and there is a set of drawings to accompany these. As usual, the estimate turned out to be optimistic, and by November 1928, 50,986 francs had been spent.

The lighting trough solution (FLC 15284) involved the use of 24 light bulbs, each of 25 watt, and must be seen as comparable to the lighting fitment of the Villa Savoye salon of one year later. The overall lighting level of the gallery was enormously boosted by the gallery fitment, and numerous lights were also added further, to a total wattage of 1,075 watts.

La Roche payed generously and regularly to maintain his house in reasonable order. Between 1929 and 1938, sums regularly averaging 10,000 francs a year were spent repairing windows, leaking roots and a

19. Dossier La Roche, Doc. 431, 9 May 1925.

lamentable succession of central heating systems. Large
sums were spent in 1931–32 installing a new oil-fired
Wayne boiler, with its oil storage tank. This fared little
better than the old coal-filled boiler originally installed,
and La Roche complained, on 23 March 1934, of the
smell, noise and low heat output of the new device. Yet
another appliance was installed in 1939. In 1936, the
cold and condensation in the gallery led to an integral
insulation of walls and ceiling with *isorel* panels, which
somewhat spoiled the purity of the surfaces, with their
intrusive beading dividers. Despite these alterations,
the La Roche house is the best preserved of the 1920s
villas, a tribute to the care and dedication of Le
Corbusier's most loyal patron.

53. Perspective of the
La Roche gallery
showing the table,
divan, lighting trough
and original version of
the shelves under the
ramp, January–April
1928 (FLC 15290)

54. Part of the living room in the Jeanneret-Raaf house

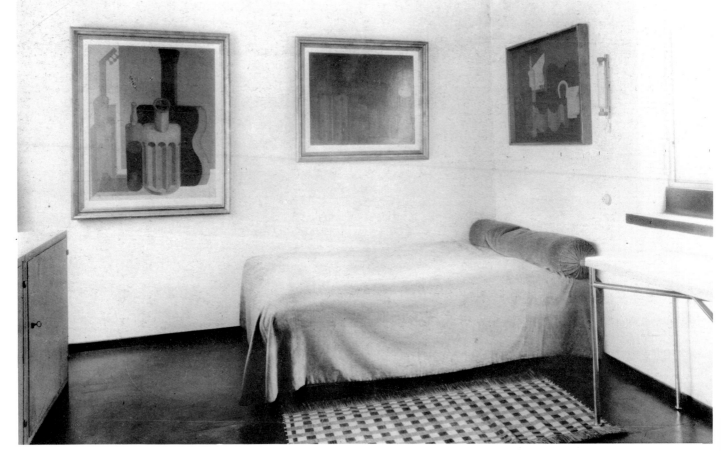

55. La Roche's bedroom, with paintings by Le Corbusier and Ozenfant.

74

56. Jeanneret-Raaf living room with painting by Bauchant.

57. La Roche picture gallery, taken in 1926, showing makeshift lighting arrangements.

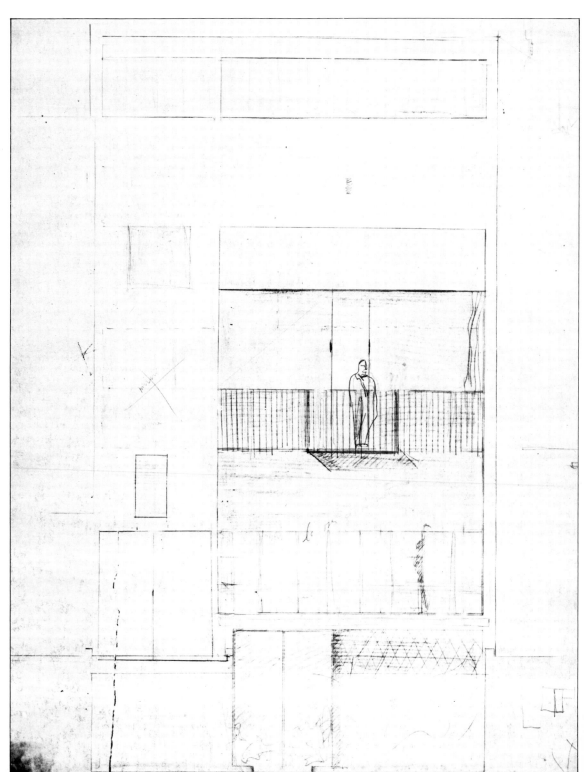

58. North-east
elevation of the house
projected for Mr. Casa
Fuerte, adjoining the
Jeanneret-Raaf house,
January 1925
(FLC 23044)

LIPCHITZ– MIESTCHANINOFF STUDIOS

Le Corbusier knew the sculptors Lipchitz and Miestchaninoff well; it has been asserted that Lipchitz and Le Corbusier spent a holiday together in Brittany. All these men, too, were involved in purchases of paintings for the La Roche collection, especially from the four sales of the Kahnweiler collection in 1921–23. Although the brief might have appeared similar to that of the atelier Ozenfant, the differences in the site led to quite different considerations and results. Because the site was open to the garden side, as well as to the street, Le Corbusier was able to place the studios at ground level, virtually essential for sculptors of large pieces anyway, with the living accomodation above (the opposite of the Ozenfant solution). But the differences between the two projects, separated in conception by only one year, are more profound than this. The Lipchitz and Miestchaninoff studios are themselves sculpturally modulated and robust, compared to the glazed fragility of the Ozenfant studio. It is difficult to avoid the conclusion that these studios included a response to the language of sculpture. Another important ingredient in the iconography of these houses is the notion of the artist's colony which ties the three houses into a sculptural unity in the early projects. An intriguing aspect of the developing composition is the use of rhyming and matching forms which enable the houses to be read as 'similar' despite very obvious differences in the plan form and details of elevation.

Two drawings (FLC 9205, 30328) which, as we have seen, must have been drawn around May 1923, (because of the transitional stage of the design of the houses in Auteil) show two houses on the Boulogne site, in the positions to be occupied by the Lipchitz and Miestchaninoff studios. The third site is shown vacant, and for sale. This drawing, unlike the one of the Auteuil site, was included in L'Esprit Nouveau (No. 18, November 1923), suggesting that, unlike the case at Auteuil, the missing client had still not been found. Little can be deduced from the outline plans of the Lipchitz and Miestchaninoff houses: they show what looks like a twin domestic block linked to a free-standing studio block, in a mirror-image arrangement. No surviving plans detail this version of the scheme, and it may well have been nothing more than a schematic indication.

It seems, therefore, that some idea for three houses on the Boulogne site was in hand in the summer of 1923, that Canale emerges as the third client at some

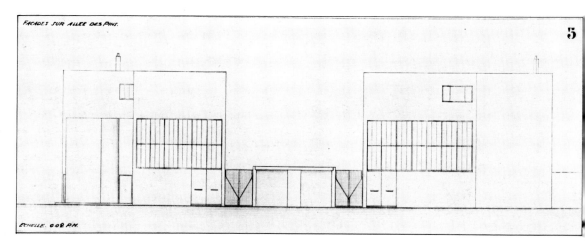

FACADES SUR ALLEE DES PINS.

5

ECHELLE. 0 0 2 P.M.

68. Elevation of Lipchitz (right) and Miestchaninoff (left) studios on the allée des Pins, first variant of the three studio scheme (including the Canale studio), c. January 1924 (FLC 8051)

point after November, and that serious design of the project only began after this date, since the first plans are for three houses. The semi-detached house plan shown in FLC 9205 is a simple repetition of the arrangement of the twin houses on the right of the private road in the early versions of the Auteuil project. This is significant, since the first set of drawings for Boulogne incorporates a remarkable degree of symmetry in the street frontage (FLC 8051). The strategy adopted was to place the living accomodation above and to one side of the studio blocks, with garages in between (as at Auteuil). The third house, for Canale, took the general form of the Vaucresson house, a long rectangle with staircase expressed in line, separated by a vertical window – 'utilising the largest dimension'.

On further analysis, the three houses in this first project are all variations on a theme, complicated by the irregular site; the theme of an exemplary display of alternative combinations of repeated elements: studio, staircase, living level. The Canale house is the simplest – a double-height atelier flanked by the stairs on one side and the garage on the other, with a mezzanine level for the maid's room, and the living area above, complete as a self-contained apartment. An important feature of this linear design was a long terrace overlooking the garden, providing some variety in the garden profile. The Lipchitz villa was complicated by being bent around an oblique angle, and by the partial enclosure of the 'expressed' staircase. In the first project (FLC 8059–62 and 8051, see p. 90), therefore, the organization of the Lipchitz villa was closer to the Canale solution than in the later versions, including the provision of a first floor terrace, enriched principally by the site and by the rounded end of the staircase and the overhangs associated with it. The Miestchaninoff solution preserved the simplicity of a cubic studio block,

with living quarters above, but the 'corner solution' was developed with the help of a staircase bent round at right angles, faced with a vertical curved columnar device which turns out to contain a water-closet, and a spectacular cantilever kitchen and servery on the top floor. Taken together, the three houses display 'what one can do' with the elements of the brief and the developing language of Le Corbusier's architectural vocabulary.

The drawings for the first project are numbered 1–8, those for the second project 9–17 (FLC 8063–5, see p. 91). The drawings for the second project must have followed almost immediately after the first. The main change was to enlarge the Miestchaninoff atelier and move it closer to the Lipchitz house, while converting the open space to the right of the Lipchitz house into a second, smaller studio. The garage lost by moving the houses closer together was resited next to the Canale house, and the complexity of the Miestchaninoff staircase was modified by incorporating it into the body of the house. It was in this second project that the extraordinary feature of the high level *passerelle* was introduced, extending the high level living area in the direction of the Canale house. The plans show clearly that there was never any intention to open any throughway onto the Canale terrace, but the *passerelle* does seem to perform a symbolic role of unifying the livng spaces of Miestchaninoff and Canale, while also embracing the garage in its new location. In virtually every other respect, the second project repeats the solutions of the first.

Two tenders were submitted for the three houses in January 1924, and we must assume that the second project formed the basis of these tenders. Kuntz and Pigeard, who also tendered for the La Roche house at this same date and who built the nearby Ternisien studio house shortly afterwards, submitted an estimate

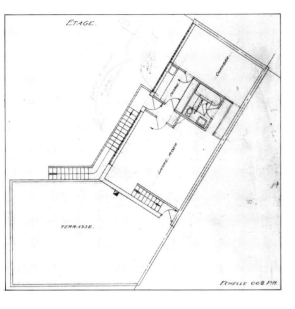

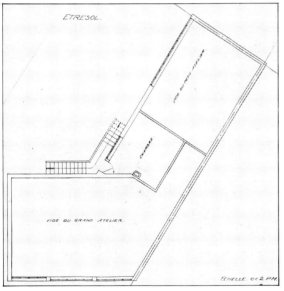

development of a dramatic rounded staircase tower, projecting as a turret on the corner, and the cantilevering of the living quarters towards the garden front, thus emphasising the notion of an independent living area detached from the studio below (see p. 113). Another element of drama was added by a store room tacked on to the back of the garage, with a triangular shed roof.

The Lipchitz studio house, however, went through two further stages of design, which changed the character of the architecture notably. The main problem was how to remove the top storey and achieve a compaction of the organs within the reduced volume. In order to fit in the living quarters, the staircase had to be removed from the interior space. Two solutions were tried. In the first variant, an open concrete stair, like those at Pessac, was tried (FLC 8014–6). The living area occupied the whole of the side block, over the little studio. An additional bedroom was suspended as a mezzanine in the space adjoining the big studio, with access from an external landing on the external

69. Lipchitz studio, floor plans of the intermediary project, c. 15 March 1924 (FLC 8016, 8015, 8014)

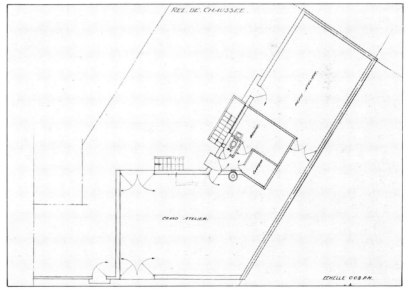

on 30 January 1924, for the three houses (112,040; 123,790; and 134,290 francs respectively). Summer's estimate, of 23 January 1924 for the three houses came out at 110,800, 95,300 and 106,700 francs respectively, but Pierre Jeanneret clearly thought this excessive and preferred to use Summer for the Auteuil site only. The tenders were submitted to the clients on 23 February, 1924. There was a delay until March 1924, during which time Canale dropped out for some time. Kuntz and Pigeard were contracted to build the two houses in March. In the March schemes for the houses, the Miestchaninoff property changed least, except for the

staircase. Lipchitz himself seems to have caused this design to be changed, after refusing to accept an external staircase as the only access to his apartment from the atelier. Kuntz and Pigeard refer to this design change in their modified tender of 15 March.

The idea of an external spiral staircase, forming a 'hinge' on the re-entrant corner, was suggested in an outline correction (FLC 8014) and this was the solution adopted in the next variant (FLC 8048–9 and 7876, see p. 113) and the final solution (FLC 8018 and 8043).

One consequence of the reduction in height of the Lipchitz block was to put stress on the symmetry of the

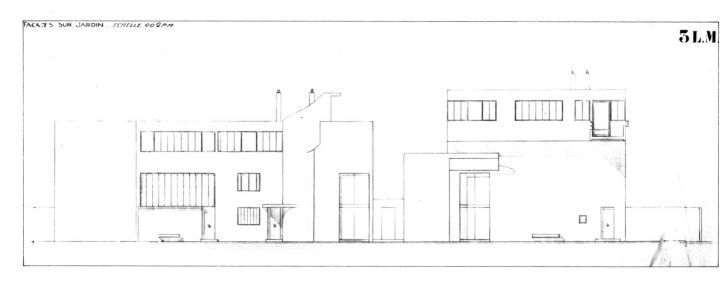

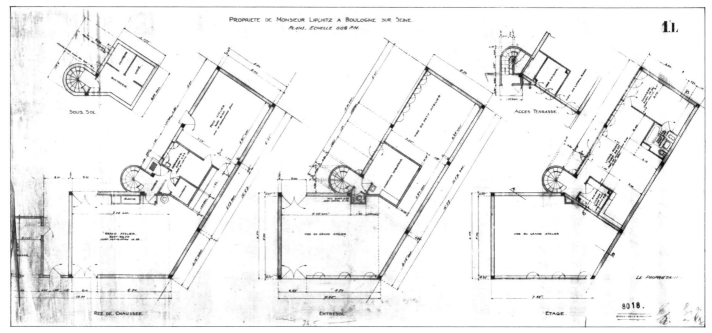

70. Top: Garden front of the Lipchitz (left) and Miestchaninoff (right) studios, 15–19 March 1924 (FLC 8049)

71. Above: Floor plans of the Lipchitz studio in its nearly finished state, April 1924 (FLC 8018)

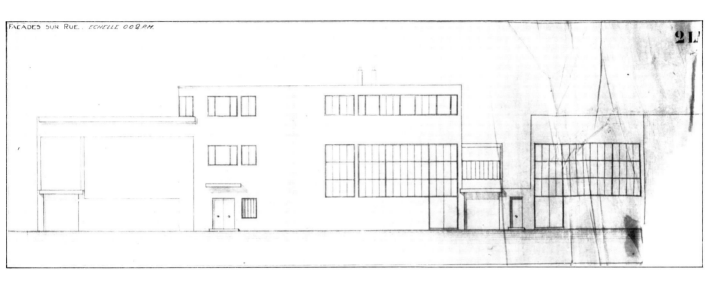

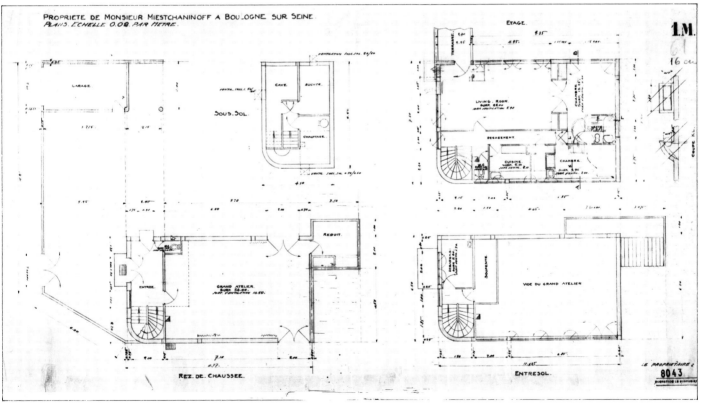

72. Top: Street front of the Lipchitz (right) and Miestchaninoff (left) studios, 15–19 March 1924 (FLC 8048)

73. Above: Floor plans of the Miestchaninoff studio, nearly as built, April 1924 (FLC 8043)

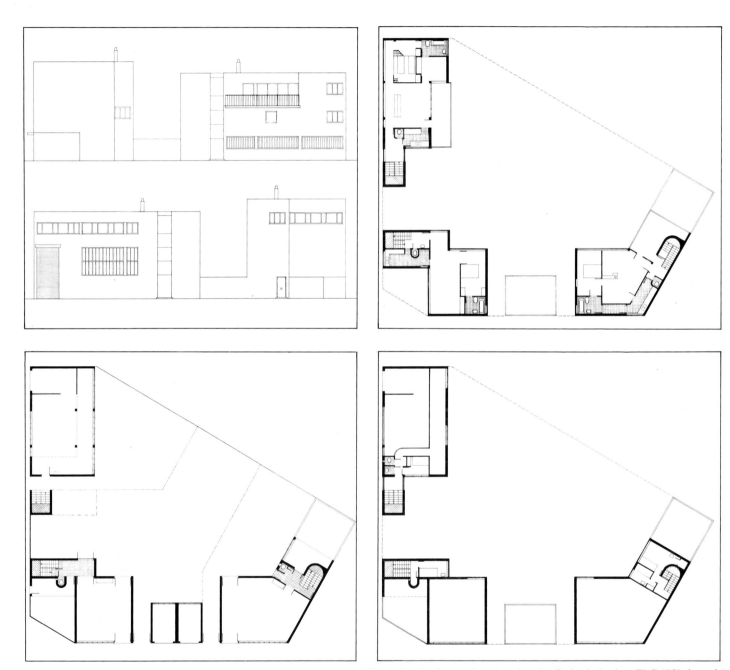

74. Redrawn elevations and plans of the studios for Lipchitz, Miestchaninoff and Canale, first project, based on Le Corbusier's plans FLC 8059 through 8062, January 1924

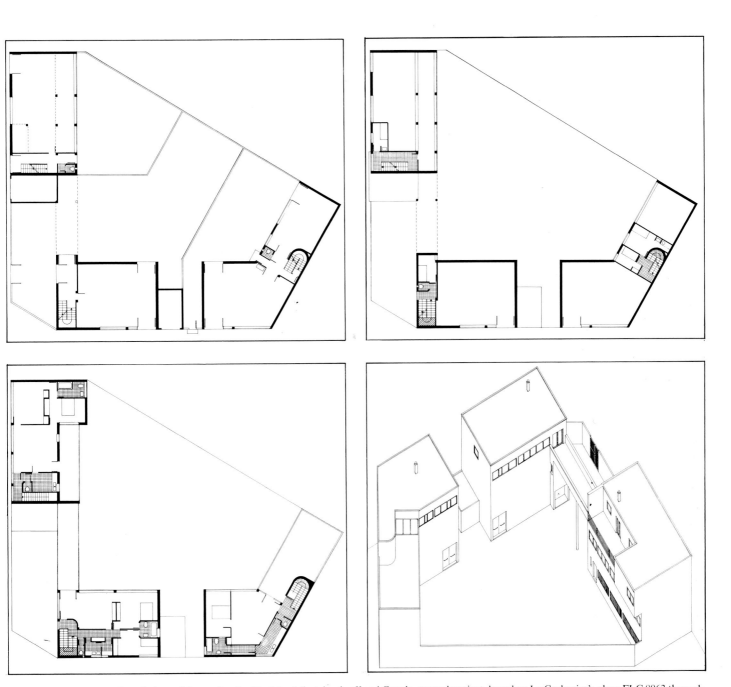

75. Redrawn axonometric and plans of the studios for Lipchitz, Miestchaninoff and Canale, second project, based on Le Corbusier's plans FLC 8063 through 8065, January 1924

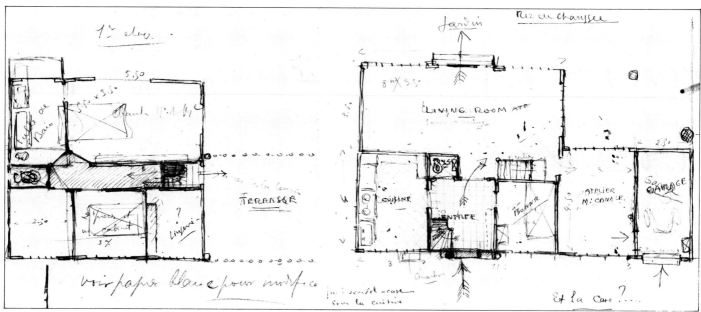

76. Top: Perspective, elevation and plan probably for a later
scheme for the Canale studio, 1926–7 (FLC 8172)

77. Above: First and ground floor plans of a project for the
Canale studio, 1926–7 (FLC 7954 and 7955)

street frontage of the Miestchaninoff and Lipchitz houses. Le Corbusier replaced the close symmetry of the two ateliers, by a set of matching rhythms which can be deduced from close observation of the whole. The two buildings help to explain each other. For example, the very clear expression of the living quarters in the Miestchaninoff house, cantilevered out from the garden front, help us to read the much more complex and compacted insertion of the living area in the body of the Lipchitz house, one storey below.

The more or less definitive drawings for the Lipchitz and Miestchaninoff houses are dated '18 March 1924' and '19 III 24' (FLC 8048–9). Estimates were sent to the client on 25 April and agreed upon. The concrete construction plans were prepared during May and June, when construction seems to have begun. Two of Kuntz and Pigeard's drawings are dated 26 May and 30 June 1924.

The houses were completed in the spring of 1925, with the usual delays occasioned by design changes. A protracted dispute with Roneo over the supply of metal doors for the two studios (as for the La Roche, Jeanneret and Ternisien houses), continued through 1925, with the architects refusing to pay the full bill, due to damage caused to the doors by their being left out in the rain on delivery, and disputes over errors in dimensioning which had caused expensive repairs and adjustment. Some of the late modifications involved the strengthening of the roof of the Miestchaninoff atelier, alterations in the flower-beds and concrete fitments, and the addition of a cornice to the Lipchitz studio (on which the client had insisted (26 April 1924), wishing to have the same as the Ozenfant studio). It is noteworthy that Kuntz and Pigeard refused to guarantee the waterproof properties of the roof slabs of both buildings, considering that the system advocated in the building programme (two coats of Pitcholine and six centimetres of gravel) was inadequate and inferior to the more expensive system advocated by themselves. It is not known how expensive any repairs to these roof slabs might have been.

Although Canale had dropped out as a firm client after January 1924, the project was resurrected in 1926–27 (FLC 8172 and 7954). A complete set of plans and elevations was prepared in May–June 1927 (FLC 7867–70). The house later built on this site, however, was not to Le Corbusier's plans.

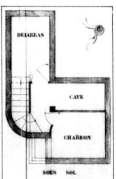

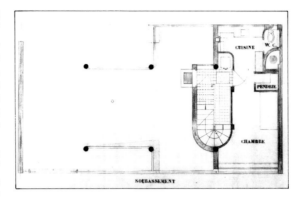

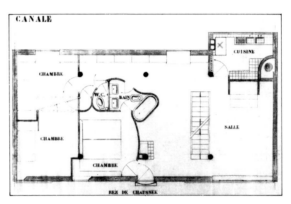

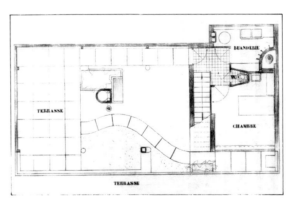

78. Canale studio project, definitive version, May–June 1927: ground floor, cellar, first and roof terrace plans. Note the tree trunk accommodated in the top right corner of each plan. (FLC 7867 through 7870)

79. Ternisien house, Boulogne-sur-Seine. Bird's eye view sketch of a proposal to double the height of the music room, 8 December 1926 (FLC 7941)

94

TERNISIEN HOUSE

An out of the ordinary problem, a wager, a *jeu de l'esprit*: how to exploit a site with a particularly difficult form.[1]

If this commission began as a *jeu de l'esprit*, it was a game which backfired, a fantasy which turned sour. Paul Ternisien, a musician, and his artist wife, apparently approached Le Corbusier:

> It was M. and Mme Ternisien who, after my Sorbonne lecture in 1923, insisted that we should undertake their plan. Dealt with by us as friends, they later came to inform us that they had new funds at their disposal and wanted us immediately to build an extension onto their house.[2]

By the time this letter was written in 1932, clients, architects and builders were involved in a legal dispute which was to culminate in Ternisien's bankrupcy and, in a bizarre sequel, the demolition of the house (apart from relics of the walls on the corner) and the construction of the present block of flats on top by the modernistic architect Georges-Henri Pingusson (1932–6). In another weird tailpiece to the story, Le Corbusier's refusal to pay the fees (2,192.50 francs) of the *architecte expert* consulted during the trial, led to a running battle which continued until 1939, when a bailiff actually laid claim to drawing equipment, plans and furniture in the rue de Sèvres atelier to the value stipulated. In the end, Le Corbusier payed the first instalment of these fees on 23 March 1939.

It is unclear, in this sorry story, how innocent the Ternisiens were in business matters. For example, they managed to persuade the debt-collector in 1938 that, despite having sold their property for the construction of Pingusson's block of flats, they remained bankrupt. It seemed that Mme Ternisien was forced to perform in a music hall to make ends meet (Doc. 91 20 May 1938).

It is certainly clear that Paul Ternisien was the more innocent of the two, and that it was Mme Ternisien who made all the decisions on money matters. She seems, also, to have been an unstable and emotional character, filling her letters with gratuitous rudeness from the period at the end of December 1927 that she fell out with Le Corbusier and the patient Pierre. For the flavour of these exchanges:

> I reproach you too for having rather abused the situation. You know that, at the wish of my husband, it was I who should take charge of everything...my husband told you himself, his artistic temperament renders him incompetent and defenceless in all questions of money. Yet you addressed yourself to him during one of my short absences...[3]

Six months later, the tone was even more strident.

> I would appreciate it if you would stop impeding my husband from coming to join me by pressurising him so. No decision will be taken before my return and the consequent examination of our position and your plans. I have written to my husband that, if you make any decisions at all in my absence, not only would I refuse to be involved in any way, which would make you very happy, but I will never return to a house which has not been made to please me. Are you prepared to carry this responsibility?[4]

One point which does emerge from the arguments around December 1927, was that, as in many other cases which we have looked at, Le Corbusier and Pierre were casual over the accounts. Although the house seems to have been largely built during the autumn of 1925 and the first half of 1926, Pierre presented no accounts to Mme Ternisien until December 1927, by which time several of the contractors were threatening to prosecute the Ternisiens for non-payment of long overdue bills. She blamed Pierre for this, with some justification, it seems.

> You have been seriously in the wrong in giving us accounts by word of mouth or letter without giving us full information. We have believed you to be well informed and sure of yourself, but we were wrong.[5]

1. Le Corbusier, *Oeuvre Complète*, I, p. 122.
2. Dossier Ternisien, Docs, 61 and 64, 8 July 1932.
3. Dossier Ternisien, Doc. 19 n.d. (c. January 1928).
4. Dossier Ternisien, Doc. 25, 25 September 1928.
5. Dossier Ternisien, Doc. 18, 2 January 1928.

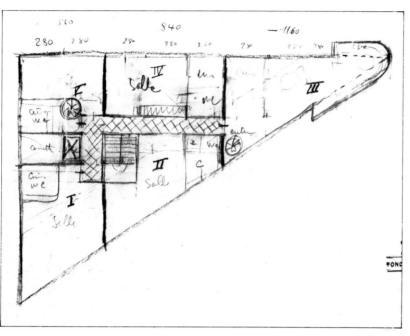

80. Schematic plan for five studio apartments on the Ternisien site, 1924 ? (FLC 7948)

This letter, and the circumstances of the legal battle of 1932–3 may help to explain why the documentation of this house is so uneven in its contents. Only a few tantalising scraps provide any references to the period during 1925 and 1926 when the house was being designed and built. The matter is compounded by lacunae in the dated drawings. The first matter to specify is when exactly construction started. Pierre remembered the construction as follows:

> Construction carried out during 1925 for Monsieur P. Ternisien, 5, allée des Pins at Boulogne-sur-Seine, by a masonry and reinforced concrete firm unaccustomed to our buildings, this with the agreement of Mr Ternisien, who did not want to exceed a certain price which only this firm could meet.[6]

Kuntz et Pigeard, the mason, had indeed tendered for a number of other Le Corbusier buildings, and had built the Lipchitz and Miestchaninoff studios a few doors down the allée des Pins. We must assume that some of the points made in these letters involved in the legal action exaggerated the culpability of the clients. On the question of the date of construction, there are some accounts from Pasquier (plumbing and central heating). which show that the main payment was made on 15 June 1925. One would expect this to correspond to the advance payment made at the outset of building work. Two other sizeable payments to Pasquier were made in August and December 1925. Fittings and furniture were being supplied by Selmersheim and Monteil in February 1926, including what looks like the front door. Payments to Lucien Bled, the painter and glazier on this job, stretch from October 1925 to October 1926, not counting the frequent later repaintings and repairs. This information is consistent with an agreement between architects and clients around May–June 1925, contracts with the entrepreneurs of the same date, and a finished house, in its essentials by the summer of 1926.

As for evidence of the drawings, a complicating factor is that the set of definitive drawings (FLC 7892–6, see pp. 100–1) which can be dated precisely, from their stencilled atelier numbers (Nos. 643–7), turn out to have been much too late (March 1926) to represent the contract drawings. All these drawings, therefore, must be seen as being produced for publication purposes. To establish which drawings were used for the contracts with builder and contractors, and how the sequence of preliminary drawings must be interpreted, we will have to work backwards.

These drawings show the house basically as built (May–June 1925). The design involved a clear accomodation with the site: a 'standard' studio (or Esprit Nouveau-type double-height living cell) on the left, for Mme Ternisien, is linked by a functional middle section for Paul Ternisien, the musician. A bedroom and shower are squeezed with some difficulty into the sharp end of this acute angled space. On the first floor, only the functional central section, and the bedroom looking down into the double height atelier, remain, although it was part of the plan of this scheme that the staircase which projects its diagonal onto the exterior could be enclosed by a filling out of the first floor over the 'piano-shaped' section and an extra storey over the atelier. The house is meant to be read as extendable, and the elevation (FLC 7894) seems to have been designed to emphasise the potential for transformation. The section (FLC 7896) emphasises the transitory nature and wayward quality of the design.

A drawing (FLC 7909, probably from the end of 1927), shows two ideas for the extension of the house, not only building over the atelier and over the 'piano-shaped' part, but also adding two rooms at the far end of the atelier. Another plan (FLC 7911) also records a scheme for building over the whole area of the house. Yet another scheme consisted of a more modest operation, in November and December 1926, doubling up on the 'piano-shaped' part but leaving the atelier untouched (including FLC 7941, dated '8 Dec 1926'). The bird's-eye view of this scheme, represents what, to

6. Dossier Ternisien, Doc. 37, 2 February 1932.

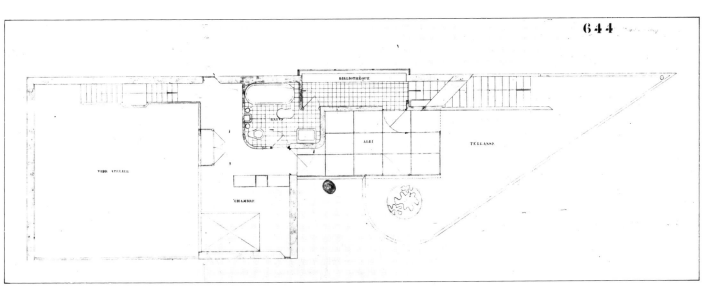

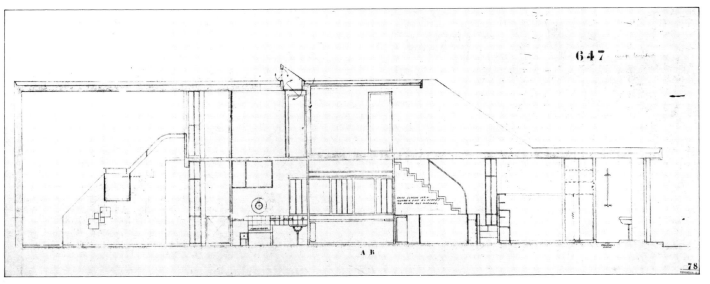

planning authorities of Boulogne. Fleury eventually prepared a large dossier for the *architecte expert* Viet (not the same as the builder of the Ozenfant studio), who estimated necessary repairs at 49,196.87 francs, to be put at the door of Le Corbusier and his builder. Kuntz et Pigeard responded with a brief statement contesting most of the allegations of structural failure, although some necessary repair work certainly was needed, including the remaking of one of the corner piers and sections of the roof slab and terraces. The *jeu d'esprit* was to haunt Le Corbusier, but the evidence shows that, in this case at least, the clients were at least partly to blame.

A rueful Le Corbusier summed up the situation in this way:

> We were payed 4,500 francs in fees for M. Ternisien's house... Now that Ternisien is bankrupt, we are called on to pay his debts, that is to subtract 2,192.50 francs from the 4,500 francs which represents payment for our labour.[10]

10. Dossier Ternisien, Doc. 80, 22 February 1925.

85. Ternisien house, Boulogne-sur-Seine. First floor plan (top) and section (above) prepared for publication, December 1925 (FLC 7893 and 7896)

86. Ternisien house,
Boulogne-sur-Seine.
Garden and studio.

87. Villa Church, Ville d'Avray. Perspective sketches of first proposal for guest pavilion, 5–11 April 1927 (FLC 8186)

VILLA
CHURCH

This undertaking consists in reality of three projects for the American couple Henry and Barbara Church. The first two coincided with the construction of the Villa Stein-de Monzie, the third with the Villa Savoye. Each scheme was, to a different degree, a reconstruction or rehabilitation of an existing structure on a large estate in Ville-d'Avray. Henry Church was described as the *apporteur* of the property, but only the tenant of the buildings constructed on it, which belonged to a company called the Société 'La Mavraysienne'. The administrator of this society was M. Moreau-Lalande, with whom much of the correspondence took place. A bird's-eye view (FLC 8078) shows the two adjoining properties which made up the site: to the south (top) the main house inhabited by the Church household, with a stable block to the west (top right). To the north and at a lower level was a neo-classical pavilion (bottom left), which belonged to the separate property. This drawing, made in late 1927 or, more probably, in 1928, shows the work on the stables and the small pavilion in progress, but nothing begun on the main house.

To make sense of these three ventures, and disentangle their chronology, we must give a succinct account of the main events. We will use the nomenclature employed by Pierre and Le Corbusier to distinguish the buildings: 'Bâtiment A' (or Bâtiment haut) for the stable block, 'Bâtiment B' (or Bâtiment du bas) for the pavilion on the lower property, and 'Bâtiment C' for the main house. The first project, to which I shall return, was mooted in April 1927 and in construction by the autumn.

The history of the second project, the restoration and partial reconstruction of the pavilion (Bâtiment B), took longer to get started. The first drawings, and the preliminary tenders came in July, 1927, but these were substantially altered in September, when two quite radically different schemes were proposed (a 'large' and 'small' version, and a compromise). The large version was costed at around 297,600 francs in one estimate, or 258,700 francs in another (15 September 1927); the smaller one at 202,200 francs (17 September 1927). The final collection of tenders and estimate was apparently agreed to by Moreau-Lalande in October, but not sent off to the client until December 1927, by which time the figure proposed was 304,200 francs (27 December 1927). Construction proceeded fitfully through 1928, with completion being around March 1929, when Church claims that only the lighting and bookshelves were needed for completion.

When it came to discuss the third project, the extensions to the main building, Church insisted that the music pavilion (B) should be finished first and that the architects should undertake the designs and estimates at their own risk, making no charge if the designs were rejected (19 March 1929). A set of drawings were sent to Church in March, but Moreau-Lalande reported that Church would not consider them unless the estimate could be substantially reduced. It appears from a later letter (Doc. 94, 2 June 1929), that a figure of 450,000 francs had been mentioned, and a set of calculations of areas and costs arriving at this figure has survived. Le Corbusier agreed to try to reduce this (25 April 1929). Not until the accounts for the first two houses were settled, (after 26 June, 1929), did progress on the third undertaking show itself.

All this helps to set the scene for the agreed programme of 28 June, 1929, in which Pierre modified the more ambitious plans of March in the light of a list of requirements supplied by the client. After further revisions, including some illuminating criticisms of the June drawings (5 July 1929) and a price limit set at 320,000 francs, a set of plans was, apparently, agreed to before the architects' departure on holiday in August. Moreau-Lalande tried to make Pierre secure signatures from all the entrepreneurs to a binding statement limiting them to a given sum and deadline (26 August 1929), but there is no sign that this was done.

The subsequent history of this building is complicated by the fact that neither Pierre Jeanneret nor Moreau-Lalande seems to have been effectively in charge of operations, and the records have few documents. As a token of this, Moreau-Lalande tried to reduce the architects' fees, from ten to seven per cent (May 1931). The documentation does show clearly that the third undertaking for the Church properties was carried out at a different level of control and, indeed, design input by Le Corbusier and Pierre Jeanneret. A large amount of work was carried out by Summer on the estate as a whole, none of which seems to have been formally presented to either Church or Moreau-Lalande for agreement. And the whole process of managing the redecoration of the interior of the old house seems to have been left to Mrs Church to supervise. Consequently, I will concentrate on the first two projects, and the preliminary drawings only for the third.

On 19 December 1928, Le Corbusier wrote out a description of the work at Ville-d'Avray, no doubt intending to publish it in the edition of the Morance album which featured the two buildings A and B. Here are some extracts from this illuminating text:

> Over a hundred years ago, some bourgeois people built decent and simple dwellings in the outskirts of Paris and surrounded them with gardens in which they had a pleasurable life. In the present case of the Church property at Ville-d'Avray, the problem situated in the above mentioned terms was markedly complicated by the fact that the original property dominated by the old house reproduced here has been extended by the purchase of a second property. Now, as good neighbours, the two original owners had used high boundary walls to build up terraces and planatations which have turned into fully grown trees, an impenetrable obstacle.
>
> What was needed here, then, first of all, was the unification of the two properties: landscape gardening. We cut down the high hedges which covered the edge of the second property with shadow and we pruned the trees. We demolished the high boundary walls. We excavated earth from some places and built it up in others, so that the lawn of the first property runs up to that of the second without a break. And since, despite everything, there was still a considerable difference of level to the right of the ruins of the second house, the architects had recourse to ingenuity: they threw a concrete walkway across this great gap, so that access to the second house is made *from the roof*.
>
> The establishment of the walkway allowed one to *see* the second property. To see, also, the large parterre of flowers (laid out like lace) on the *south* side the very side which originally had been the back of the house. Beside the old house where the owners live, the architects used the substructure of a demolished stable wing to create a *'Summer house' for guests*. The bedrooms are like an intimate inn while, for recreation, there is a great Hall-Salon and dining room, flooded with light and opening its North bay window to the tree-covered horizons of Ville-d'Avray. From the library, considered as an attic storey, you pass through to an astonishing roof garden sparkling with flowers.[1]

What is remarkable about this account is the dual insistence on the continuity of history (side by side with radical change) and the leitmotif of natural, organic growth and the use of plants and trees. When we come to study the drawings, it is important to bear in mind this *paysagiste* strand running through all the designs, and the profound sense of continuity with the neo-classical buildings.

To return to the beginning of the story, the plans of the English architects Falconer, Baker and Campbell of the mainhouse and outhouses have survived (FLC 8109–11). It seems that Le Corbusier's first solution (FLC 8080, see pp. 50–1) was to leave the substructure of the main block untouched, concentrating on the block at the southern end and a roof garden in concrete running right along the top of the main block. On 5 April 1927, Le Corbusier sent Church two sheets of sketches (FLC 8186, 8067), of the attractive kind often shown to clients to prompt a quick response to which can be associated an elevation sketch (FLC 8082). These have in common the selection of the central section of the stable block, symmetrical and tripartite in the original, as a rigorously formalised and classical motif, facing across towards the old house. The perspective sketches show the declaratory power of the big Citrohan window of the salon and the stark 'T' shape of the guest wing, both intended to be seen from a distance in juxtaposition to the main house. A set of drawings traces the gradual metamorphosis of this solution towards a more or less complete rebuilding of the whole complex. The idea of the suspended concrete garden above the old building is transformed into a suspended first floor *fenêtre en longeur*, housing the guests' rooms.

It can have been on the basis of little more than these presentation sketches that Pierre drew up estimates (230,410 francs) for the cost of carrying out the work on building A, on 11 April. After Church had specified some additional features, Le Corbusier wrote to Church with an estimate of 300,000 francs, on 21 April, but reserving five to ten per cent as a margin for eventualities. Church replied (with the cheque for the first 10,000 francs fees) that this sum was far too high (25 April 1927). Thus began the strained relations between client and architects, with the relationship deteriorating as the actual costs rapidly mounted. After the radical

1. Dossier Church, Docs. 211–4, 19 December, 1928.

redesigning of the project in May and June, the contracts issued to the entrepreneurs already came to over the substantial 405,500 francs, (23 June 1927), while the further revisions to the plans, of June and September, (plus the usual unforeseen circumstances), led to the agreed eventual cost of 502,985 francs (March 1929).

In Church's letter of 25 April 1927, he asked for a new set of plans in which the changes he had asked for could be assessed. These plans duly materialised in May (FLC 8195, 8198, 12 May see p. 112). Matters are complicated by the fact that a number of minor adjustments in the design were carried out during May, using these drawings as the basis, and often preserving the same atelier numbers and dates. What emerged from this work during May was a scheme with a clearly expressed spiral staircase in the servants' quarters and an external staircase from the roof of the main block down onto the roof of the servants' block, where some of the drawings showed a *bain de soleil* (FLC 8198). The three guest bedrooms were, as Le Corbusier's explanation makes clear, modelled on the American apartment-hotel type. The three rooms are 'standardised' as much as possible, even to the extent of reproducing the effect of the curved wall of the shared bathroom in the water-closet of the bedroom on the left. The basic arrangement of the salon, with its staircase rising up through a double-height space to give access to the roof garden, along with the first floor dining room and adjoining kitchen, remained virtually unchanged through the subsequent redesigning process. The main changes during May and June concerned the servants' quarters, which began as a relatively short, double storey block, with a staircase contiguous to the wall of the main block and rectilinear. By 19 May, the staircase has been resolved as a spiral, clearly expressed in the exterior (FLC 8076, see pp. 50–1) and the service block has been reduced to a single storey, with its roof served by a lengthened open staircase from the main roof terrace. This latter feature was eliminated for cost-cutting reasons in June. The balcony in the middle of the guest bedroom floor appeared on 19 May and the roof terrace canopies now echo the symmetry thus invoked. The tenders were sent in between 30–31 May 1927, and these were altered and signed between 8 and 20 June 1927, including Summer's estimate.

Contracts were signed between 24 and 29 June, so many of these revisions were barely in time. In September, another round of corrections marked the beginning of construction, with plans of drainage and services, and details of the kitchens. The lighting of the dining room and aluminium cupboards were not installed until June 1928.

In Pierre Chenal's film on Le Corbusier's architecture, Church and his guests are shown exercising on the roof of Bâtiment A, and this terrace forms a definitive image of the luxurious, sun-filled existence of the modern spirit. The building has a curiously loose-fit feeling to it, partly because of the constraints of the given plan form, which allowed for a certain spreading out of functions, and partly because of the simplicity of the brief. The double-height salon, with the bridge spanning the space in front of a monumental north facing window reminds one more of the Garage Marbeuf than of any other Corbusian interior. Surprisingly, despite Le Corbusier's interest in interior design at this time, coinciding with Charlotte Perriand's arrival in the atelier in the autumn of 1927, there are no known photographs of the interiors of the Bâtiment A, and the whole scheme had a quality of rhetoric about it – a folly in the modern movement spirit, intended to be seen from the outside, rather than lived in.

The story of the Bâtiment A was that of a first flirtation with a 'dialogue' between old and new, resolved in the vent in a building which to all intents and purposes is completely new, despite the retention of the basic plan forms and some of the old walls. The refurbishing of the neo-classical pavilion (Bâtiment B) presented a different order of problems. Cost constraints were much in evidence in the design stages, no doubt exacerbated by Church's observation of Le Corbusier's attitude to estimates on Bâtiment B. A complication here was that the wooden ceiling of the ground floor of the old building had been used as formwork for a new concrete slab, installed by another builder, Villesuzanne, to the orders of a different architect, Leveque. This new roof was not fully waterproof, and as the autumn of 1927 progressed, it became urgent to at least protect the ground floor rooms from the rain. All this became the subject of litigation in 1925–6, when the ceiling began to deform and leak catastrophically, and Church tried to obtain redress from Summer and Le Corbusier.

The July scheme for Bâtiment B (FLC 8168, 8210, 8017, see p. 51) was an ambitious proposal, involving extensive changes to the ground floor plan and the north façade, as well as a completely altered façade to the South. This scheme incorporated the idea referred to in Le Corbusier's text of December 1928 – the *passerelle* to the higher ground of the neighbouring property, but this footbridge was sited differently to the finished solution. On the ground floor, large windows

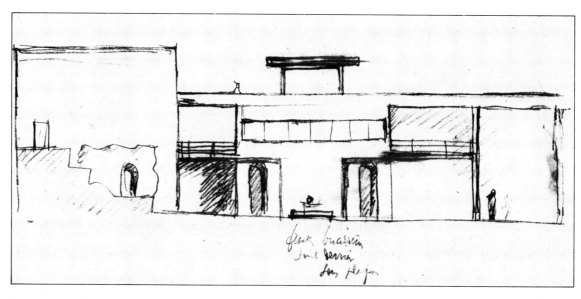

88. Villa Church, Ville d'Avray. Elevation of guest pavilion, 5–11 April 1927 (FLC 8082)

to the north would have been installed in the library and study. These were included in Louis's tender of 27 July 1927, and that of Celio along with the large glazed bay in the middle of the south side, illuminating the salon. The idea was clear enough, to give the existing masonry building a cement render skin all over while piercing large apertures in the exterior surfaces to reflect the opening out of the space inside. In the event, although the demolition of the internal partitions went ahead, the opening out of the large windows did not take place, for economy's sake. In this first scheme, however, the upper storey was treated in a minimal fashion, including only a small servery to the west, presumably for meals on the terrace, and a small room on the left which acted as lobby for the footbridge. All the rest of the upper floor was either terrace (covered or open) or space around the staircase and its landing. The impression of arriving 'by air' and descending through this space into the music salon must have been an evocative idea. The south elevation, in this first scheme, was an expressive device to highlight the space of the music room and add mystery to the route of access along the footbridge. The effect of surprise, passing through a little door in the high wall to venture on this narrow footbridge is celebrated by a viewing box, halfway along, from where the ornamental garden could be seen below. In this way, the rigidly hierarchic symmetries of the old building were given a dramatic shift by the eccentric approach, and this asymmetrical twist to the given platform was to develop progressively in each subsequent project.

After one variant which proposed to place the *passerelle* on the east side (FLC 8177), Le Corbusier worked up a scheme for Church's return from holiday,

in which the basic arrangement of the final solution was discovered: *passerelle* extended from the west side of the house before striking south to the neighbouring property, balcony in the middle over the south door and level with the landing from the stairs, the retention of the existing walls, faced with chanelled stucco and painted a dark colour (FLC 8215–6). In this version, the central balcony was treated as if it was an abbreviated *passerelle*, or as a place for one man to stand and welcome visitors. In the revisions which followed Church's return, this balcony became wider. From this point onwards, there is virtually no interest by the architects in the north front of the pavilion at ground floor level. The interior perspective of the music salon defines this space in a way which does not substantially change from now on (FLC 8075, see p. 50).

A new round of tenders, (all around 14 September), from Summer, Giullameau, Louis, Celio, seem to have been intended for this version of the project. On the last page of Summer's tender, Pierre worked out a total estimate of 258,700 francs, which he labelled 'grand project', and 'chiffres remis à M. Church'. Two days later, Summer submitted a reduced tender, on one side of paper, for a 'third' project for the Bâtiment B. On this sheet, Pierre worked out a rough sum for a reduced set of tenders, which totalled 202,000 francs, and which he labelled 'petit Project'. These words also appear on two drawings (FLC 8158, see p. 123) which show the top floor reduced to nothing but the staircase housing and one small room.

The decision was quickly taken to go for the larger scheme, which was further slightly modified by changing the pantry on the terrace into a small bedroom (21

September 1927). On the basis of this scheme a large number of drawings were made. From a drawing made after November 1927 (FLC 8165), it is clear why the *passerelle* was moved to the west end of the pavilion, so that it could line up with the terrace at the end of an orangery on the main house's property. A detail shows the connection between footbridge and orangery more clearly, and there are drawings showing a curved extension of this terrace at the point where the footbridge lands, looking down on the site of the lawns levelled down to the lower level of the pavilion. In addition to the main salon, two smaller rooms on the ground floor were refurbished, the study and the downstairs library. Two vigorously drawn axonometrics of the main staircase show details of a curved section handrail placed low down on the banister rail, as if for children. The fittings for the upstairs library, including the bookcases with their aluminium sliding fronts, do not seem to have been designed until 1928. Duflon's tender to carry them out dates from 19 March 1928. The other unfinished work was the painting, and it is clear from the correspondence that neither Henry nor Barbara Church appreciated Le Corbusier's ideas on colour. On 9 July 1928, when Celio was beginning to paint the second building, Church wrote:

> I discovered this evening that you have caused the painters working on the stable block (Building A) to paint part of the wall of the lower building in black... Needless to say, I do not want that colour anywhere at all... In the interior, I want neither blue nor umber. Please let me know if you have something else to suggest. Otherwise, we propose, with your agreement, to start from the proposition that the second building will be painted white inside and out, at any rate unless by common agreement we decide on other colours.[2]

Blue and burnt umber were the staple colours of Le Corbusier's interiors, and featured in the interior perspective of the salon on Bâtiment B (FLC 8075, see p. 50). Whether Church's antipathy for black was connected with the serious illness of his mother in January 1928 is uncertain, but the old parts of both the buildings

2. Dossier Church, Doc. 250, 9 July, 1928.

89. Villa Church, Ville d'Avray, guest pavilion. Bird's eye view of preliminary project shown to the client, 5 April 1927 (FLC 8067)

90. Following page: Roof terrace of guest Pavilion

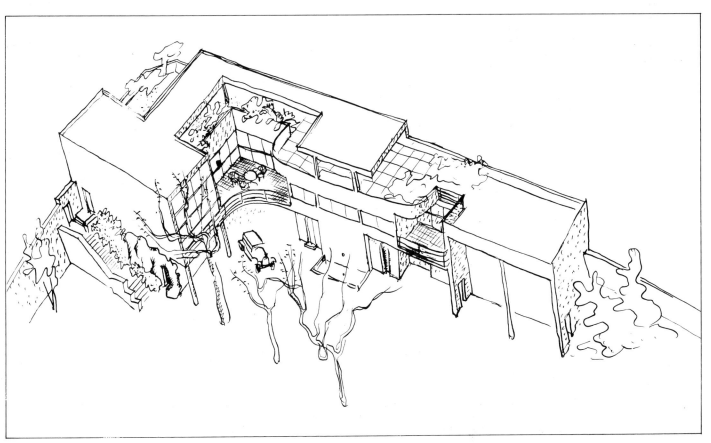

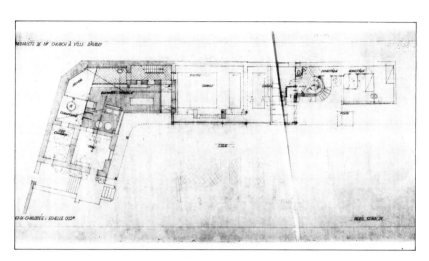

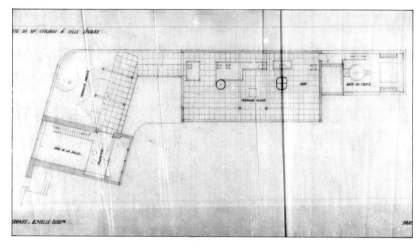

91. Villa Church, Ville d'Avray, guest pavilion. Top: Ground floor plan, intermediary project 12 May 1927 (FLC 8195)

92. Above: Second floor plan, intermediary project, 12 May 1927 (FLC 8198)

commissions from wealthy clients, but in order to keep up with the revolution of interior design in Paris which, increasingly after 1927, was taking on the glossy and glittery shine of tubular steel offset against exotic veneers and fabrics. When Pierre wrote to Church to persuade him to accept the more expensive alternative in Duflon's estimate for the cupboards (aluminium rather than tin), he gave two reasons for choosing aluminium:

1) The sliding panels will be easier to handle, due to their weight.
2) We will be dealing from the outset with a finished material, needing no painting; in addition we believe that this whole wall of aluminium in the library will make a splendid impact and will constitute the only luxury of our decorative scheme.[3]

Clearly, Pierre was exploiting not only Church's antipathy to coloured interiors, but a sophisticated notion of the term 'luxury', similar to the argument Le Corbusier used with that other American William Cook, on the plate glass windows of his house (see p. 159). The library on the first floor of Bâtiment B became earmarked by Le Corbusier to represent a showcase of modern design. All the new items of furniture designed with Charlotte Perriand were to be displayed in it, the *chaise grand confort* (about which Le Roche had complained), the *dossier basculant* and the *chaise longue*, all three marketed by Thonet, were put on show in conditions designed to show them off to best advantage.

Interestingly, Le Corbusier became involved in yet another fees dispute over precisely the question of the rights on the furniture for the library. Moreau-Lalande tried to force Le Corbusier to accept a lower royalty on the items of furniture which, although designed by the partnership, were manufactured by Thonet and were in no sense unique to the Church project. This issue clearly annoyed Le Corbusier, since he took the trouble to send Moreau-Lalande a copy of a letter from someone in New York detailing American rates of architectural fees. But in the agreed settling of account, by Moreau-Lalande in his letter of 26 June 1929, the furniture was accounted for separately (146,000 francs) on the basis of five per cent honoraires.

The early stage of the third undertaking for Mr and Mrs Church, the proposed revision of the main house

A and B were painted in dark green, rather than black, which corresponds to coloured renderings of the exterior of Bâtiment A made considerably before this dispute (FLC 8076, see p. 50).

A comparison between the coloured rendering of the grand salon in Bâtiment B, before the introduction of the aluminium faced fitments under the windows, and the photographs of the upstairs library, with its wall of aluminium bookcases, represents a major shift in Le Corbusier's aesthetic of interior decoration.

The effect of working on a succession of luxury house projects had certainly worked a change in Le Corbusier's attitudes to interior design. The 'problem of luxury' had to be faced, not only for extracting large

3. Dossier Church, Doc. 185, 18 June, 1928.

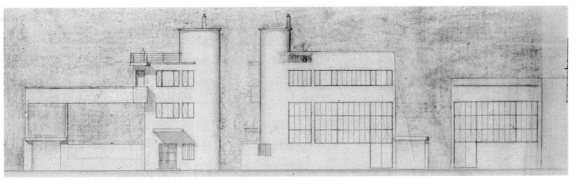

7. Atelier/Studio Miestchaninoff (FLC 8058)

7876

FONDATION LE CORBUSIER

8. Atelier/Studio Miestchaninoff (FLC 7876)

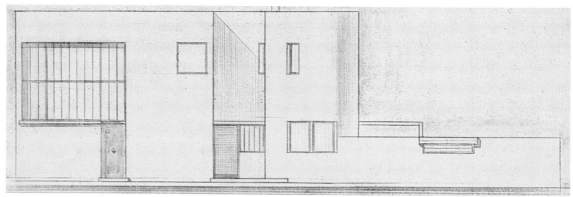

9. Maison/House/Haus Ternisien (FLC 7918)

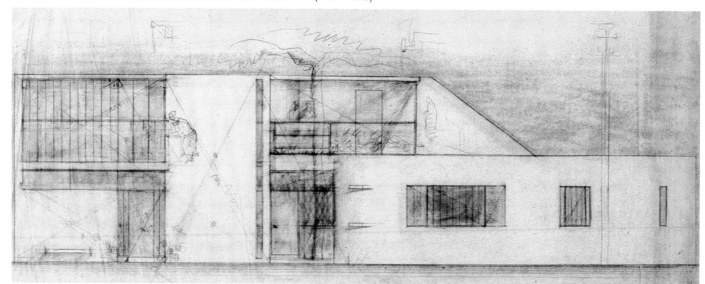

10. Maison/House/Haus Ternisien (FLC 7942)

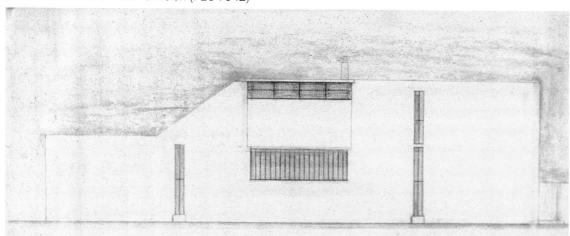

11. Maison/House/Haus Ternisien (FLC 7903)

12. Maison/House/Haus Ternisien (FLC 31573)

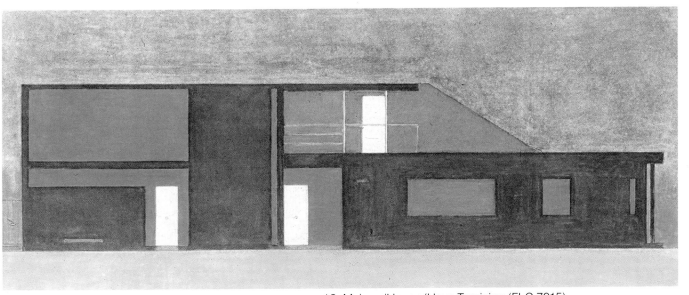

13. Maison/House/Haus Ternisien (FLC 7915)

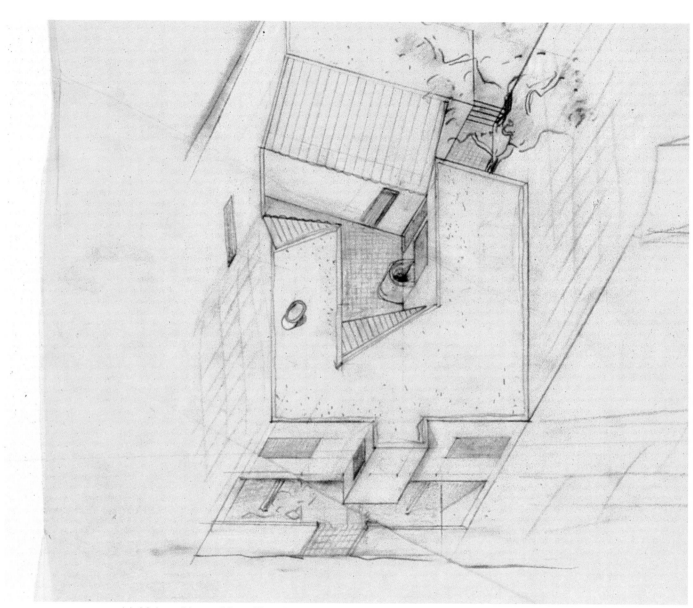

14. Maison/House/Haus Planeix (FLC 8908)

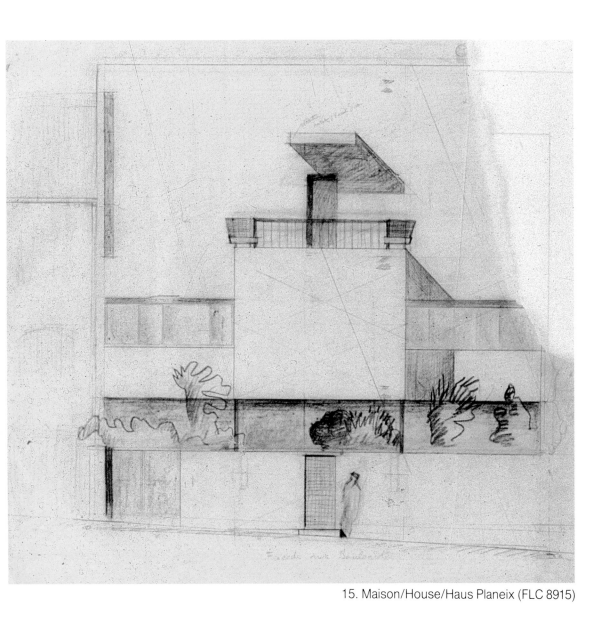

15. Maison/House/Haus Planeix (FLC 8915)

16. Villa Cook (FLC 8350)

17. Villa Cook (FLC 8309)

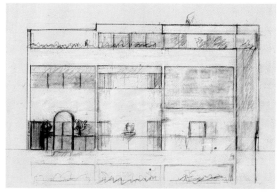

18. Villa Meyer (FLC 10377)

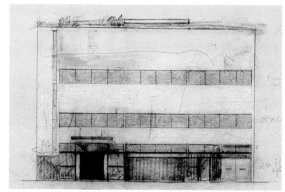

19. Villa Meyer (FLC 10585)

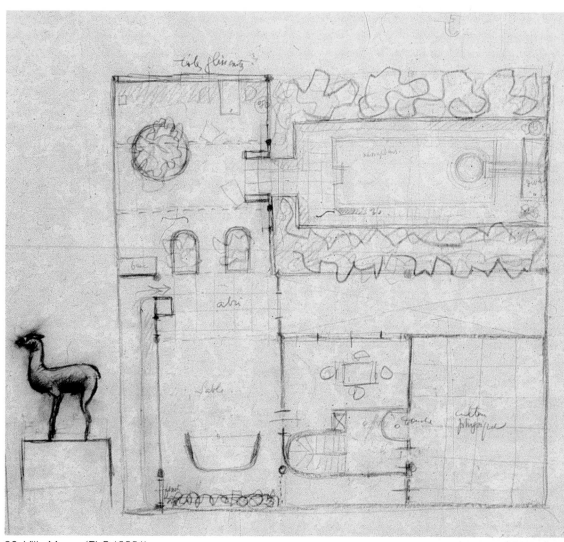

20. Villa Meyer (FLC 10391)

93. Villa Church, Ville d'Avray. Guest pavilion, view from upper landing of staircase hall. 121

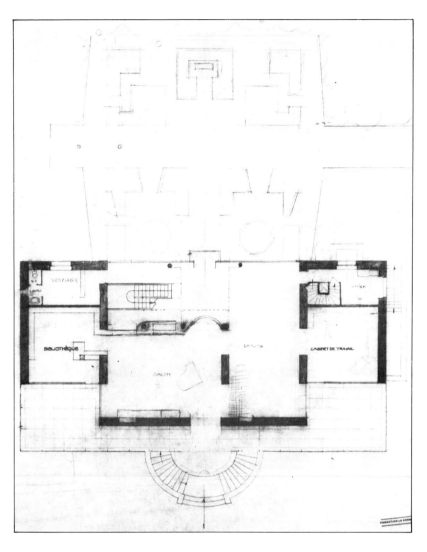

Minor work was carried out in the old house during the other building operations, but I can find no firm discussion of the main operation on the main house until 1929. In February 1929, Moreau-Lalande asked for details of all the work remaining to be done and shortly afterwards a set of drawings was prepared which can be dated to 11 March 1929. What is not clear, however, is when the preliminary drawings for these plans were prepared, nor when the clients' brief was written. Finally, the architects have made it difficult to identify the different projects with either the clients' brief, or, indeed Pierre's own description of the work to be carried out (28 June 1929), since no drawings correspond to this description.

The old house is illustrated in one of the set of drawings by the English architectural firm of Falconer, Baker and Campbell (FLC 8111). On the north side, facing the grounds, was a formal external staircase, leading up to the piano nobile, and on the north east corner an annexe used for the library.

An undated brief, probably in Barbara Church's hand, lists 18 points for attention in Bâtiment C. Many of the points seem to fit the later schemes rather than the earlier ones, but this may be due to Le Corbusier's casual reading of the document and the later insistence of the clients. The list is headed by an underlined statement:

> All these alterations are not to change the exterior of the house, at least on the façades.

And this would seem to contradict one at least of Le Corbusier's rough sketches, (FLC 8098) which showed a completely new three storey encasing of the west front, and a new block extending towards the stable block.

All one can say about the date of this sketch is that it must postdate the solution of the driveway in front of the Batiment A, and probably predates December 1928. Already visible in this drawing are the raised terrace on the north side and the large 'hall' which took up the whole space between the house and the road on the south side. The west side is used for the main entrance, with a large *porte-cochère*, as at the Villa Stein-de Monzie.

Mrs Church's brief refers to the re-use of the library annexe, and this poses a problem, since most of the early studies demolish this annexe completely, in order to give the raised terrace a clear sweep, and no doubt on the assumption that the functions of the library could be subsumed in the vast area of the salon to the south. She also referred to converting the existing

94. Villa Church, Ville d'Avray, Music pavilion Ground floor plan of existing building with proposed modifications, July 1927 (FLC 8168)

95. Facing page, from top to bottom: First floor plan, 27 July 1927 (FLC 8210)
First floor plan, 'small project', 17 September 1927 (FLC 8158)
First floor plan, variant of definitive project, September – November 1927 (FLC 8162)

(Bâtiment C), are obscured by the long period (1927–29) in which discussion and designing of the project might have taken place. We know that, by December 1928, the basic idea of the renovation, which was to build a large double-height salon onto the south side of the old house, was clearly in Le Corbusier's mind, since he included a description in the text from which we have included extracts earlier:

> And, by way of conclusion, the old house too (also with an orientation to the north) has need of sunlight. At the back of the house, to the south, we're going to build a huge salon-winter garden, where the most up-to-date (!) furniture will be juxtaposed with terraces of great plants and even exotic trees. Onto this salon-garden will open the original rooms, retained in their present form.[4]

4. Dossier Church, Docs. 211–14, 19 December, 1928.
5. Dossier Church, Doc. 2, 2v.

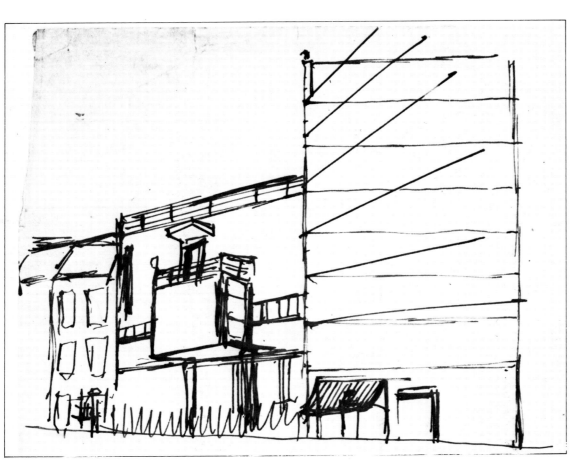

verso of FLC 8966 contains Planeix's sketches accompanying detailed notes in his letter about the down pipes and drains. The second half of the letter includes the brief for the extension on the ground floor, to be added before the main building was even finished, accompanied by two pages of his sketches; and his description, to ascertain precisely how much of the finished scheme owes to his specific planning.

I have more or less decided on this arrangement because otherwise you could only provide either *more expensive* and *more inconvenient* shops, in an area where they could not be profitable for a long time, *or* only one passable studio for a sculptor (difficult to let) *or* two pretty poor little ones, *or* an industrial workshop (equally expensive) which would take up more space and be more of a nuisance.
Could I not expect about 10,000 francs in rent from these two small apartments?
Would the construction cost over 60,000 francs?

Of the two drawings by Planeix which accompanied this letter, one shows the mezzanine floor and section,

the other the ground floor, and two sections. Pierre's first design in response, labelled 'Ier Project', (FLC 8959) kept the basic parti of a central space for the garage and two duplex apartments either side, but he introduced the formula of the Citrohan II, with stairs at the back and a double-height atelier at the front.

In February, Pierre drew up his plan for the two storey additional apartments to be inserted into the ground floor space of the Planeix house (FLC 8930) and this plan was used to obtain tenders from Summer, and the others. Planeix's hopes of carrying out the whole scheme for around 60,000 francs were quickly dashed. Summer's tender alone (11 February 1927) came to 61,650 francs, not counting extras such as the use of tiles for the garage-hall. Planeix developed a feud with Summer at around this point, so that he refused to accept this tender, turning to another builder, Camille Barbier, to carry out the heavy work of clearing the site of several tons of earth and gravel.

Dealing with Mr Summer over the ground floor seems impossible. Another builder must be asked to

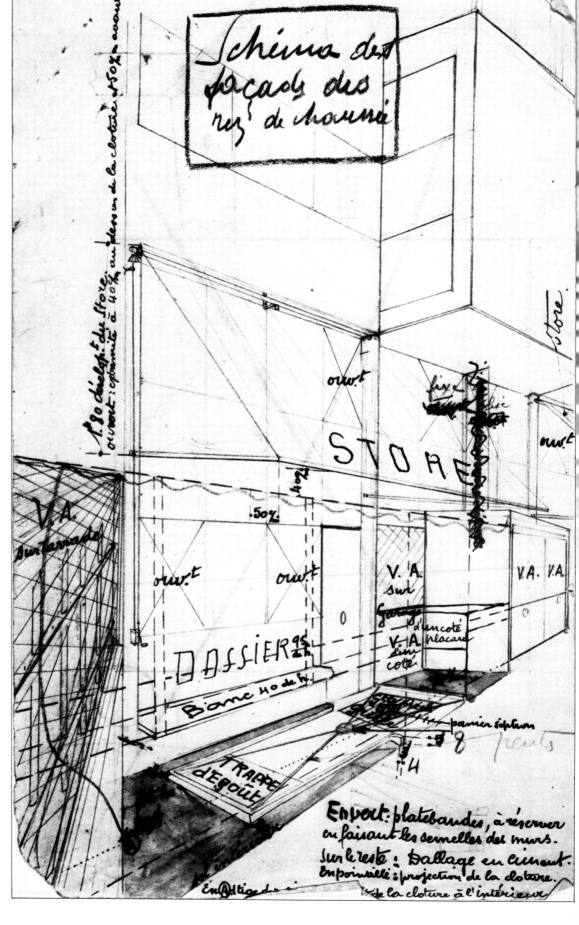

112. Planeix house,
boulevard Masséna.
Perspective drawn by
Planeix of street front,
showing the two new
studio apartments,
16 February 1927 (?)
(FLC 8968)

tender for a start, and, secondly, the tender must be based on the project which I submitted to you on my own drawing . . .

In my opinion, the tenders should not exceed 30–35,000 francs for the masonry and as much again for all the rest.[6]

Accompanying this letter was a drawing (FLC 8968), in which Planeix showed how he saw the treatment of the windows of the ground floor apartments, with wired glass for the garage doors as well as the other doors. The perspective also showed the place of the trap for the sewer, an expensive item now that the ground level had to be dug out. In March, Pierre revised the plans (FLC 8901, 8882), using a distinction in the glazing to divide the central section of the elevation (industrial glazing) from the windows of the two studio apartments (large panes, this was not executed). Unfortunately, some of the drawings from this period do not survive (e.g. LC Nos. 835–7, 846, 847, 857), depriving us of evidence of any steps taken to economise in the design. By April 1927, the cost estimates had reached 100,500 francs. Whatever the difficulties, however, work proceeded slowly throughout the rest of 1927, interrupted temporarily by refused building permission again, from the Prefecture (6 July 1927). Reasons given were the incompleteness of the plans submitted and the insufficient height of the mezzanine floor rooms (less than 2.80 metres).

On the 20 July, Pierre declared having sent Planeix new plans of the extension, in which he had reduced the floor area of the mezzanine storey, in order to improve the ratio of window survived, nor does any significant change to the existing plans seem to have been carried out.

On 6 September, Planeix declared himself nearly certain of a loan of 50,000 francs, and that he was following up the address of a source of funds which Summer had given him. From this point onwards Planeix's shortage of funds featured prominently in the correspondence. By 31 October 1927, Planeix was forced to offer promisory notes to the entrepreneurs. By January 1928, finishing was advanced, with the supply of gas and electricity being discussed in February and March. But numerous delays held up proceedings during 1928, so that the painting of the house was undertaken only in the summer. Planeix's money problems continued into 1929. Summer wrote on 26 March 1929 furiously demanding his outstanding fees and declaring once again what a disaster the whole undertaking had been for him (Doc. 89).

Le Corbusier, too, had still not been paid. Curiously, the tone of the letter was more respectful and sympathetic than that of his usual request for fees:

Let us remind you that we have been working for you since 1924, that is, nearly five and a half years! You are also well aware how difficult this work has been, due to the continual delays which have been occuring. You have been living in your house for nearly a year. It only seems right, therefore, that our fees should be paid forthwith. We were glad to allow you reasonable deadlines, but we must now insist on concluding this matter and so we are asking you to prepare three credit notes of equal value, scheduled for the end of May, June and July. We are confident that this procedure will be to your satisfaction.[7]

Planeix at last managed to obtain a loan in July 1929. The final cost of the house, including the two extra apartments on the ground floor, but excluding all the furniture and fittings, worked out at about 345,843 francs, giving Le Corbusier and Pierre fees worth 34,584 francs. This modest house, therefore, with its many detailed and difficult problems, earned the architects more than the Cook house.

6. Dossier Planeix, Docs. 60–1, 16 February 1927.
7. Dossier Planeix, Doc. 133, 3 May 1929.

113. Villa Savoye, Poissy. View of north corner, showing the site still unencumbered.

'CLASSIC' HOUSES

The final flowering of the modest but passionate effort of 1918–25: the first round of new architecture to be *manifested*. I use the term manifested to mean in full bloom, open to the eye as to the soul (poetry, technology, biology, human scale). This week I saw Garches again, 32 years on, white (inside and out) behinds its trees. It's an exquisite site, at an *exquisite* scale, the adjective is justified here. This drawing is decisive testimony. (FLC 31480, 20 July 1926, annotated 25 July 1959.)

114. Villa Meyer
project, Neuilly.
Perspectives of second
project and 'letter',
October 1925
(FLC 31525)

VILLA MEYER (AND OCAMPO PROJECT)

Neuilly had been one of the areas investigated by Le Corbusier for possible sites for houses since 1922. In 1925, April–May, he was investigating a number of sites in Neuilly, of which the front runner appeared to be one on the corner of rue de la Ferme and rue Windsor. One client in mind for this site, as we have seen, was Mongermon, but Pierre Meyer was definitely approached in 15 April, with information about two sites, the rue de la Ferme one and another at Neuilly, between rue de Longchamps, rue Saint James and rue Chézy (more expensive). On 4 May 1925, Le Corbusier wrote to Mme Meyer about the rue de la Ferme site, claiming that he had found another client (Mongermon?) to share the purchase of the rather large plot. But the site the Meyers chose was the other one, on a new road running east from rue Longchamp.

The pre-history of the purchase of the plot on the avenue Madrid is potentially of use to us in identifying the sources of a mysterious undated project which has been identified as part of the Meyer group (FLC 8338, 10401–3, 32000). If it could be established that this design, which shares many of the features of the Meyer programme, including the elaborate roof garden, was intended for the rue de la Ferme site, it would help to establish a date around April or May 1925. Unfortunately, the dimensions of this site are not known, and these plans approximate closely to the dimensions of the avenue Madrid site. And a sketch held with the Esprit Nouveau documents (published in Gresleri, *L'Esprit Nouveau*, Electa, 1979, Fig. 113) would confirm that this project was indeed for the avenue Madrid site. On quite circumstantial grounds, I associate this 'first' project with the rushed and aborted plans for Mongermon of April 1925, where the obsession with a central ramp was manifest. An alternative hypothesis might look to locate this design rather later than April 1925, possibly after the October scheme, given the closer affinities with the project of April 1926, in some points. Some rather mysterious sheets of sketches conserved among the archive documents seem to relate together ideas of a straight ramp, taking a zigzag path through the building, and a curved one. One drawing (Meyer dossier, doc 33v) shows a particularly 'picturesque' ramp which enters at an angle, turns right round and exits to a raised terrace in the garden. It is difficult to find anything specific to say about these sketches except that they form some kind of link between the Mongermon studies in April 1925 and the April 1926 scheme.

The circumstances in which the October 1925 scheme was prepared are not illuminated by the documentation. All we know is that a set of floor plans was drawn, fairly schematically (FLC 29843, 8339, see p. 146) of a house 9 metres deep and 15.50 wide and these seem to have been accompanied by the famous illustrated letter (FLC 31525 dated October 1925) which was published in *L'Oeuvre Complète*. This scheme, too, could be referred back to the Casa Fuerte and Mongermon schemes. The first and second floor plans can be described as an Esprit Nouveau Pavilion plan, with an extra bay added on to the side (with 'Ch.Bébé'). Like the Casa Fuerte scheme, which also had a double-height space over the salon, the service staircase was a spiral, but here the main staircase was simply pushed out of the main plan, in a way which is reminiscent of the Immeubles Villas and the Esprit Nouveau Pavilion. Far more interesting than the plans, however, is the illustrated letter to Mme Meyer, written in the flirtatious banter of an experienced raconteur.

> Our dream was to make you a house which would be smooth and clean like a well proportioned casket, one that would not be spoilt by multiple effects creating an artificial illusion of the picturesque, making light impression in sunlight and merely adding to the surrounding tumult. We are against the present fashion, here and abroad, for fortuitously complex houses. Our view is that unity is stronger than the parts.[1]

This is a statement which marks a watershed between the composition of La Roche-Jeanneret and Lipchitz-Miestschaninoff (and Ternisien) and introduces the 'classic' designs of 1926 and later (Cook, Stein-de Monzie and Savoye). Further on in the letter, Le Corbusier referred to the *tambour de service* in the first floor living area. This was to be a servery made of a curving wall of cork bricks, but it has to be taken together with a dumb waiter and spiral staircase as forming the service artery passing right up through the house. Again, this idea was to be particularly poignant for the later designs, in which spiral service stairs would frequently recur with a similar meaning, carrying the biomorphic analogy, whether arterial or arboreal, to quite specific conclusions. The romantic connotations of the roof garden are also spelled out, with strong indications as to how the roof terrace should be used:

> Behind the swimming pool and service rooms, you would take breakfast... From the boudoir, you have gone up onto a roof with neither slates nor tiles, but a

1. FLC 31525, dated October 1925.

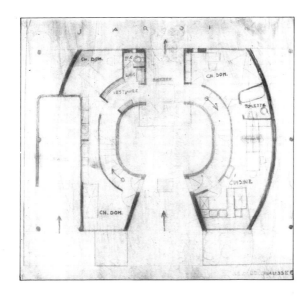

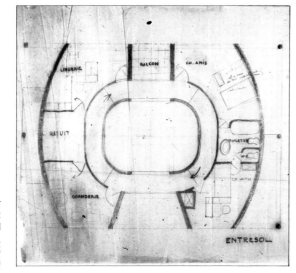

115. Villa Meyer project, Neuilly. First project, ground and mezzanine floor plans, April–May 1925 (FLC 8338 and 10403)

Corbusier had a very interesting notion of the private, and in letters like this it is clear that this idea of the private life of his (female) clients interested him. Finally, the letter looks forward to the later designs for Mme Meyer, and to other projects like the Villa Stein-de Monzie in stressing the three-way dialogue between structure (and its potential for economy), lyricism (and the dangers of complication) and the need to *faire rentrer dans le rang*:

> These ideas . . . these architectural themes which bear within them a certain poetry are subject to the most rigorous constructive laws . . . Twelve concrete piers, equally spaced out, carry the floors at little expense. In the concrete framework thus constituted, the plan is deployed with such simplicity that one might be tempted (how easily tempted!) to consider it naive . . . For years we have grown accustomed to plans which are so complicated that they have the air of men with their viscera on the outside. We have insisted that the viscera should be on the inside, classified, tucked away, and that only a clear form should be apparent. Not as easy as it sounds! To tell you the truth, this is the great challenge of architecture: to form ranks again (*rentrer dans le rang*). These architectural themes require the resolution of difficult problems of juxtaposition, if the result is to have any poetry in it. Once achieved, all looks natural and easy, and it's a good sign. But at the outset, putting the first lines of the composition on paper, all was confusion.[1]

It would be intriguing to know whether there actually were any other drawings for this variant of the project, but the text of the letter suggests to us that: 'This project, Madam, was not thrown together by the hurried pencil of a studio draughtsman in between telephone calls. It has matured slowly, with tender loving care, during days of perfect calm in the presence a site of High Classicism.'[1] And the sketch accompanying this shows a beach and rocky outcrop in the sea, probably referring to the location of his summer vacation.

With this letter, as much as the plans, the scene was set for the next two variants, of the spring of the following year, in which the key themes of the Villa Stein-de Monzie were tried out. Clearly, Mme Meyer was a careless client; Le Corbusier had had no reply by February 1926, and wrote back in the tone of an offended troubadour:

> My paternity is suffering! You are cruel, Madam, to make us wait so long! I have told you the infinite trouble we have taken with your project and we were celebrating to see it emerge into the light of day. A house which remains on paper is a stillbirth. Let me

solarium and swimming pool with grass growing between the paving slabs. Above you is the sky. With the surrounding walls, no one could see you. In the evening you would see the stars and the sombre mass of the trees in the Folie St. James. Like Robinson (nearby on the Seine), rather like Carpaccio's paintings. A *divertissement*. . . This is not at all like a garden in the French style but a wild wood where, thanks to the tall trees of the Park St. James, you could imagine yourself far from Paris.[1]

This, too, was a theme of the later 1920s, the constant stress on a nature abstracted from incident and removed from the prying ideas of neighbours. Le

tell you that my suffering is truly that of an expectant father.[2]

Given that the young Meyers were expecting a child themselves, this is powerful language. And Le Corbusier called on the newly acquired site to plead for him:

Meanwhile, in the Folie St. James, the birds are singing at this moment in the bushes and some of the groves are already in leaf. I can promise you that when your roof garden is ready, you will listen to them next year and you will be greatly moved by them: your roof will be something 'the like of which we have not seen'. But you are down in Monte Carlo among the mimosas; what is the song of a rooftop garden in Paris to you... But Paris has never been abandoned by her children. Everyone returns to Paris and it is only the blocks of flats built by our colleagues which can make Paris gloomy. Now, we have created an architectural poem rather like an '*Innovation* trunk'. Open the trunk, the suitcase, and inside is a box of surprises.
 Your site at Neuilly is admirably situated. I often look for sites for first class clients and they're unfindable in Paris, even paying 1,000 francs the square metre. And even then you can have neighbours six floors up who can look right down onto your roof garden, not so charming after all.[2]

He clearly thought that there was a good chance of the Meyers proceeding with the project, since he continued, still in the rhetoric of the jilted lover: 'To be honest, your silence pains us. Not that we're anxious, since you declared so categorically to me that we have well and truly made up, for which I was delighted'.[2]
 Whatever Mme Mayer's answer was, Le Corbusier and Pierre Jeanneret did produce another set of plans, the most complex and complete set for the clients, in April. Three variants can be identified in these drawings, of which the last carry the atelier numbers 663–9, dated 21 April 1926 (FLC 10394). The middle group (FLC 10389, 10391, 10377) may be dated by the presence on two of the drawings of the words '10 Av' (FLC 10393). What makes these three phases of the April scheme particularly interesting is that they represent a conscious discourse on alternative geometries for the grid of *pilotis*. If we can talk of an 'A' bay of around 5 metres, a 'B' bay of roughly half that and a 'C' bay varying between 1.25 and 1.50 metres, the three variants can be described as having the following grid layouts:

2. Dossier Meyer, Doc. 5, 24 February 1926.

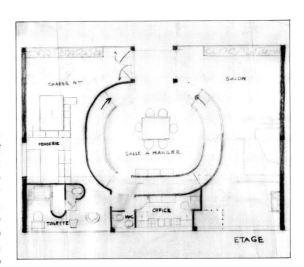

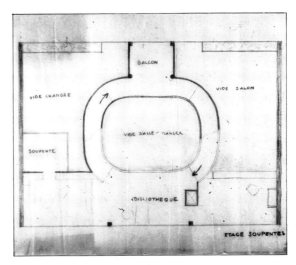

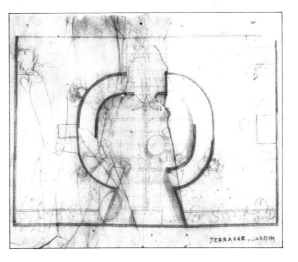

116. Villa Meyer project, Neuilly. First project, first, second and third floor plans, April–May 1925 (FLC 10402, 10401, 32000)

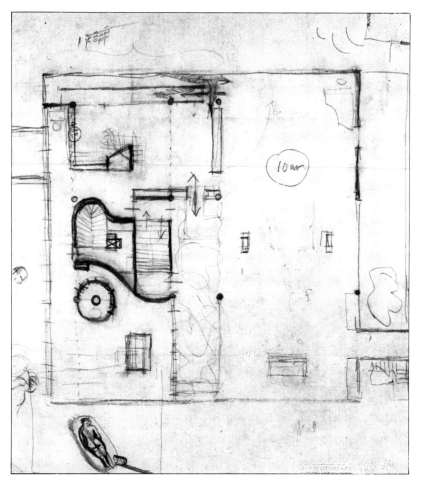

117. Villa Meyer project, Neuilly. Second project, floor plans, October 1925 (FLC 29843)

118. Second variant of floor plan, 10 April 1926, entrance front on the left (FLC 10393)

1) CABAB (width); CABBA (depth). (FLC 10397 etc.)

2) CAAA (width); CAB (B + A). (FLC 10389 etc.)

3) CAAA (width), CAB (A + B). (FLC 10394 etc.)

The project is roughly 17 metres square (compared to the October 1925 scheme's 15.50 × 9). It was an inordinately extravagant design, with a large part of the cube taken up by a hanging garden based on that of the Immeuble-Villa. The grid helps to give richness to the associations. The thin slice of space along the side, as in the case of the Citrohan II cell houses, carries the circulation, but instead of an external or internal staircase, this is to be a ramp. The 'C' bay along the front of the house is a cantilevered bay intended to display the *fenêtre en longueur* in its purest form, a portent of the Maison Cook (see FLC 10385). Each variant employs different subtleties in the juxtaposition of the service staircase (a vertical spiral) contrasted to the ramp. The two staircases are aligned with the middle 'B' bay in the grid, while the transverse 'B' bays are seen to be subservient to the others. The right hand 'B' bay is given most of its point by the garage. It is the first variant, then, in which a free-hand association of functions with a geometrical order is clearest. In the second variant, the detailed complexities of planning become more insistent (FLC 10389). Here the grid takes second place. On the first floor, too, compared to the first variant, the more relaxed CAAA grid is exploited to make the plan freer and more curvilinear than before (FLC 10393). The association of

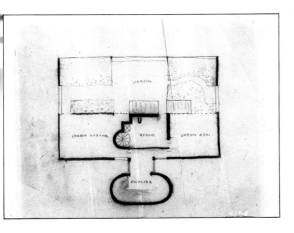

Corbusier's letter to Mme Meyer's mother, Mme Hirtz, who, it transpires, was to pay for the new house, mentioned the figure of 350,000 francs as a maximum (discounting furnishings). A sheet of sketches (FLC 10404) based on the general scheme suggested in Pierre's list of economies is dated '20 May 1926'. Again, an extreme curiosity as to the possibilities of organising grids can be seen in these sketches. The overall size in the drawings which follow has been reduced to the grid ABAA × ABA (c. 17 × c. 12.50 metres). Not only has the 1.25 metres cantilever been removed on the street front, but also the extra 2.50 metres towards the garden. In three drawings (FLC 10381–2, 10386), all rather tentative and heavily based on ruled grid lines, a variety of solutions for the two staircases are investigated. The solution which would later be adopted in the Villa Stein was chosen here: a special staircase, with a lot of space about it, for ascending from the ground to the first floor, followed by the service staircase and a narrow spiral to mount onto the roof terrace. A lot of

119. Villa Meyer project, Neuilly. Left: Second project, plan of roof terrace, October 1925 (FLC 8339)

120. Second variant of third project, ground floor plan, 10 April 1926, entrance front below (FLC 10389)

the *tambour de service* and the service staircase, reminiscent of the October 1925 scheme, is brought out clearly. A similar loosening up process takes place on the bedroom floor. The roof plan FLC 10391 expresses in the clearest possible way the agenda for the modern spirit life of luxury: a breakfast room indoors, or out on the terrace, a suspended swimming pool surrounded with its own verdure, a more sheltered terrace for less kindly weather, a solarium like open air Greek theatre, with a sandy area in front of a stage, and a screened off area for *culture physique* with an open air shower. And yet, despite all these intimations of luxury, this project rests more closely than any other on the basic thinking of the Immeuble Villa standard cells, and the garden front (FLC 10377) makes this clear visually too. The house is an Esprit Nouveau Pavilion, with an extra bay at the side and extra floors above and below. The drawings for the final variant differ little from the second, except in details of resolution in preparing the presentation drawings, most of which were published in the *Oeuvre Complète* (I, pp. 87 and 90–1).

Despite the apparently unrealistically grandiose nature of this project, real tenders were obtained from the usual Corbusian entrepreneurs (Selmersheim and Monteil, Pasquier, Guillaumeau, Celio, Summer, etc.). The whole thing came to around 514,000 francs (12 May 1926), according to Pierre's computation, but he also worked out a lower figure making a number of economies, in which were included scrapping the swimming pool, part of the superstructure of the roof terrace, the ramp bay, 1.25 metres towards the garden, all the expensive treatments (cement, render, oil painting, etc.) and so forth. This calculation gave a putative figure of 405,800 francs. Two days later, Le

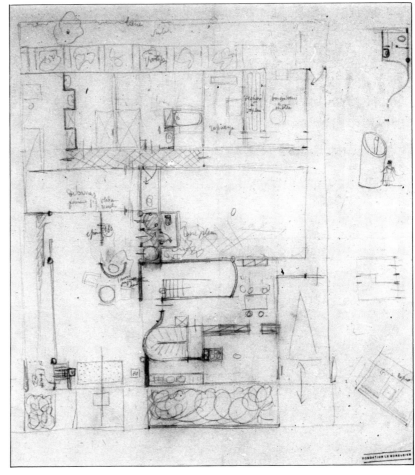

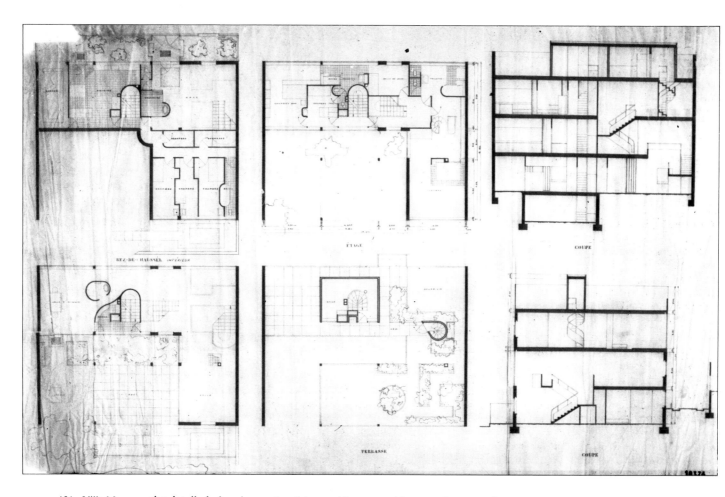

121. Villa Meyer project, Neuilly. Definitive version of the fourth project, plans and sections, 11 June 1926 (FLC 10374)

the detailed planning, rather laboured here, would pay dividends when it came to the Villa Stein-de Monzie. The finished drawings for this scheme (FLC 10374, 11 June 1926) represent a compromise in some ways but a considerable tightening up in others. The elevations, represent an intriguing set of discourses. The 'B' bay on the street frontage, for example, is picked out not only by changes in the fenestration, but a balcony and incision in the roof parapet. The staircase hall, too, is expressed in a double height window on the left. On the garden front, the integrity of the Esprit Nouveau cell module is made clearer.

Unfortunately, before these drawings were finished, Mme Hirtz had decided to break off relations with Le Corbusier and Pierre, at least for some time. An element of mystery surrounds the letter she wrote, because it was undated and received during Le Corbusier's absence in Bordeaux. She wrote:

Dear Sir,
Given the monetary crisis through which we are passing, I find myself under the obligation of breaking off our discussions. I am very sorry about this, but I hope that it will eventually be possible to reopen them – this is my sincere wish – on my return from holiday.[3]

Le Corbusier wrote back on 26 May, hoping that her expressed wish to meet them could be followed up soon, and declaring that, following her expressed wishes to proceed with the house (at the time of the letter of 14 May), they were proceeding with a fourth project for Mme Meyer. On 19 June, he wrote announcing the completion of the plans of the fourth project, which had been put out to the entrepreneurs for tender. He hoped for a meeting next week. Mme Hirtz later (13 December 1926) claimed that she presented herself on 23 June but that, after waiting for more than an hour, had left, and that she had considered this the end of their relationship. Although some effort had been made to estimate the cost of the fourth project, Le Corbusier and Pierre had clearly not followed up on the Meyers, since it was not until 9 December that Le Corbusier wrote to Mme Meyer trying to enforce a take-up of the scheme. He asserted that the 'fourth project' had been finished on 19 June and that it was 'particularly interesting', due to its 'happy birth'. He enclosed the drawings with his letter.

The most extraordinary thing about this seems to be that Le Corbusier does not even seem to have sent the June plans off until six months later, either through sheer inefficiency or because he knew perfectly well that Mme Hirtz would block it. Le Corbusier would

122. Villa Ocampo project, Buenos Aires. Perspective of the final project, 18 September 1928 (FLC 24235, detail)

suffer again at the hands of the parent of a young married couple, in the case of the Maison Canneel, but there is a peculiar appositeness in this circumstance, since it was exactly the romance of the site and its client which encouraged him here to develop some of the key ingredients of his mature luxury houses.

Of course, the first beneficiary of the Meyer designs was the Villa Stein-de Monzie. But the third project was dusted off again, and reused, almost without change, in the summer and autumn of 1928, for another glamorous and very wealthy lady, Mme Ocampo. And André Lurçat produced a 'Villa Moderne' at Meudon in 1930 in which a mushroom-shaped external staircase similar to the October 1925 version was used. On the site adjoining the Meyer's one, 17, avenue Madrid, Gabriel Guevrekain built a house, the Villa Heim,

3. Dossier Meyer, Doc. 19, n.d. (May 1926).

149

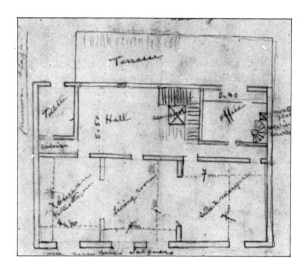

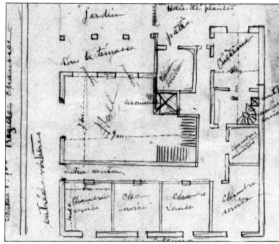

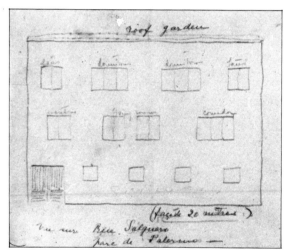

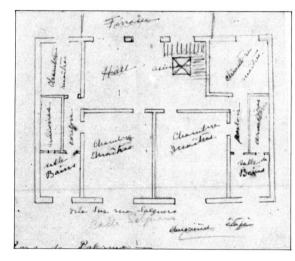

which shares some features with Le Corbusier's Meyer projects of April and May 1926, and also with some of the early elevation drawings for the Villa Stein-de Monzie. So Le Corbusier's use of his own drawings might seem less egocentric than at first appears. The circumstances, furthermore, required speed.

On 27 August 1928, the Comtesse de Vera wrote to Le Corbusier asking him to prepare some plans for her friend Mme Ocampo for a site in Buenos Aires, rue Salguero. The site was twenty metres wide, forty-three metres deep. Mme Ocampo had clearly seen the Villa Stein-de Monzie, because she specified the same kitchen and had prepared herself some plans for her house, (FLC 31043) which was due to begin construction on 1 October, so the Comtesse Vera wanted plans from Le Corbusier in fifteen or twenty days at the most.

123. Villa Ocampo project, Buenos Aires. Three plans and an elevation sent by Madame Ocampo with her brief, 27 August 1927 (FLC 31043)

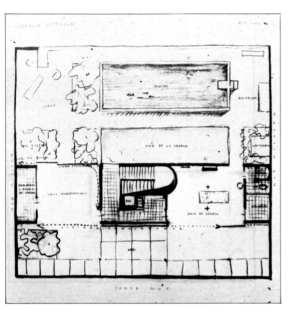
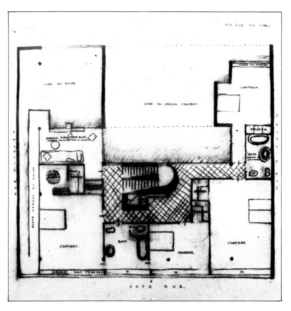
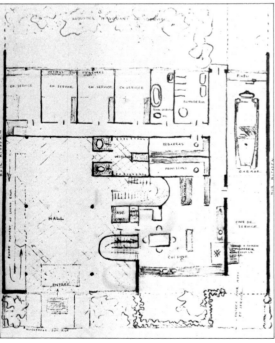
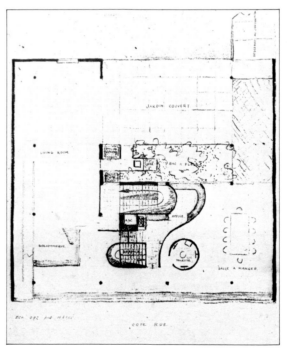

124. Villa Ocampo project, Buenos Aires. Floor plans of
definitive project, 18 September 1928 (FLC 24231)

125. Villa Ocampo
project, Buenos Aires.
Interior perspective
of salon on first floor,
18 September 1928
(FLC 24235, detail)

As well as a list of eleven items forming the brief, Adela Cuevas de Vera finished her intercession with the following line of encouragement: 'My friend has good taste and a keen perception of your architecture; she will carry out your plans to the letter'.[4] On 6 September, she wrote again, delighted that Le Corbusier would take on the plans for her friend's house and asking for a first study as soon as possible, so that she could radio her with her opinion. This letter was written from Anglet, Basses Pyrénées, but by the 24th she was in Eastbourne, England, telegraphing for the plans.

Given this extraordinary introduction, it was clear that Le Corbusier can have had little serious hope of securing a commission. Mme Ocampo became quite a good friend, helping to organise his lecture tour in Argentina in 1929. She was well known in international literary and artistic circles, editing the most respected Argentinian poetry journal and spending most of her time travelling between Paris, London, New York and Buenos Aires. The plans must have partly been aimed, therefore, at the potential publicity and propaganda effect they would have in the hands of someone as well placed and supportive as Mme Ocampo.

FLC 31043 illustrates the four ground plans sent to Le Corbusier via the Comtesse de Vera in her letter of

4. Dossier Ocampo, Doc. 11, 27 August 1927.

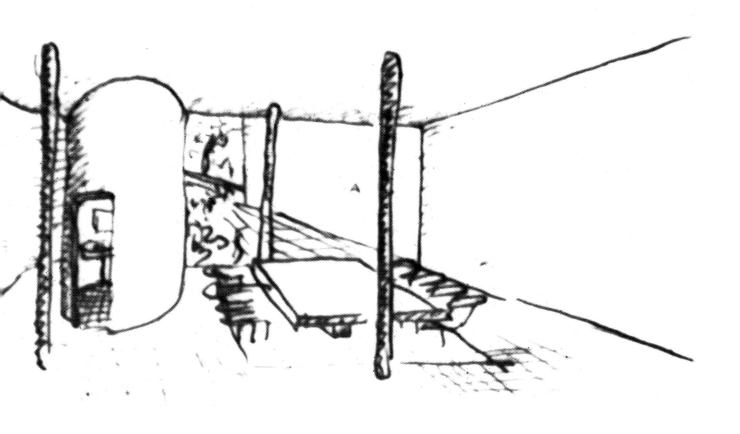

27 August, along with a photograph of Madame Ocampo's beach house. These plans lent themselves well to incorporation into the Meyer scheme. The outline sketches on FLC 31046 are probably connected with the Ocampo project (the bottom right drawing is for Baizeau, as is a rather strange plan in FLC 31044 (top right) which appears to have no staircases or ramp marked in. The presentation drawings, (FLC 24231, 18 September 1928) begin with the third project for Mme Meyer, of April 1926, and add an extra half-bay to the side. Instead of CAAA, the grid now read CAAB, and this 'B' bay is used to introduce one of the discoveries of 1928, the idea of placing a mezzanine space along the side of a double-height terrace or salon (see Wanner

apartments, Baizeau projects of February and March 1928, and so forth). Apart from that, the changes are minimal, a through passage for the cars to the back of the property, a more clear-cut division of spaces on the second floor, and, above, all a more robust and rugged look to the exteriors. The interior perspectives (FLC 24235) incorporate the new furniture designed earlier in 1928: the *chaise longue*, the *grand confort* and Charlotte Perriand's 1927 dining chairs. This design already has some of the feel of the Algerian projects about it, and along with the Villa Baizeau projects, must be seen as pointing forward to some of the solutions of the 1950s Indian buildings.

154   126. Villa Cook, Boulogne-sur-Seine. View of living room on second floor.

VILLA COOK

William E. Cook and his French wife Jeanne came to know Le Corbusier at a particularly fruitful point in the development of his architectural style. He was an American in Paris, a journalist who also practised painting in his spare time. He knew the Steins, not only Gertrude, who wrote a poem dedicated to him, but also Michael and Sarah, whose house was being designed and built at the same period as Cook's, and who came to visit it, in March 1927.

The contacts with the Steins and the Cooks seem to coincide: 7 May 1926 for the decisive meeting with the Steins (and Gabrielle de Monzie), 28 April for the brief from the Cooks. The houses are very different, however, not only in size and complexity, but in the manner of their designing. The Stein-de Monzie house went through several successive phases of substantial re-design, after the first dated scheme of 20 July, taking nearly a year before construction began in earnest. In the case of the Cook house, the basic features of the design were settled on a scrap of paper on 1 May and, despite a few variations on a theme, remained substantially the same when construction began in July. The Cook house was inhabited in March 1927, before Summer had even submitted the estimate for building the Stein-de Monzie house.

The site was on the rue Denfert-Rochereau, Boulogne-sur-Seine, not far from the Lipchitz-Miestchaninoff and Ternisien sites. The owner had sold the neighbouring plot to Mme Colinot, who was having a house built to the designs of Rob Mallet-Stevens. The plots were ten metres wide with a *non-aedificandi* of ten metres depth along the street and an imposed servitude of eleven metres overall depth for the house itself. The neighbour also stipulated that any roof balconies had to fall two metres below the roof balcony on the Mallet-Stevens house and that the topmost point of the Cook house should not exceed the height of the full balustrade of the large terrace of Mme Colinot's house.

A page from a tiny notepad contains a record of the brief, and is dated '28 avril'. Three days later, this brief was worked up on three pages of a sketchpad (FLC 8588), of which one is dated '1 Mai 1926'. This sheet, shows the outline of the Mallet-Stevens house on the left, and a roof terrace on the Cook house which would have been overlooked from Mme Colinot's house. Another sheet concentrates on this problem, studying the angles of sight and coming up with the solution of a curved roof slab to keep the Cook terrace private. The third sheet in this set consists of four floor plans in which the basic arrangement of the house is resolved, apart from the first floor containing the bedrooms and bathroom. The ground floor solution is particularly

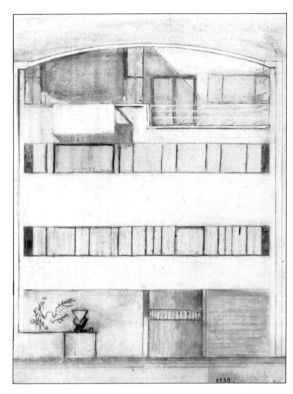

127. Villa Cook,
Boulogne-sur-Seine.
Elevation to the street,
with vaulted roof, May
1926 (FLC 8330)

follow the 1 May plans quite closely, shows the basic idea for the street frontage. The Mallet-Stevens house is indicated, with the positions of the floor heights, as if the consideration of the servitudes was still foremost in Le Corbusier's mind. There are two sets of ground plans, in a similar technique (charcoal on a pencil grid, at a scale of 1:20), which have to be distinguished. One set (FLC 8322, see p. 159) differs from all the other ground plans in that they are based on a depth of under nine metres, whereas the agreement with Mme Colinot allowed a depth of eleven metres. I take this 'short' version to be the first detailed set of plans, in which we can see for the first time the plan of the first floor worked out. The second floor plan, too, shows an approximation to the end result, with the projecting D-shaped extrusion of the roof terrace balcony thrusting into the space of the salon, like the inverted cone of the acacia in the November scheme of the La Roche house. We also see in this plan and in the next, the system of skylights which would have lit not only the water-closet and 'office' on the second floor, but also the dining table (FLC 8324). Other details, such as the dumb waiter which, as in the Mongermon project, would have traversed the house from bottom to top, are fixed at this early stage. The other set of charcoal-drawn plans (FLC 8323, 8327), based on the correct depth of eleven metres, used the extra space to expand the organs of the plan, particularly necessary on the crowded first floor.

An intriguing elevation (FLC 8330) retains the curved roof slab but includes the balcony and cut-away parapet of the roof terrace, as well as the ground floor low wall and sculpture plinth, none of which were shown on the charcoal plan sets. Another very similar one, (FLC 8350, see p. 118), shows the curve in pencil only. The curved roof has gone, however, from the set dated '1 June 1926' (FLC 8293, see p. 160). This set represents to all intents and purposes the basis of agreement between client and architect, although minor modifications were made on another print of this drawing which was the drawing actually signed by Cook (and dated 22 June 1926) on the day of the application to the mayor of Boulogne-sur-Seine for permission to build.

On the basis of the drawing of 1 June, estimates were

clear, suggesting that the phrase, *sur pilotis*, showed Le Corbusier decided to deploy the central *piloti* and aircraft nacelle solution from the start. As in the second storey, the top floor plan would have been divided into quarters, each representing a different kind of space: open air (covered), open air (uncovered), enclosed (single storey), enclosed (double-height space over the salon). These formulaic distributions would become quickly more subtle and complex, but they show the lineage of this design from the 'aunt's house' on the La Roche site, and the first designs for the Casa Fuerte site.

An elevation drawing (FLC 8329), which I take to

submitted by Summer and the other contractors and contracts issued within a few days. The estimates in June add up to around 200,000 francs, and the final cost was not too much in excess of this figure (about 265,057 francs by December 1927). This house was built under Pierre's supervision, with a charge of ten per cent honoraria, as opposed to the seven per cent fees (and global contract with Summer to supervise the other tradesmen) as carried out in some of the earlier houses.

Summer's set of concrete drawings have been preserved (Dossier 390, 29 June 1926) and are in a particularly well-printed set. Unlike most Le Corbusier houses, important changes to the plans were not introduced after the estimate stage, so that most of the extras (11,500 francs) charged by Summer were to do with decorative finishes and some minor work to the garden walls and plinths. The slab making up the floor of the first storey was a particularly complex one, including a shallow recess for the double bed of the Cooks, and a built-in concrete bath in the bathroom. The preliminary drawings for the definitive set (FLC 8299 24 June 1926), show how complex the section became under the pressure of fitting the service functions into the tight band of space at the back of the building. One ingenious solution, (FLC 8342), also dating from June 1926, shows how the coal cellar was organized under a mezzanine rear entrance which also served to load goods onto the dumb waiter for raising up to the kitchen. The play with levels along the back of the house also allowed a shift at the top, so that the strip along the back of the library forms a raised shelf. The definitive set of drawings (FLC 8288–9), prepared between 19 June and 22 July, include one set inked for publication in the *Oeuvre Complète*.

FLC 8306, dated 2 July 1926, shows the kitchen with its built-in cupboards, dumb waiter, and roller blind fitments flanking the landing door (p. 161; see also the modified drawing FLC 8321, 'Oct 26'). The materials used were the standard Le Corbusier ones: small ceramic tiles for the service areas, library, stairs, either in black or yellow, Euboolith flooring in the bedrooms, parquet (second choice timber) in the salon and dining room. In the bathroom, Cook seems to have envisaged the possibility of a built-in bath *en piscine* from an early stage (28 April). The plans continued to

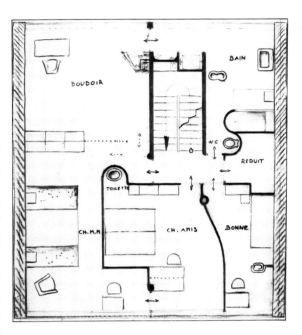

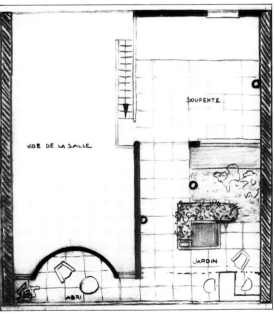

128. Villa Cook, Boulogne-sur-Seine. First floor (top) and third floor (left) plans of intermediary project, May 1929 (FLC 8323 and 8327)

show either a cast iron bath or a concrete one, and Summer's work on it was listed as an extra (FLC 8317, dated 25 September 1926). This is one of the first of the built-in baths (Villa Savoye, de Mandrot were other well-known examples) with which Le Corbusier brought together ideas of Art Deco luxury with his notion of *un seul corps de métier*. The fact that very expensive specialist art ceramics had to be used on these baths does not detract from the place of this detail within an 'architectural' conception of furnishing. The *fenêtres en longueur* were an important feature of the main façade and a key ingredient of the 'Five Points'. Each long window represents a living storey: bedrooms on the first floor, reception on the floor above. The *fenêtre en longueur* suggests a standard solution, the automatic resolution of the equation: façade, lighting, interior functions. Far from being standardised sliding windows, they include four categories: fixed, sliding, casement and centrally hung. Not only did they pose problems in design, but in manufacture. Pierre broke the contract with the carpenter Louis in September, when the latter went on holdiay without arranging for the window frames to be installed in time. He turned to his other favourite firm, Selmersheim and Monteil, with an urgent order at twelve days' notice (20 September). The frames were made of oak, with bronze runners for the sliding windows, and bronze fittings for the casements. One detail, the provision of drainage holes and pipes to catch condensation, which had appeared in the La Roche-Jeanneret houses and ever since, caused trouble once more:

> We would like to bring to your attention that the drainage holes on the second floor windows have been forgotten. It is essential to provide them, since water is dripping onto the window-sills.[1]

Another recurring problem was connected with the glazing of the long windows. Le Corbusier and Pierre seem to have deliberately allowed the painter and glazier Celio to misrepresent his estimates in all their houses, leaving the quality of glass to be used (wired, frosted, rolled or plate glass) open to later negotiation. Yet, invariably, they specified the more expensive plate glass for all visible windows at a later stage of the proceedings. The Cook house bears witness to the obsessive interest which both men, but particularly Le Corbusier, paid to this question. This example also shows clearly the differences between the two men's approach to business. Pierre drafted the following letter:

> Dear Sir,
> This afternoon on the site we established, just as we told you, that the street façade of your house was totally compromised by the glass. We have decided today to replace the glass with plate glass, and this at our expense, if you yourself are not prepared to remedy this serious state of affairs.[2]

On the same piece of paper, Le Corbusier's draft was more forceful and operated at a different level of discourse:

> We visited your site today. Your windows had been glazed with window-glass... Window glass is quite out of place in this kind of construction and not only spoils its appearance, but places it in an inferior category of buildings...
> My colleague informs me that you took this decision while I was away on holiday. It is this which prompts me to intervene and to ask you immediately *as a matter of utmost importance*, to have the glazing of the principal facade replaced by plate glass. I attach to this request a decisive importance. I am

1. Dossier Cook, Doc. 108, 10 February 1927.
2. Dossier Cook, Doc. 16, 11 December 1926.

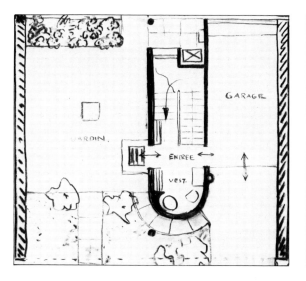

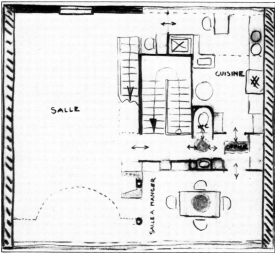

129. Villa Cook, Boulogne-sur-Seine. Ground floor (far left), second floor (left) and first floor (below, left) plans of 'short' variant, May 1926 (FLC 8322, 8324, 8348)

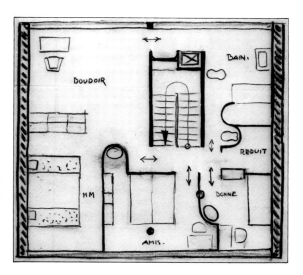

convinced that you will readily agree to it so as to avoid a serious blemish to your property. For you we have made the best of our houses, and one with which we have taken particular trouble. Alas, I fear that you do not appreciate it for what it is, or the distressing incidents which you have caused us would not have happened.

Le Corbusier went on to stress that the charge of replacing ordinary with plate glass, at 2,400 francs, represented a mere one per cent of the total cost of the building. And he finished with an argument calculated to touch the Anglo-Saxon mentality, as he understood it (through the eyes of Adolf Loos): 'A fine gentleman setting out for a ball would never wear a paper collar with his dinner jacket.'

The period immediately following the *succès de scandale* of the Esprit Nouveau Pavilion was one of a bifurcation of Le Corbusier's housing and urbanistic

159

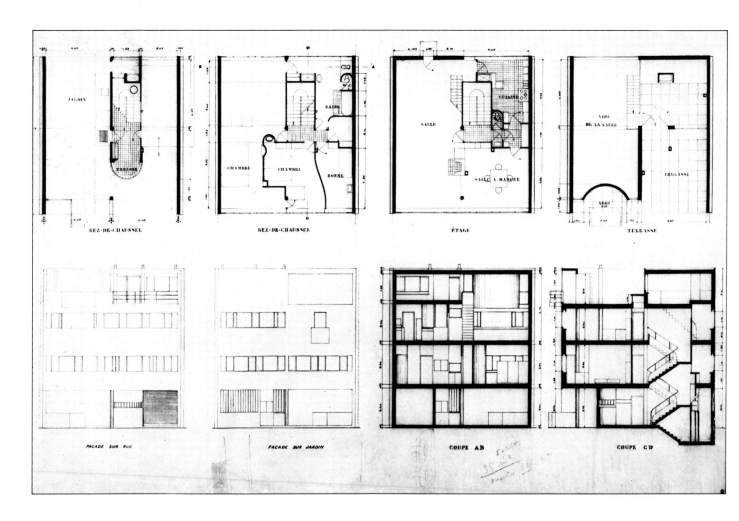

BEZ-DE-CHAUSSÉE   BEZ-DE-CHAUSSÉE   ÉTAGE   TERRASSE

FACADE SUR RUE   FACADE SUR JARDIN   COUPE AB   COUPE CD

130. Villa Cook, Boulogne-sur-Seine. Plans, elevations and sections, 1 June 1926 (FLC 1926)

concerns from those of 'Architecture'. The series of projects, maisons Cook, Stein, Savoye, and Church, re-flects a confident professionalism in which the imagery of functionalism is never allowed to divert from the precision and glitter of the truly luxurious modern house. As we have seen, Pierre and Le Corbusier repeatedly encouraged clients to embark on houses on the basis of estimates far below the eventual cost. Normally, the client's own interests in these matters diverted attention from the architects' strategy, but here is a case where the architect attacks the client in the most wounding possible way – in order to enforce the required change.

The axonometrics of the Villa Cook are intriguing because they match in style those drawn for the Esprit Nouveau Pavilion a year earlier (FLC 8309, see p. 119). They remind us how ambiguous the language of Le Corbusier's architecture could be: the Cook house sits uncomfortably between a mass housing prototype and

a bourgeois luxury villa. In one degree, the Cook house followed a tradition established with the La Roche and Jeanneret houses: the furniture was custom-built to Le Corbusier's designs by Louis, according to an estimate added to the plans (12,800 francs, 23 November 1926). Particularly impressive among Louis's work were the cantilevered fitments in the dining room housing the sideboard and backed by a mirror (FLC 8320, March 1927). The basic idea here, of suspending the drawer units across an alcove on tubular steel supports, matches the structural principle of the garden seat at the front of the house. The interior photographs show the tribal rugs and Maples chairs of the early 1920s interiors. Curtains were in white cotton or linen, and the lights, mostly simple bulb holders, were attached directly to the walls. Unfortunately, any correspondence about the popularity of these arrangements, or the functional efficiency of the house as a whole is missing. We do, however, have a telling detail of the cost of securing a client's happiness: 'Provision of a vase of flowers for Mrs Cook...50 francs.'[3] This bill seems to have referred to the inauguration of the house in March 1927, when William Cook remarked: 'We are more and more pleased with the house day by day. Mrs Cook was delighted with the superb arrangement of flowers which she received yesterday evening. The living room is full of them, like a field in springtime.'[4] And his wife confirmed her thanks for the flowers, adding: 'We are very happy and grateful that you have managed to produce not only a great house, but a very pretty one, with so much light and sunshine.'[5]

A year after the final settlement of accounts for the house (24 March 1928), the Cooks decided that they would like to build on a maids' room at the back of their house, with an outdoor bedroom and sports room above, for themselves. Summer's estimate for the masonry is dated 11 May 1929 and the other tradesmen also submitted estimates at the same time. The total cost seems to have been around 27,000 francs (again with ten per cent honoraria) and the work was substantially complete by autumn.

3. Dossier Cook, Doc. 202, Crepin's bill, 25 June 1927.
4. Dossier Cook, Doc. 19, 9 March 1927.
5. Dossier Cook, Doc. 24, 9 March 1927.

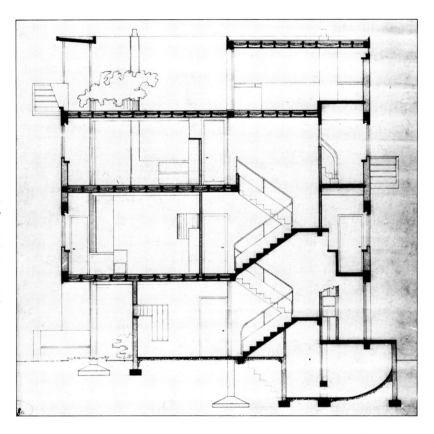

131. Villa Cook, Boulogne-sur-Seine. Above: section, definitive version, 24 June 1926 (FLC 8299)

132. Plan and elevations of kitchen, 2 July 1926 (FLC 8306)

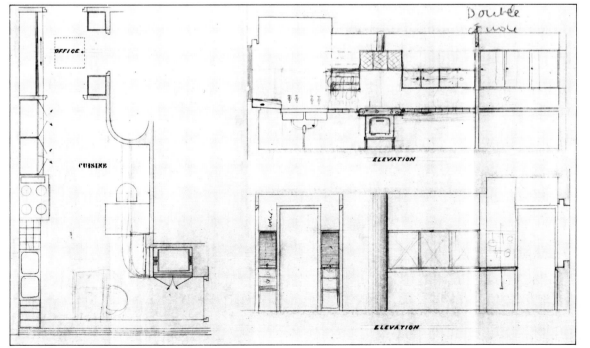

161

133. Villa Cook, top: garden side, before alterations; above: street front, facing page: terrace balcony and entrance

given first access to the site, carrying out quite extensive transplanting and landscaping work in December 1926 and January 1927, four months before construction on the house itself began. Before the house was completed, 67,893 francs were spent on Crépin's bill, testifying to the interest both architects and clients must have had in this feature of the house. From this point on, the Stein-de Monzie house incorporated a play of levels on the terraces which linked, at least conceptually, the garden and the roof terrace. Another feature which remains is the turning place at the end of the drive, the low wall and plinth which defines it and some sort of piercing of the ground floor area at the east end.

The preliminary drawings for the 20 July project are surprisingly tentative, but all of them have a thin service wing projecting to the north, on the west side.

The ground and first floor plans (FLC 10514, see p. 173) show the key developments. Some marginal sketches, by Le Corbusier on FLC 10509, show a dramatic extension to the *promenade architecturale* on the first floor terrace, sketched out in perspective, and in plan (FLC 10515, right). A complex route was contrived in a set of steps and walkways within the screen walls of the terrace, and then passing out through a 'window' in the north façade, to continue up to the roof in steps attached to the outside of this façade.

The result was a dramatic gesture, perceived on arrival along the drive: the two left-hand bays formed an 'empty' screen with a square hole in the middle of the upper part, from which a staircase rises to the roof. The house proper, then, was confined to the westward part of the site, clear of the pine trees, and this emerges most clearly from the garden front (FLC 10586). At this stage of the design, the importance of the trees on the east side of the site emerges clearly from FLC 10514, as does the programmatic alignment of a little formal garden in front of the main entrance in line with the driveway. The first floor shows a fascinating transition

between the first drawings, with the dining room on the right and the salon (now replaced by the terrace) to the left, and the main stairs in the middle. The plan is still essentially tripartite, despite the rhythm of five equal bays plus a thin 'extra' bay for the attached service wing. And yet, a key idea for the finished building is clearly visible here – the transparent vertical space around the main staircase, allowing views down into the hall from the first floor. This is yet another clue as to the continuity between this scheme and FLC 10410 in October.

The top floor plan (FLC 10512) provides us with a key poetic image of the luxury houses, which will remain a theme in large domestic buildings right up to the *Unité d'Habitation* (1945). Not only is the D-shaped roof of the Steins' bedroom developed as a solarium (as well as serving the sculptural function of the Miestchaninoff staircase tower), but the free plan of the roof line, and the eighty-two-metre running track, create a mixture of associations – Purist sculpture to Matte-Trucco Fiat factory racetrack – which ties together several Corbusian ideas. Michael Stein made his fortune out of the San Francisco tramways, rather than automobiles, but it was a consistent theme in Le Corbusier's attitude to the very rich that athletic exercise, sun and vigorous sculptural forms should be brought together at roof level, like some kind of deliberate commentary on puritanism and the rise of capitalism. The houses for Henry Church and the Savoyes would have similar forms and associations,

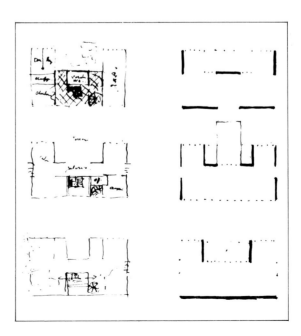

138. Villa Stein-de Monzie, Garches. Elevation and plans of the project of May–July 1926 (FLC 31049)

169

Villa 'Les Terrasses'

and it is a fascinating exercise to watch how these ideas were metamorphosed but never occluded in later developments of the designs for the Stein-de Monzie house.

The project of 20 July[3] clearly represented a serious proposal for the clients' consideration, given the formal nature of the presentation drawings. And yet the scheme has a number of surprising shortcomings. There is no garage, apparently no lodge indicated for a concierge, a remarkably wasteful use of space, with the very large wall surfaces represented by the service extension and, in the end, disappointing development of the spaces of the main living areas. I see the whole project as part of a vigorous 'loosening up exercise' intended to precipitate a decision, or at least a commitment, on the part of the clients. Like the similar drawings for Mme Meyer, they benefit from the in-attention to the finer points of planning in order to change the level of discourse, to raise the emotional temperature. A key ingredient in achieving this is the dramatic organisation of the *promenade architecturale* around a series of linked terraces. An essential pre-requisite was the extravagant use of space, bursting open the confines of the box to extrude the service functions in a separate wing, realising the geometrical rigour of the ABABABA grid. This expressive element was what Le Corbusier rediscovered in the scheme in 1959.

This drawing (it's the original) expresses the first flowering of the modest but passionate effort of 1918–25 – the first round of new architecture to be *manifested*. I use the term 'manifested' to mean in full bloom, open to the eye as to the soul (poetry, technology, biology, human scale). This week I saw Garches again, 32 years on, white (inside and out) behind its trees. It's an exquisite sight, at an *exquisite* scale, the adjective is justified here. This drawing is decisive testimony.[4]

Is it possible that this project, with its effortless manipulation of exterior perspectives, could have preceeded the painstaking researches of the other drawings we have been looking at? It is clear that almost all the ingredients of the final scheme have been introduced to us, needing only to be reorganised, synthesised, condensed (both in size and cost) and clarified.

What is not in doubt is the next dated step (FLC 10410, 7 October 1926, see p. 172). Here we have a combination of the ABABA grid of the earlier sketches with the dramatic *paysagiste* development of terraces, transferred to the west side of the house. If we return to FLC 31048 (p. 168), the top left sketch shows the basic idea; instead of of large central space,

flanked by two projecting wings, both 'wings' are joined together on the left side, with the terrace on the west. This idea is clearly legible in FLC 10410, but we also have the stark expression of the ABABA grid across the site, and an ABA grid in depth. After the explosion of expressive energy represented by the 20 July scheme and its preliminaries, these drawings return to the discipline of the enclosed area, within a plan of approximately 20 × 12.5 metres. The 2.5 metre wide bays run across the depth of the house and are clearly marked, not only in elevation, but in plan: the easternmost strip serves service functions on each floor. The elevations would have been clearly marked to show the 'B' bays, both in width and depth. The transverse, 'B' bay (east-west) was picked out clearly by free-standing *pilotis* and marked indentation in the flanking walls. One intriguing link between this drawing and FLC 31048, which refers back to the 'brief' of 7 May 1926, is the marking in of the Steins' antique furniture in the dining room. It is likely that the discussion of the 20 July scheme would have reasserted the interest of the clients in the reuse of their furniture.

What is clear, however, is that, whatever the precise sequence of events, the October scheme represents the basis of some kind of agreement with the clients, which was sealed by the legal contract between the architects and Gabrielle de Monzie on 10 November 1926. The contract deals only with the architects' services, honoraires fixed at ten per cent, and no mention of the forms of the house or the scale of the undertaking. The first estimate as to the eventual cost of the building was an ad hoc one, in April 1927, based on a rule of thumb (the mason's estimate representing sixty-two per cent of the total), which came out at 779,000 francs. We must assume that the clients were not putting much pressure on the architects for firm assurances of specific target budgets. Nevertheless, between FLC 10410, in October 1926, and the commencement of construction in April, a large number of detailed drawings and revisions were made, in which several key changes were introduced. One variant (FLC 10541, 10506, 10588 and 10582) enlarged the area of the first and second storeys by adding on a curious triangular balcony at the north-east corner, adjoining the kitchen. It is clear from this variant, not only that Le Corbusier felt highly con-strained by the physical limits of a rectangular plan form, but that he wanted to bring back into the scheme some of the drama and variety of the 20 July project. In both the October and November variants, a small external staircase was provided to link the second de Monzie bedroom (on the west side, second floor) to the roof, rising up through the space of the terrace. In an

3. *Oeuvre Complète*, I, p. 140.
4. FLC 31480, 20 July 1926, annotated 25 July 1959.

170

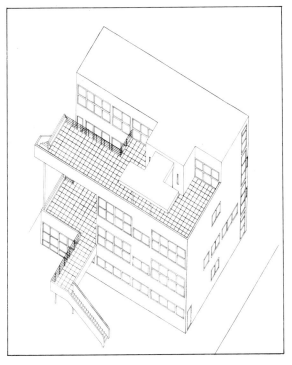 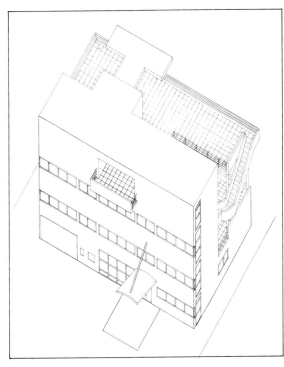

supplied by St. Gobain, which he proposed to mount in oak. A special bid had to be obtained from a local man, E. Henry, for a well and septic tank. The floor surfaces were typical; tiles in most of the public spaces (white or black), oak parquet *à l'anglaise* for the salon, dining room and library on the first floor, and the main bedrooms on the second.

None of the vagaries of design changes seem quite to account in this case for the very large extras submitted by Summer and the other tradesmen which must at least in part be attributed to the estimate of the client's worth and willingness to pay. Summer's *Memoire II*. 28 March 1928, runs to over 100 pages and 110, 353.75 francs, and did not count the 70,000 francs for the lodge of the concierge. Among the extras were some repairs and reinforcements to the *pilotis* on the north façade, to which reference was made in a letter by du Pasquier, one of the Swiss assistants, on 30 June 1927. A sketch in the letter confirms that the two streamlined section *pilotis* next to the main entrance were among those

altered, and they are mentioned on p. 60 of Summer's *Memoire*.

But most of the extras concerned simple details of finishing cupboards, concrete tables, sills, planters and borders, all of which could presumably have been specified in the plans if more time had been taken. The facts are stark enough. After a rough estimate of 779,000 francs in April 1927, the total by March 1928 had risen to something close to 984,251 francs, and Le Corbusier's request to Mme Colaco Osorio (Gabrielle de Monzie's maiden name) for the second two thirds of the fees was based on a total of 1,000,000 francs (9 March 1928), (66,666 francs, plus 2,000 francs towards the Lodge). Other accounts or pages of sums show the totals mounting through 1929–9, culminating in a letter of 2 January 1929 to Mme Colaco Osorio in which the total figure used for, calculating the fees, was 127,783.71. From a careful analysis of the records, I believe the figure should be raised slightly to 1,497,606 francs which, at roughly 1.5 million francs, makes it by

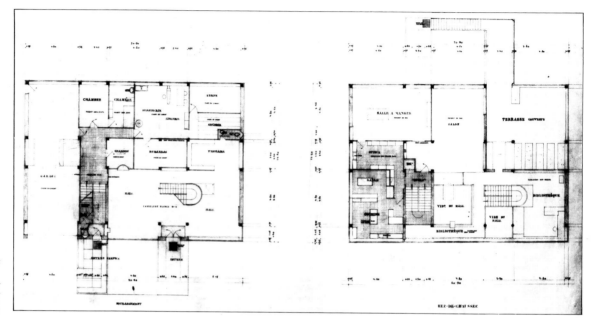

143. Villa Stein-de Monzie, Garches. Ground and first floor plans, 8 January 1927 (FLC 10417)

a fair margin the most expensive single house built by Le Corbusier before the war.

The house was occupied at some point before 2 January 1929, when Pierre writes to Mme Colaco Osorio at 'Les Terrasses' for the first time. Great care was taken with the publication drawings for the Villa Stein-de Monzie. The plans were redrawn in September 1928 for publication in the *Oeuvre Complète*. There were some drawings in March 1928 for metal sheet folded bookcases for the library, but there is nothing on any major repairs until December 1935– March 1936, when the house changed hands, being bought by a Danish banker called, surprisingly, Steen. Drawings record the initiatives associated with the purchase by the new client. First, there was the addition of a fireplace in the salon, faced in Italian cippolino marble (FLC 10457, December 1935 and FLC 31462, 24 March 1936). This fireplace and its surround can be

seen in some interior perspectives, in which the antique furniture of the Steins and de Monzie households is banished and replaced by Charlotte Perriand–Le Corbusier tubular steel designs (FLC 10494; pp. 184–5). It is notable, in fact, that although the Charlotte Perriand chairs, as already seen in her *Bar sous le Toit* of 1927, are very prominent, the armchairs are not of the *grand confort* type. A curious detail is the survival in the drawing of the Matisse nude belonging to Sarah Stein (FLC 10495; p. 165), on the concrete tablette designed for it. Three drawings record a scheme, presumably from the same period, to face the whole house and lodge with marble. Nothing came of this extraordinary proposal (FLC 10530; p. 165).

The history of the lodge reflects, in many ways, the history of the latter stages of development of the main villa. As we have seen, the 20 July 1926 scheme had no apparent provision for a lodge at the entrance, and the

21. Villa Stein (FLC 10587)

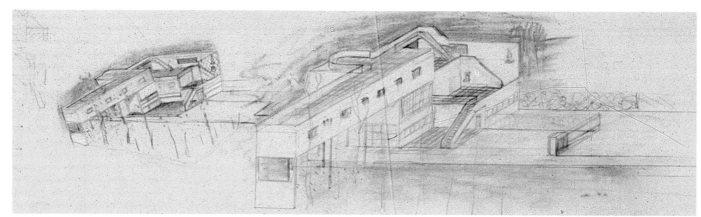

22. Villa Stein (FLC 10584)

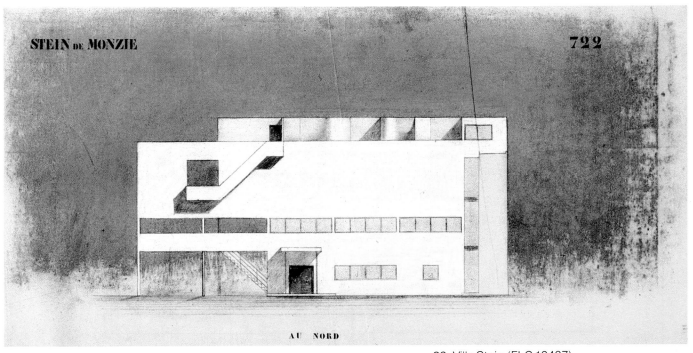

23. Villa Stein (FLC 10407)

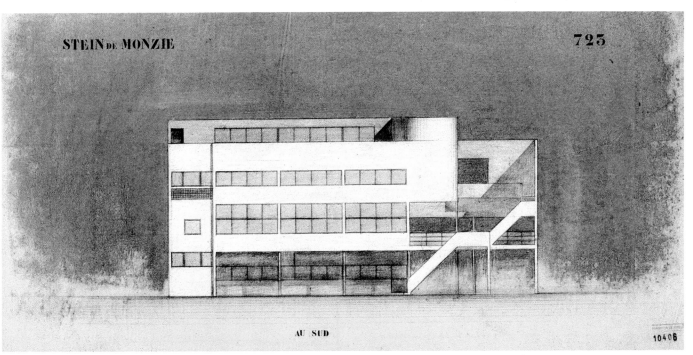

24. Villa Stein (FLC 10406)

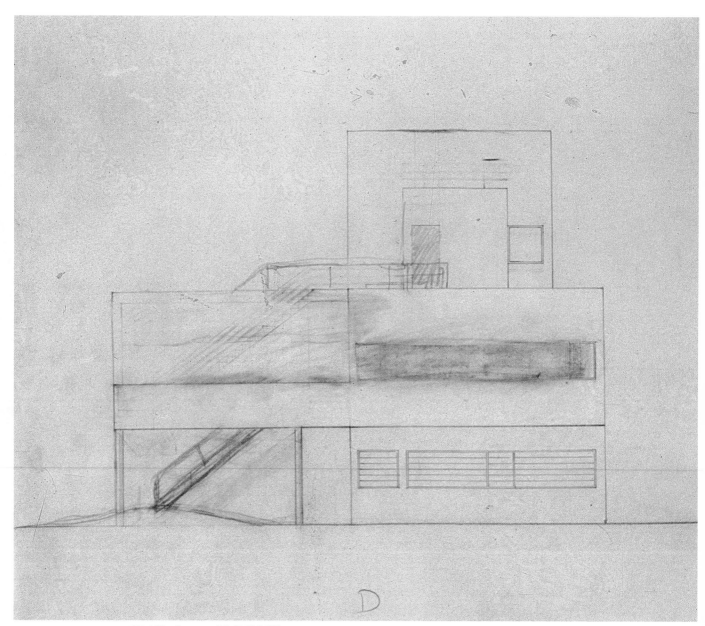

25. Villa Savoye (FLC 19549)

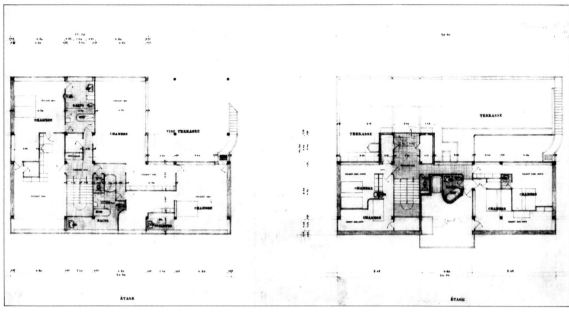

144. Villa Stein-de Monzie, Garches. Second and third floor plans, 8 January 1927 (FLC 10416)

first sure sign of one can be dated to November 1926. We must interpret its necessity as occasioned partly by the decision to eliminate the extruded service wing of the 20 July scheme, and partly, no doubt as a way of imposing a framed and controlled access to the main villa. It is clear from the photographs taken under Le Corbusier's supervision that the lodge was an important addition to the house. Both this one and the one for the Villa Savoye stand in relation to the main houses as units of mass housing to the luxury house derivatives. They have, therefore, a programmatic message. It is instructive, for example, that the first idea for the lodge

(FLC 10510 and 10411, 13 Nov. 1926), should have involved spanning the drive with a concrete slab, since this arrangement was a reminder of the 20 July scheme which would have presented a similar image of penetration in the main building. A note on FLC 10510 refers to the use of this roof slab as a reservoir of water for irrigation purposes. A drawing which reuses the idea of a concrete triumphal arch approach, possibly again in the context of some sort of water tank (FLC 10478), reverses the siting of the lodge. Instead of placing the drive close to the east side of the site, with space for a garden to the west of the entrance, this drawing and all

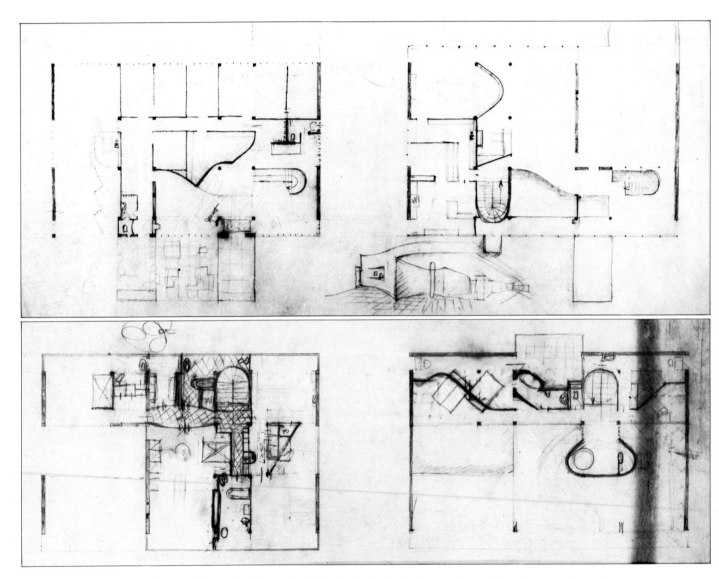

145. Villa Stein-de Monzie, Garches. Floor plans showing Le Corbusier's revisions before March 1927 (FLC 10518 and 10517)

subsequent ones place the drive in line with the service entrance, and the lodge to the west of this, aligned with a circular planter and small tree. The next datable lodge drawings do not follow until September 1927, but there are several earlier designs, presumably from the summer of 1927. The connections with Pessac became clearer in one of these schemes, which includes several drawings by Le Corbusier himself (FLC 10539). Here an external staircase led to the roof, while projecting L-shaped canopies over the door gave a hint of the organic, spreading analogy which informed the main building. The lodge was always conceived as more than an example of proletarian housing, but an 'introduction' to the main house. Thus an ABAA rhythm was introduced in some of these drawings as an introduction to the geometry of the main house. The L-shaped canopy over the door served to signal this 'B' bay in the smaller house, rather as the larger canopy over the principal entrance to the main building signalled one of the 'B' bays there. In these drawings, there is already a lot of attention to the functioning of the gate. Instead of masonry gate posts and traditionally hung gates (ironically sketched in on FLC 10480), the entrance gates would declare the theoretical principles of the *fenêtre en longueur*: they would roll sideways and be suspended under variously contrived steel scaffolding.

The group of drawings most closely associated with the set dated 5 September 1927 (FLC 10435) have in common a changed parti, compared to the earlier ones with the service functions grouped together at the north end of the lodge and a large sheltered porch on the west side. From the street, the north front of the lodge would have presented a rhythm of two five metre bays (porch on the right, lodge in the middle) followed by a 2.5 metre accent (formed by the canopy over the entrance). Thus, the syntax of the main house was introduced quite programmatically by the lodge.

In November 1927, the L-shaped porch on the west side of the lodge seems to have been dropped, along with the clear expression of the ABAA grid. As the form of the lodge became more modest and retiring, so

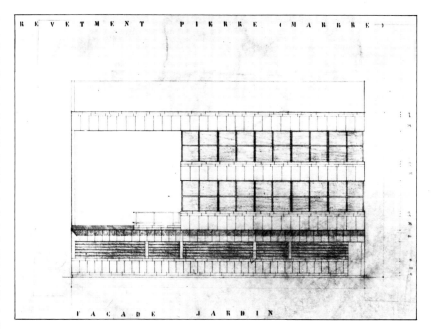

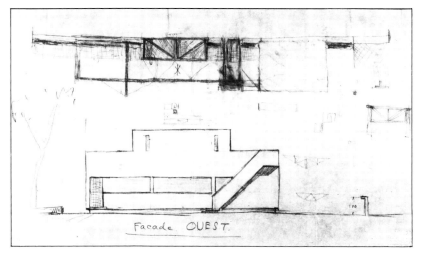

146. Villa Stein-de Monzie, Garches. Top: South elevation showing proposal to face the house in marble for Mr. Steen, 1936 (FLC 10530)

147. Above: South and West elevations of gatehouse lodge, May–September 1927 (FLC 10539)

183

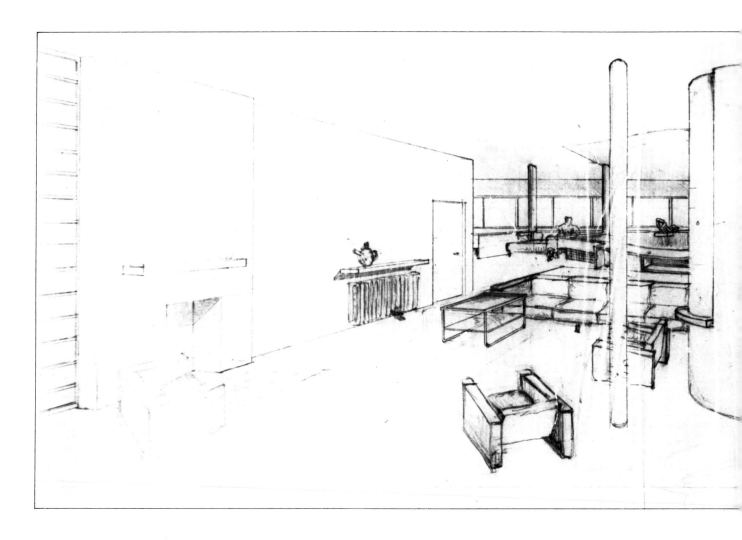

148. Villa Stein-de Monzie, Garches. Interior perspective of dining room and living room, showing proposed changes and new furniture, March 1936 (FLC 10494)

149. Following page: View of entrance hall

the ironmongery of the gate became lower and more discreet, still within the theory of a horizontally rolling mechanism. A number of drawings record the changing solutions to this expensive item.

The Villa Stein-de Monzie was not only the most expensive house built by Le Corbusier between the wars, it was one which raised and raises issues of principle, connected with what Giedion called the problem of the luxury house. Le Corbusier wrote a book about it, *Une Maison Un Palais*, in which he tries to show how all architecture, from the fisherman's cottage, built with his own hands, to the most 'important' palace (such as the League of Nations competition project), share the same fundamental values and material constraints. The Villa Stein-de Monzie can be read as an extension of the Esprit Nouveau Pavilion (like the Vitruvian hut extended into the Doric temple), or like a modernist re-analysis of the large bourgeois

pavilion, or as a more universal statement, an idealist affirmation of a new spirit. It is in the latter sense that the ever perceptive du Pasquier represented the building, writing to Le Corbusier on 30 June 1927, with the raw carcase of the building still emerging from the coffering:

I was enthralled on my return from the site on Tuesday evening... What a marvel the upper terrace is. You feel such joy on it that you put off the moment of coming down. What would the League of Nations terrace be like? The delegates would install themselves there and abandon their meetings![5]

5. Dossier Stein, file C, 30 June 1927.

150. Villa Stein-de Monzie, Garches. Above: Living room towards dining room; below: garage

151. Above: Roof terrace; below: garden front

152. Villa Savoye, Poissy. View underneath *pilotis* showing entrance on north-west side.

VILLA SAVOYE

Here then is the villa, born in 1929. It was happy in its limpid clarity. So was I. Thirty years have passed, years heavy with hair-raising struggles[1].

The Villa Savoye certainly looks limpid, clear and smiling, even today. Few other Corbusian buildings make such a powerful and startling first impression, befitting a villa with the name *Les Heures Claires*. It is interesting that Le Corbusier remembered the house as witness to a serene and untroubled period of his life. He can hardly have been remembering well, if by this he meant an uncomplicated and smooth daily routine, lacking *bagarres perilleuses* – the documents reveal that the building history of the Villa Savoye was as stormy, anguished and controversial as any, with the client eventually forced to threaten legal action. But I believe that there is an inner truth in the old architect's memory of this time. I read the design of the Villa Savoye as being the product of an uncharacteristically 'easy' birth, the almost automatic expression of the synthesis of ten years' research. Whether we call it the last Purist villa or the last ideal attempt at the reconciliation between Platonic absolutes, nature and man, it is clearly classifiable as the last of a series of Parisian villas sharing a certain vocabulary of forms and syntax of detailing. The next house to be undertaken, for Mme de Mandrot, at Le Pradet, Var, introduced very different ideas and forms.

There are two aspects to this. In the material sense, Le Corbusier and the atelier were overwhelmed with work between 1929 and 1933. Large and complex problems like the apartement de Beistegui, the Centrosoyus building (Moscow), the Cité de Refuge, the Cité Universitaire, the flats rue Nungesser et Coli were all actually built, while many other schemes went through numerous design stages. For a start, this work removed one factor in the design of bourgeois villas, the need to earn some money. In an intellectual and ideological sense, however, the work of 'research' which dominated the 1920s had come to an end. I have argued that what characterised the domestic work of the 1920s was its insertion, often against the grain, into the single, unified inquiry which Le Corbusier called, in *Précisions* 'L'Architecture en tout, Urbanisme en tout'. All the little problems of the house – the window, the fireplace,

1. From dedication of a copy of *Oeuvre Complète*, II, sent to M. Touhladjian, Mayor of Poissy, 15 July 1960.

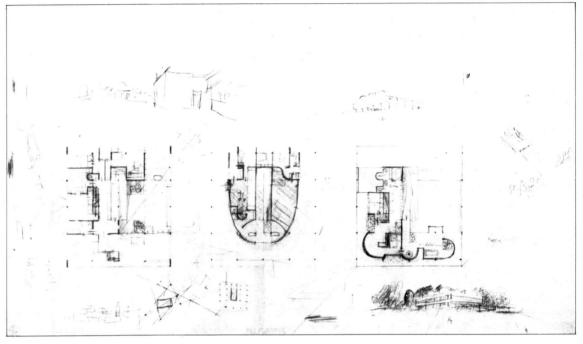

153. Villa Savoye, Poissy. Plans and perspective sketches of first variant of the first project, September 1928 (FLC 19583)

concrete detail profiles – were tackled again and again as if they were part of a single solution: the victory of Modern Architecture. Every feature, *pilotis*, roof garden or whatever, had to be justified both in individual and in urbanistic terms. This is why the standard housing cell types – Dom-Ino, Citrohan, Immeuble-Villa and, after 1928, Maison Loucheur – underpin the thinking and indeed the actual forms of all the 1920s villas. After 1930, Le Corbusier's thought diversified considerably. The urban plans, especially those for Algiers, became increasingly free form creations in their own right. The forum of CIAM encouraged this extension of urbanism as autonomous creation. Meanwhile, just as Le Corbusier's painting had begun to lead a separate path from that of Purism since 1928, so the domestic architecture began to free itself, to become more 'personal', more biomorphic and organic.

He considered that the work he had done in defining the 'certainties' of machine-age architecture allowed him to step onto a higher plane than the functionalists: 'But I will only allow a poem made of "freestanding words". I want a poem *made of solid words with defined meanings and a clear syntax*. For art is nothing but an individual manifestation of freedom, of personal choice; through it, a man can feel alive.'[2] And again, in even stronger language: 'The architectural idea is a peremptorily individual phenomenon, inalienable. It is good to push an idea to a state of purity.'[3]

I see the Villa Savoye as the spontaneuous expression of the *mots solides* and the *syntaxe claire* developed over the previous ten years at the precise moment at

2. 'Ou en est l'architecture?' in *Le Corbusier et Pierre Jeanneret, I serie, L'Architecture Vivante*, n.d.
3. *Precisions, Sur L'Etat présent de L'Architecture*, 1929, p. 134.

which a unified language of Purist architecture was about to be discarded. I see it, furthermore, as an 'easy' design, rather like the Villa Cook, benefiting from a number of circumstances which removed the kind of obstacles which had usually complicated and upset the design process in the earlier villa. All the villas we have looked at so far were complicated either by cramped sites, awkward clients or shortage of funds over expectations. At Poissy, the site was an idyllic one, open to a spectacular view to the north-west, shielded from the road by high trees. Problems of access, lighting, and the compression of functions in a pre-scribed space were here made redundant. Secondly, the client appeared to be amenable. Le Corbusier described the Savoyes as 'quite without preconceived conceptions, either old or new.'[4] Unlike the case with many of the clients, the Savoyes had few criticisms to make of the design drawings (but plenty of the construction!). That the design history of the Villa Savoye is as complex as it is can be attributed to quite different, but characteristic factors. Once again, the first project, (p. 194, right) turned out to be too expensive and it was simply the difficulties in cutting the first scheme down in cost which led to the bizarre excursions of November 1928. The final designs marked a return to the arrangement of the first project, with apparently minor modifications, but with the accretion of a number of new features which add richness and complexity to the building we see today.

Before tracing this bizarre sequence of events, we should analyse the first project for the Villa Savoye, and investigate its origins.[5] Unusually, there are no drawings conserved among the Villa Savoye set which trace the gradual emergence of the key features of the design. On one sheet (FLC 10583), Le Corbusier worked out not only the details of the three floor plans, but also several of the perspective views. The many preliminary drawings for this first project can be shown to follow after this key sheet, leading up to the presentation set of October 1928. But, fortunately, some drawings have been preserved, filed among the drawings of other schemes, which allow us to trace

some of the background ideas with precision. There is a group of tiny marginal sketches, added to a drawing for the Villa Baizeau which can be securely dated to March 1928 (FLC 24983), and we can suggest that they derive from the generalised substratum of Corbusian idealism running behind all his projects. These sketches show a horizontal box, raised off the ground on *pilotis*, with a *fenêtre en longeur* running right round it. There are no clear plans, just perspective sketches. And yet these sketches look undeniably like the Villa Savoye, at a time when the Poissy project was at least six months away. Now, the Baizeau scheme, too, was for a site with a view and on a hill, or at least a cliff top, and I explain these sketches as simple developments of the Baizeau idea without the constraints of the Tunisian climate or Baizeau's site, which was long and narrow.

Another general theme which could be extrapolated from the 1920s work is the obsession with circulation and how the paths traced by automobiles can be integrated into the form of the architecture. Again, Maison Cook provides one kind of precedent: the ground floor entrance hall shaped to act as divider between car access and the curving pedestrian path.

This should be considered together with some sketches on two pages of sketchbook mounted with a third (top right), the latter being for the Villa Ocampo scheme (FLC 31044). A set of drawings for Mme Ocampo were prepared on 18 September 1928, and it is likely that this one belongs to the same period. The other two sheets, however, have nothing to do with the Ocampo scheme and are on the contrary clearly identi-fiable as for Savoye. One of the sketches shows the corner of the Poissy property quite clearly, and the section shows the characteristic tall trees flanking the site. Now if ever we needed proof that Le Corbusier made a mental connection between the circulation of automobiles and that of people moving round the interior of a house, these drawings supply it. Here we

4. *Oeuvre Complète*, II, p. 24.
5. See Tim Benton, 'Villa Savoye and the Architect's practise', *Le Corbusier*, vol. 7, Garland, for a fuller account of these developments.

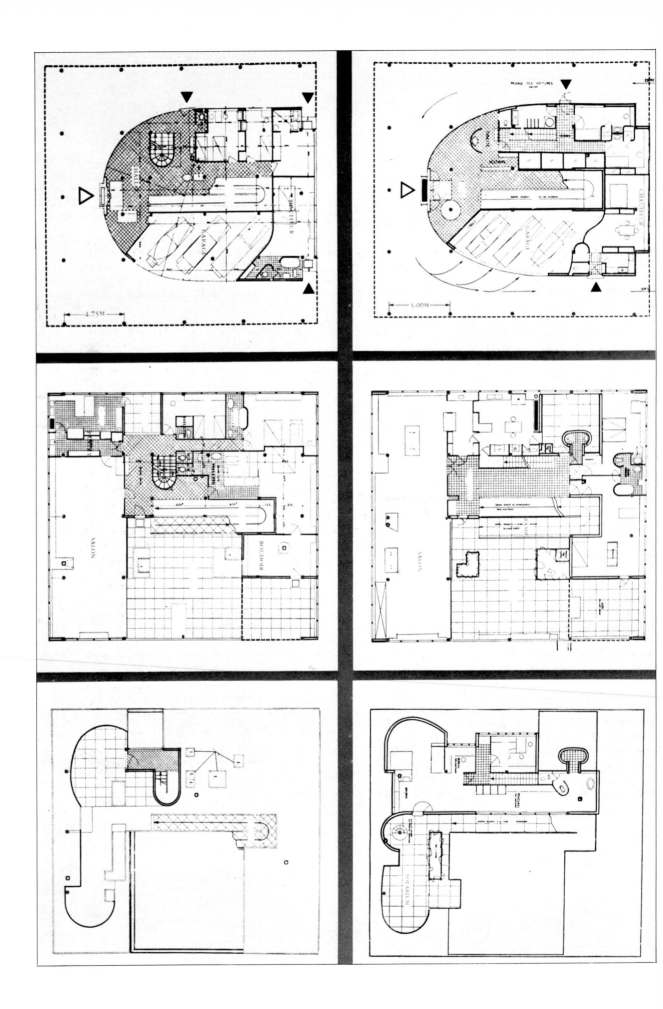

have a plan in which the driveway literally takes off and enters the house at first floor level, an idea which was only given partial form after the War, in the Carpenter Centre in Boston or the Mill Owners house, Ahmedabad. But what makes this external ramp even more relevant to the Savoye scheme as we know it is the internal ramp which follows. The cars, having deposited their occupants at a *porte-cochère* projecting from the main building, plunge down through the centre of the house. Le Corbusier clearly had difficulty imagining what could happen next, but the plan shows a bifurcation, with a garage to the left and an exit drive to the right. Another plan adopts a more moderate approach, with a turning place for cars in front of the house (south-east side) and what looks like an external pedestrian ramp rising up to the first floor. Only the internalisation of this ramp, and the superimposing of the curved form of the drive to become an integral part of the ground floor plan were required for the basic ideas of the Villa Savoye to be complete.

It is clear from these sketches that the point of departure is the first floor plan. These sketches already show the *salle* facing the view on the north-west side, a terrace garden to the south-west and the other rooms deployed around them. Again, this corresponds to our expectations of what an 'ideal' living area would be for Le Corbusier. In his town houses, he had frequently been forced to place the living areas as high as possible to catch the light. In the first Villa Savoye project developed in September (FLC 19583), the one large floor plan could accomodate all the main living functions, with the master bedroom and its apurtenances placed above so that it, too, could share the view to the north west and, most importantly, so that it could register on the exterior as that bold, voluptuous and anthropomorphic curved volume which had already been an image in Le Corbusier's mind since March. Given freedom to classify the plan in Cartesian manner, Le Corbusier deployed the four sides of the house in response to the view and the orientation of the sun. The *salle* faced north west, occupying the whole façade. The terrace faced the sun, with a sheltered portion at the south-east end. The son's and guests' rooms faced the

south east, while the kitchen, pantry and service terrace were left on the north-east side.

In his explanation of the raised living area, Le Corbusier expressed more clearly than ever before the almost pathological anxiety he felt about the ground level and the desirability of raising human habitation to a level from which nature could be contemplated 'as in a Virgilian dream'.

> Standing in a field, you cannot see very far. What's more, the soil is unhealthy, damp, etc... To live in it, consequently, the real garden of the house will not be at ground level, but above it, 3.5 metres up: this will be the hanging garden whose surface is dry and healthy, and from it you will get a good view of the landscape, much better than if you had stayed below.[6]

But at Poissy, several ideas came together. The *jardin suspendu* of the Immeuble-Villa, an inner-city solution to the flat dweller's garden, could here pose as a viewing platform, and as symbol for the function of the whole living area floor – the contemplation of nature. In the first project, the terrace garden is emblematically linked to the earth by a staircase, as it had been in the Villa Meyer projects and the Villa Stein. At the same time, this kind of link between urban man on his terrace and pure nature at his feet was echoed by the symbolism of the ramp which picked up the concept of motor car travel and projected it into a pedestrian ramp which begins indoors and finishes up externally, reaching the roof.

In this second role, the ramp picks up that imagery of the earth ramps of Middle Eastern architecture which seems to have lain behind the Maison de Weekend at Rambouillet, at the 1924 Salon. To lend some support to this, it is only necessary to read again from the architect's description in the *Oeuvre Complète*:

> Arab architecture has a precious lesson for us. You appreciate it on foot, *walking*. Only on foot, in movement, can you see the developing articulation

6. *Oeuvre Complète*, II, p. 24.

154. Villa Savoye, Poissy. Redrawn plans contrasting the project of 6–10 October 1928 (facing page, right) with the final scheme of 12 April 1929 (facing page left)

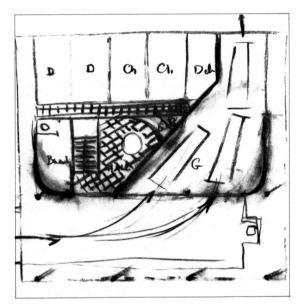

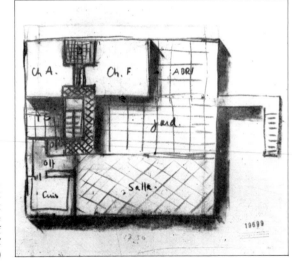

155. Villa Savoye, Poissy. Ground and first floor plans of first variant of the intermediary scheme of 6 November 1928 (FLC 19659 and 19699)

already encountered in the earlier work. Not only was the body of the ground floor withdrawn from the outer edges of the box, as in Cook or Baizeau, but the form could be made to accomodate the whole arc of vehicular circulation within itself. On three sides, the ground floor almost disappears, but on the entrance side, the arrival and departure of cars is celebrated in a T-shape which is an effective sign of welcome.

The *pilotis* in the October project are set out in the simplest arrangement compatible with the centrally placed ramp and the intrusion of the garage. The 'standard' five metre intercolumniation is used, as in so many 'ideal' schemes we have looked at. This was to be sacrificed for the sake of planning details, as the design progressed.

The October project looks so close to the villa as it exists today (see p. 194, left), that the question of design changes would appear to be simply a matter of detailing. But, although Le Corbusier clearly thought that this scheme would satisfy his clients, since more drawings (including 1:20 scale interior elevations of most of the principal rooms) were made for this scheme than for the final project, a snag emerged. A full set of contractors' tenders were called for and came in by 5 November. But when Pierre worked out the total cost, despite every effort to reduce individual estimates, the total came out at around 785,600 francs, which was clearly more than the Savoyes had intended to pay for a summer villa.

To prefigure the changes initiated after 5 November, it is only necessary to contrast the plans and south-west elevations of four of the variants: that of 6 November, 7 November, 26–27 November and the penultimate scheme of 17 December 1928 (see p. 198–9).

At first sight, this sequence of plans seems incomprehensible, a monstrous deviation from the straight path which leads from the October scheme to that of 17 December. The project of 26–27 November, above all, seems almost for a different building, especially if you look at the ground floor plan and south-west elevations. Where is the horizontal 'box in the air, pierced all around', the U-shaped ground plan formed by the path of an automobile, the ramp, the regular grid of *pilotis* spaced evenly five metres apart? And yet, a study of the first and second floor plans shows a more steady progression from one plan to the next. The first floor plans in the November projects make room for a large staircase which, when the staircase was made much smaller in December, allowed room for the guest bedroom and son's bedroom on the north-east side. A 'discovery' in the November 26–27 scheme was the possibility of putting the kitchen and pantry on the north-west side next to the salon, and this was the key feature which made the December scheme workable. It is the disappearance of the master bedroom on the

of the architecture. It's the opposite principle to that of Baroque architecture which is conceived on paper, from a theoretical viewpoint. I prefer the teaching of Arab architecture.[6]

Once arrived at the top floor, there is a typical appendix, redolent of marine architecture. As in the Villa Stein, there was to have been a spiral staircase to climb yet again onto the roof of the bedroom. FLC 19639 marks the introduction of this idea, as well as the addition of external stairs from the terrace to the ground. The ground floor, too, synthesised ideas second storey plan in December (the November projects have an essentially identical programme for the second storey) which was intended to produce the economies demanded by the client, as we will see.

What can we make of this project of 26–27 November? One impression is that violence has been deliberately done to the limpid clarity of the first project. The brutal contrast between vertical staircase block and the remaining portions of *fenêtre en longeur*, the schematic deployment of solid against open on the south-west front, like a two-dimensional graphic exercise, the introduction of the industrial *pan de verre* for the staircase window facing the terrace: all these things suggest some act of destruction. And yet, in each case, we will find traces of these changes in the finished building. For example, the vertical/horizontal contrast, almost absent from the first project, was reintroduced in the final scheme in the form of the spiral staircase. A sketch in *Précisions*, and the accompanying text, make this clear: 'The spiral, pure vertical organ, is inserted freely into the horizontal composition.'[7]

The verticality of this spiral staircase is made externally powerful through the curved staircase housing on the roof, turned round only in the last stages of the design (April 1929), so as to make an impact from the terrace. Another last minute change was to remove the screening wall which had enclosed the spiral staircase in the penultimate scheme (17 December, 1928). This made the supposed function of the service staircase obsolete, but greatly enhanced its compositional value in counteracting the overwhelming horizontality of the house. Le Corbusier often referred to the conflict between horizontal and vertical, male and female, as one of the fundamentals of art. The *pan de verre*, in the 26–27 November scheme with its incredible lighting effect through the staircase hall to the ground floor north-east window of the entrance hall, also had a lesson for modifying the first project. The ramp had originally been enclosed, apart from the one triangular window lighting the first floor landing. But in the finished scheme, every effort was made to open up the ramp to the terrace garden with a second triangular window. Where, in the first project, the ramp had also been enclosed on the ground floor by cupboards lining the ground floor servants' corridor, in the final scheme it was exposed as an object of contemplation, thus making it possible to see down into the entrance hall and out onto the terrace, as you move up or down the ramp. It was always paradoxical that the same *fenêtre en longueur* should run uninterruptedly round four sides of the box, irrespective of what was behind; but Le Corbusier very carefully showed that, in fact, the terrace window was a screen wall only. He

profiled the *pilotis* on this section in an aerofoil shape, not only to house a down pipe from the lintel above, but also to make this one *piloti* thinner than the others. A similar aerofoil profiling took place with the *pilotis* of the ramp, to help give the sense of imperceptible movement. Above all, it was the solution of placing salon, kitchen and pantry in line on the north-west side in the 1 November projects, which allowed Le Corbusier to solve the problem of economising on the first scheme.

To understand all this, we must see how and why the scheme of 26–27 November emerged. We noted that the cost of the first scheme was estimates around 785,060 francs by Pierre Jeanneret. This was on 5 November. In the next two days, he and Le Corbusier tried out a drastic reduction of the area of the building, the most obvious way to reduce the size. Three drawings (FLC 19659, 19698–9) show the first attempts to eliminate the ramp and thus make size savings on the first floor. They worked with a grid of *pilotis* (still 5 × 5 metres but only three bays square) with inexorable consequences. There was now no room for cars to make the U-turn under the house, so an L-shaped circulation route was investigated. This created a number of problems as to how the ground floor plan should be organised.

The first and second floor plans proved relatively easy. Working on these, between 6 and 7 November, the tripartite division of the plan imposed by the grid and the presence of the staircase in the centre of the north-east side, began to become increasingly dominant (see pp. 198–9, first two rows). In one drawing, (FLC 19700) Le Corbusier resolved all these details by exploding the ground floor into fragments grouped around a central staircase. Interestingly, in this first

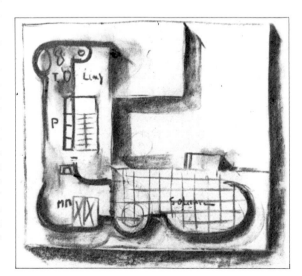

156. Villa Savoye, Poissy. Second floor plan of first variant of the intermediary scheme of 6 November 1928 (FLC 19698)

7. *Précisions*, pp. 135 and 138.

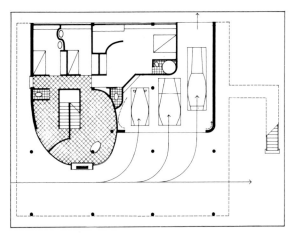
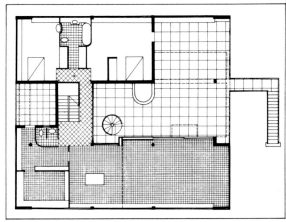

157. Villa Savoye, Poissy. Redrawn ground and first floor plans based on Le Corbusier's drawings (FLC 19660, 19635 and 19636) dated 6 November 1928.

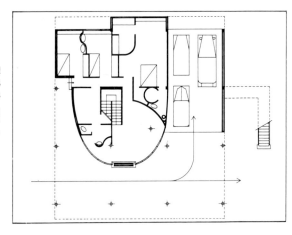
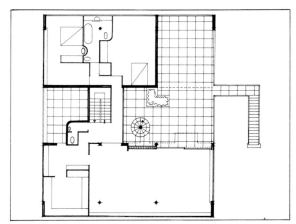

158. Redrawn ground and first floor plans based on Le Corbusier's drawings (FLC 19662, 19714 and 19661) dated 7 November 1928.

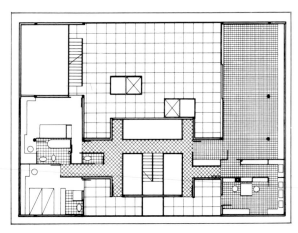

159. Redrawn ground and first floor plans based on Le Corbusier's drawings (FLC 19427, 19428, 19429 and 19430) dated 26–27 November 1928.

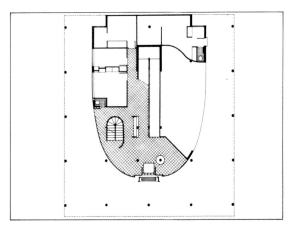
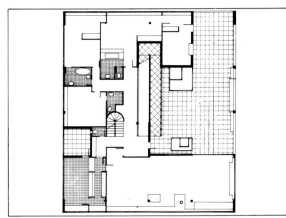

160. Redrawn ground and first floor plans based on Le Corbusier's drawings (FLC 19432, 19431, 19434 and 19435) dated 17 December 1928.

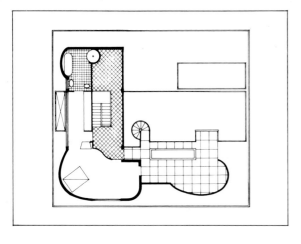

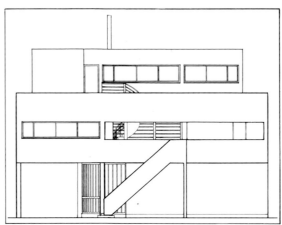

161. Villa Savoye, Poissy. Redrawn second floor plan and south-west elevation based on Le Corbusier's drawings (FLC 19660, 19635 and 19636) dated 6 November 1928.

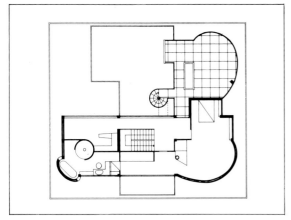

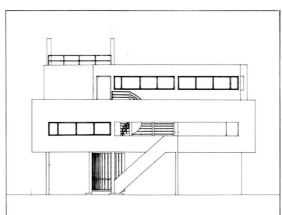

162. Redrawn second floor plan and south-west elevation based on Le Corbusier's drawings (FLC 19662, 19714 and 19661) dated 7 November 1928.

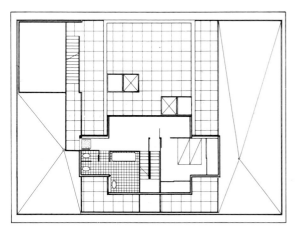

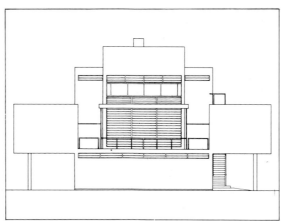

163. Redrawn second floor plan and south-west elevation based on Le Corbusier's drawings (FLC 19427, 19428, 19429 and 19430) dated 26–27 November 1928.

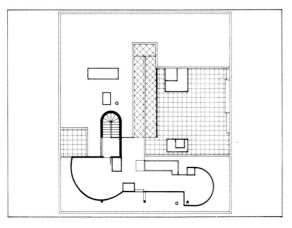

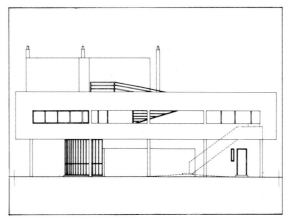

164. Redrawn second floor plan and south-west elevation based on Le Corbusier's drawings (FLC 19432, 19431, 19434 and 19435) dated 17 December 1928.

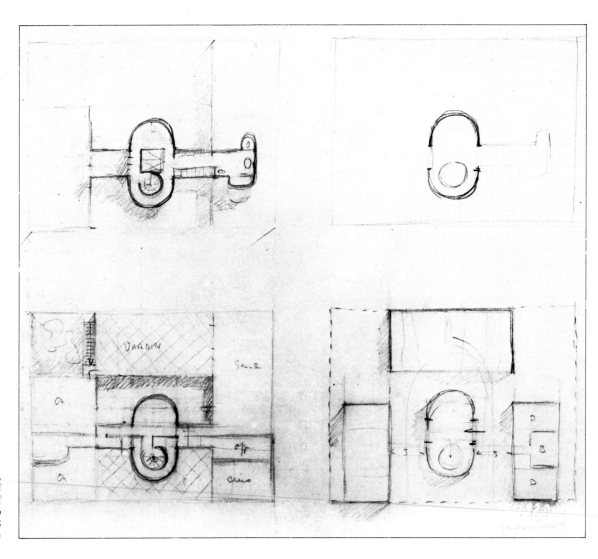

165. Villa Savoye, Poissy. Floor plans of preliminary version of the project of 7–26 November 1928 (FLC 19700)

drawing for what became the 26 November project, the staircase was conceived as a spiral, as in the finished building. It was the dismemberment of the ground floor plan into separate garage, staircase, chauffeur's apartment and servants' rooms which, in turn, led to the decomposition of the masses of the exterior. The interaction between exploded ground floor and first floor plan can be seen clearly (FLC 19491; p. 203). The garage had to be pushed out to the edge of the box. Some of the excitement of this radical departure can be seen from the vigorous drawing style of FLC 19485.

I believe that the rest, the filling in of the south-west ends of the salon window and the covered terrace to make rhetorical screens, and the opening out of the terrace wall so as to give greater impact to the *pan de verre*, must all be set in relation to the one decision

to change the ground floor plan. Interestingly, the projects of 6–7 November included no elevations or sections, nor indeed does the attempt to reconstruct them from the plans do more than show how unresolved these variants were. The story of the November projects, then, appears to do little credit to Le Corbusier and Pierre. But it demonstrates the power as well as the inflexibility of their methodology. They found it difficult to compromise with decisions. Once the whole idea of enclosing the car circulation within the body of the house had been discarded, the whole of the rest of the design went with it, apart from the basic arrangement of the first and second floors. But the solution was so simple: cut down the *cube*, not the *area*, by moving the master bedroom onto the first floor, compromise over the dimensions and reduce the area by ten per cent, giving a bay of 4.75 metres, instead of the more satisfying five metres. That this was exactly how the architects saw the matter emerges clearly from a page of calculations connected with the December scheme. In this Pierre simply marked *Suppression 1 étage* and *Reduction 10% surface*, as items for cutting the total. The resulting estimate, 487,000 francs, was enough for them to go ahead and present the clients with the worked-out scheme in December. The presentation drawings are dated 17 December and were sent to the client on the 20th. We can trace the development of the December projects, which had variants in which the intercolumniation varied from 4.5 to 5 metres and a variety of planning solutions to the arrangement of rooms on the ground floor and first floors, in eighty-one drawings. One drawing, for example, (FLC 19558), shows the service stairs straight, as in the October project, but the other planning changes as in the December scheme. Several drawings (e.g. FLC 19555) show the staircase oriented in either a south-easterly direction (to make more room in the hall at ground level) or towards the north west, where a curving screen wall could give some semblance of discretion to the service function. FLC 19557 (p. 202) show first and second floor superimposed, and seems to have clinched this discussion.

It must be said that another ingredient in the solution was to practise a conscious and systematic deception on the client as to the eventual cost of the building, leaving out several important items and including always the cheapest estimates, using materials and finishes that they would never have contemplated accepting in the finished building. Thus, the estimates presented to the client on the basis of the December drawings, on 15 February 1929, amounted to 558,690 francs, but left out any proposed estimate of the lodge, the landscape gardening and numerous other large items. A large number of details and interior elevations accompany

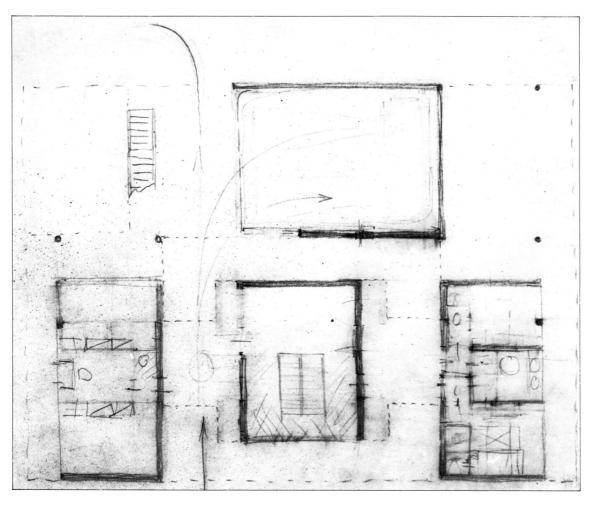

166. Villa Savoye, Poissy. Ground floor plan of project of 7–26 November 1928 (FLC 19485)

167. Villa Savoye, Poissy. The roof terrace in construction, summer 1929.

this penultimate stage of the design, mostly prepared between the December plans and the tenders and contracts with the entrepreneurs in February and March 1929 respectively.

The total eventual cost (815,000 francs) was made considerably larger by the fact that fundamental changes were introduced in a new set of drawings prepared in April 1929 and continuing until the summer. Some changes were minor, but expensive to correct: a difference in the height of the ground floor led to alterations to the windows of the hall, which had been ordered in March to the wrong dimensions. The service staircase was turned round through 90°, causing innumerable changes in detailing to the plans. A second corridor was added in the first floor plans for access to the guest and son's bedroom. The apartment for the chauffeur, which had always been placed next to the garage, was exchanged for a bedroom suite for guests, with the intention that the chauffeur would be accomodated in a double house with the gardener and concierge. Designs for this double lodge were prepared through April, May and June, 1929, as we will see, but abandoned as too expensive in July. By this stage, the ground floor guest suite, with bathroom but no kitchen, had been long since completed. The chauffeur's apartment had to be reinstalled, with modifications including the construction of a new wall. The plan illustrated in the *Oeuvre Complète*, volume II, does not correspond to the ground floor after this alteration, nor do any plans survive which show it.

The design of the lodge, like that of the Villa Stein-de Monzie, forms an interesting commentary on the history and meanings of the house itself. Some apparently early site plans had shown various indications of some kind of lodge next to the entrance gate (e.g. FLC 19544). Some of these plans may well have been redrawn or altered later, however. Although Mme Savoye had mentioned *logements* for a chauffeur and

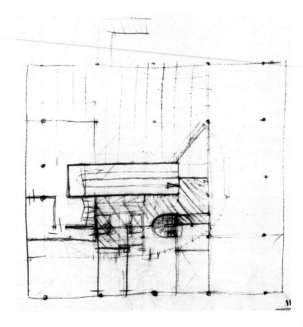

168. Villa Savoye, Poissy. The house in construction, summer 1929.

for a gardener in her brief and in the note made by Pierre (September 1928), all the early estimates, including that of February 1929, had simply allowed a guess estimate of 30,000 francs for its provision. No serious design work on the lodge can be dated before April 1929, and it is significant that the entrepreneurs had not tendered for it in February. After two rather tentative drawings, (FLC 19720 and 19612), the April designs relate closely enough to the dated drawings (FLC 19610, 27 April 1929). This drawing shows a double lodge, quite close in conception to the Maison Minimum houses of 1926 or the Loi Loucheur plans of July and August 1928. The plan shows the house lying diagonally across the old estate road, which was to be removed at this point, but two sketches show the next idea; to turn the lodge round at right angles, bridging the road and expressing clearly the chauffeur's function, above his automobile. In this form it was drawn up in May, and presented in a finished scheme on 6 and 7 May (FLC 19450). After another two variants in June, the parti was changed for that of a single lodge. An estimate of 76,300 francs for the 'double' lodge probably caused this change of mind, and although we find a reference to a 'medium' lodge, it is clear that greater economies than this were going to be needed. The first version of the 'single' lodge (FLC 19717) followed the arrangement of the last double lodge, placing the building across the road, while the later versions took the final solution of setting the lodge back next to the estate wall, partially behind a tree. (FLC 19471, 7 July 1929).

With all these changes and additions, the bill of extras from the Maison Cormier ran to eighty pages for the house and lodge and involved a total of 414,884 francs, nearly double the original contract of March (276,000 francs). Although Pierre did what he could to contest the claims for extras from all entrepreneurs, the changes in the plans made it impossible to do so effec-

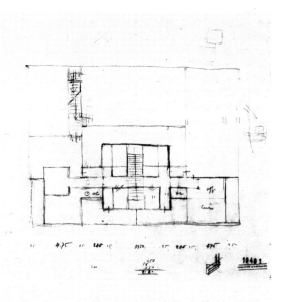

169. First floor plan, project of 7–26 November 1928 (FLC 19491)

Far left: Villa Savoye, Poissy. First floor plan, penultimate scheme, December 1928 (FLC 19557)

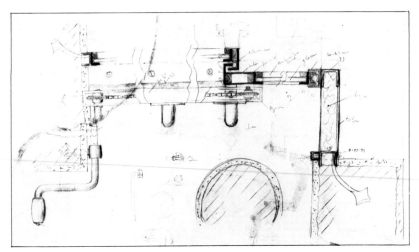

170. Villa Savoye, Poissy. Detail plan and section of streamlined concrete *piloti*, April–June 1929 (FLC 19531)

171. Detail plan of the mechanical device for opening the salon window, February–March 1929 (FLC 19637)

tively. A factor in the final arguments about the payment of outstanding bills was the urgent need for repairs which already began to manifest themselves in 1931–32. Every autumn, throughout the 1930s, there were cries of distress from the Savoye family with the first rains: 'I must admit that I am not *au fait* with this (a complaint about the central heating), which was a matter between Mme Savoye and my associate Pierre Jeanneret... Never having followed this affair, it is difficult for me to offer an exact opinion...'[8] Whatever the defects of the building, however, and whatever methods used to get it built, the Villa Savoye continues to fascinate by the direct power of its imagery. It requires, perhaps, a special kind of obstinacy to pursue an idea through so many difficulties, but if Le Corbusier saw the world largely in terms of a struggle between idea and material obstructions, like his analogy of the meander, then this is one case where the river ran nearly straight to the sea.

It is evident, furthermore, that the certainties and convictions, on which the first designs were based, in 1928, were giving way to strange doubts by the time the house was nearing completion. In January 1930, for example, Pierre carried out a number of designs to direct Crepin's landscape gardening work. One of these designs, (FLC 19539), completely demolished the classic arrival and departure scheme of the drives leading to the house, in favour of an organic and picturesque arrangement of flower beds. A month later, he designed a monumental stone dog kennel, to form and odd contrast with the crisp prism of the lodge just behind (FLC 19481). This is already the world of a very different project, being worked on at exactly this time, the country villa at Le Pradet, Var, for Mme de Mandrot. The first drawings for this house, in December 1929 and January 1930, had been in the form and technique of the Maisons Loucheur (all dry construction with central stone walls, steel frame and zinc sheet walls). By March, however, this scheme had given way to the organic stone structure with a large raised terrace curving round the sloping site and a separate guest room (not unlike the Savoye dog kennel) which marks the beginning of a completely new chapter in Le Corbusier's architecture.

8. Dossier Savoye, FLC Doc. 313, 7 September 1936.

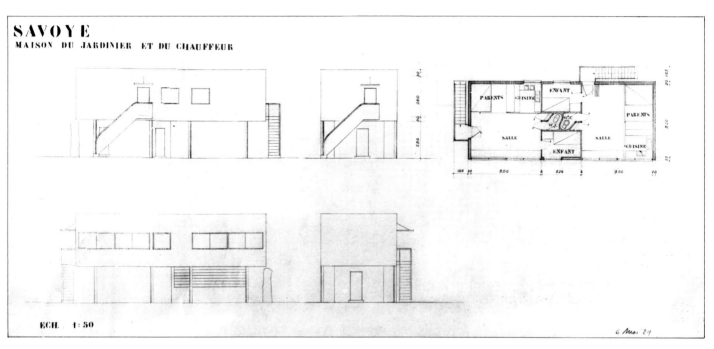

SAVOYE
MAISON DU JARDINIER ET DU CHAUFFEUR

ECH. 1:50

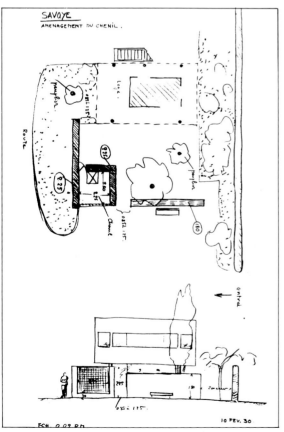

SAVOYE
AMENAGEMENT DU CHENIL.

ECH. 0.02 P.M.   10 FEV. 30

172. Villa Savoye, Poissy. Plan and elevations of double lodge for gardner and chauffeur, 7 May 1929 (FLC 19450)

173. Plan and elevation of single lodge in its definitive form, with the wall, bench and dog kennel, 10 February 1931 (FLC 19481).

205

174. Villa Savoye, Poissy. Above: Living room and terrace; below: lodge and kennel; facing page, top: terrace; below: living room

175. Beistegui apartment, Champs Elysée. View of terrace and Arc de Triomphe.

DE BEISTEGUI APARTMENT

The interaction between the architect of the Villa Savoye and the cosmopolitan millionaire Charles de Beistegui produced one of the most exotic and puzzling of Le Corbusier's works. In many ways the apartment on the avenue des Champs Elysées can be represented as a further break-up of the certainties of Le Corbusier's 1920s work. The fact that de Beistegui transformed the interior with his suffocatingly plush furniture and Surrealist imagery further confuses the issue. What is clear, however, is that Le Corbusier began the commission from a position of convinced Modernism, asserting:

> Your brief interests us because it is a shop-window programme (Champs Elysées), because it proposes a solution for the rooftops of Paris which I've been talking about for fifteen years... As for me, my campaign has been running for twenty years. Now, the victory has been won. I am famous; what I do is known. Every day I am trying to bring it to perfection. I have one idea only, to make of each of my problems a pure, unbeatable, correct work.[1]

And in a letter to the Italian modernist P.M. Bardi in 1933, Le Corbusier had no qualms in setting the apartment de Besitegui alongside the Pavillon Suisse as paradigmatic examples of his urbanistic principles.

In one sense, the de Beistegui apartment is a classic expression of Corbusian dogma: the roof garden as a prototype for a Plan Voisin or Ville Radieuse. In another sense it is an absurdly grandiose expression of *art décoratif*, with its electrically driven partition walls and hedges, its periscope camera obscura, its built-in cinema with metal screen which unfolds automatically as the chandelier rises up on pulleys to allow a clear angle of projection. To detail these complexities, these paradoxes, demands more space and the introduction of more new ideas than this book has room for. De Beistegui's own ideas on decorative art, his career as entertainer and *bon viveur*, the interaction with surrealism itself, cannot be dealt with. But a summary study of the development of ideas between June 1929 and the summer of 1930, through six clearly defined and differentiated projects, reveals that, rather as in the case of the Villa Savoye, this undertaking forms a coda and critique of the 1920s villas. Themes which have preoccupied us throughout this book recur in a particularly interesting way.

1. Dossier Beistegui, Le Corbusier letter to Beistegui, 5 July 1929.

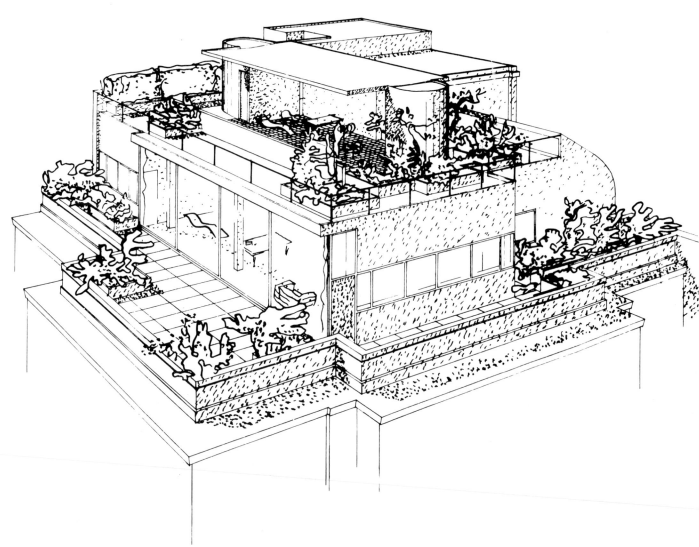

176. Beistegui apartment, Champs Elysée. Above: Axonometric view, first project, 4 June 1929 (FLC 17435)

177. Right: Section, first project, 4 June 1929 (FLC 17434)

The first scheme, prepared in plan section, elevations and axonometric (3–4 June 1929) has a classic simplicity (FLC 17431, 17434–5). The design is based on a salon with full-height window overlooking the Champs Elysées. Two symmetrically disposed spiral staircases provide main and service access to the top floor, which provides a simple solarium, as well as two maids' rooms. The rear wall of the library is treated like an attic wall, curving upwards to provide clerestory lighting from the terrace. This is a statement of faith in the essential joys of sun and air, with no apparent trace of the *jeux d'esprit* to follow. In a letter of 31 August 1929, Le Corbusier is talking earnestly about prefabricating the apartment off the site, so that assembly can be swift and cheap. De Beistegui had shown himself reluctant,

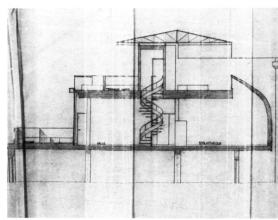

in July, to commit himself to Le Corbusier, agreeing an arrangement whereby he would pay the architects 2,000 francs for a worked out set of plans before making up his mind. This arrangement was only dropped in December. As we have come to expect, Le Corbusier's first estimate (190,500 francs) was absurdly below the reality.

From September to November, Le Corbusier was in South America on the lecture tour which produced the content of *Précisions sur l'Etat Présent de L'Architecture*. In the meantime, Pierre discovered that the project was going to be immensely difficult. The owners of the property made all sorts of difficulties and the entrepreneurs proposed to charge high supplements for raising the building materials and working in such cramped circumstances. On 14 November, a set of plans was produced in which a characteristic explosion of the arrangement took place (FLC 17646–7, 17436). Instead of a simple iron staircase rising through the salon, there were now two staircases, one internal, rising up through two sides of the library, and one external, riding on the back of the other round two sides of the exerior wall. This elaborate *promenade architecturale* continued on the roof terrace, on three levels: a lower level over the dining room and bedroom and a higher level above the projection housing the lift mechanism of the apartment block. This top level was now laid out with a croquet lawn, while another set of steps rose to a place of command above the staircase housing (p. 212).

This restless play with circulation reminds us of the Villa Stein-de Monzie. On 30 November, some of this baroque complexity was renounced, with the reintroduction of the spiral staircase in the salon, displaced into the library and rising to an apse-shaped staircase housing similar to the first scheme. The external staircase remained as in the scheme of a few days earlier, however. But when, after December, a firm agreement to proceed on the basis of a figure (now around 300,000 francs) was obtained, the first result was a reintroduction of the double stairs, this time turned through 90°, parallel to the Champs Elysées (FLC 17565, 17567). The section shows the interior staircase rising in two flights within the library, while the exterior staircase creates a corresponding diagonal in the back wall. An interesting consequence of this arrangement was the arrival at a form for the top flight of steps which rises to the croquet lawn which was later to be adopted verbatim for the north façade of the Villa de Mandrot. This design, too, was revised rapidly, between 10 and 24 January, 1930 (FLC 17441, etc.), and with yet another return to the spiral staircase, this time housed in a free-standing oval projection on the roof terrace, now without means of access to its roof. Two plans develop this scheme to the basic arrange-

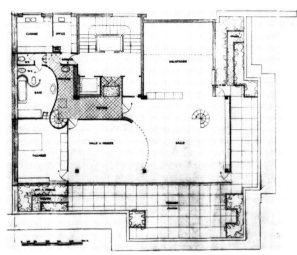

178. Beistegui apartment, Champs Elysée. Lower floor plan, first project, 3 June 1929 (FLC 17431)

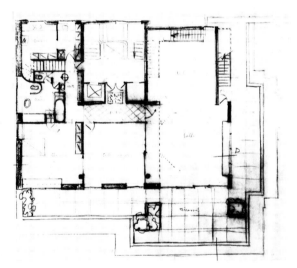

179. Lower floor plan, second project, 14 November 1929 (FLC 17646)

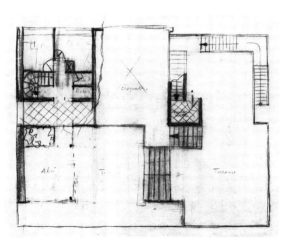

180. Upper floor plan, second project, 14 November 1929 (FLC 17647)

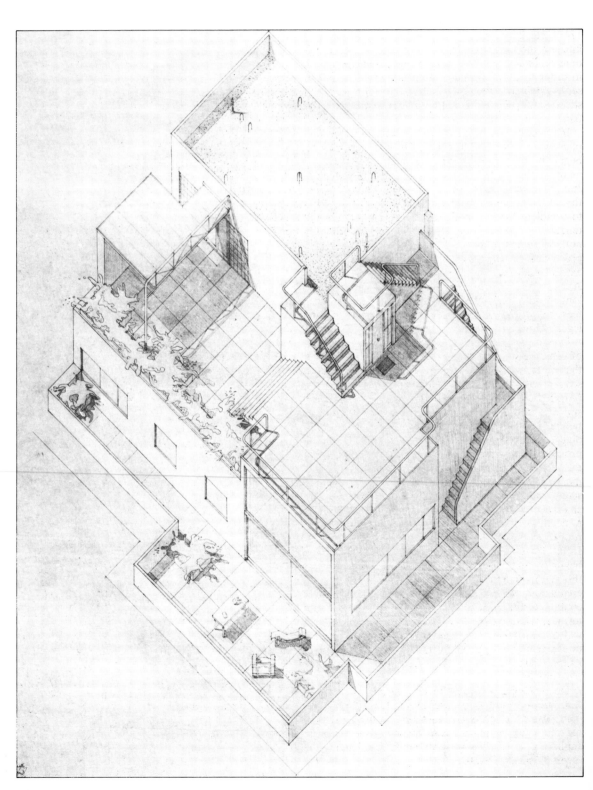

181. Beistegui
apartment, Champs
Elysée. Axonometric,
second project, 14
November 1929 (FLC
17436)

182. Facing page, top:
Axonometric, fourth
project, c. 8 January
1930 (FLC 17565)

183. Facing page,
below: section, fourth
project, c. 8 January
1930 (FLC 17567)

ment of the finished scheme on 14 February (FLC 17447, etc.). To improve lighting to the bathroom and kitchen, the top terrace is now restricted to two thirds of its original extent, losing its function as croquet field, in order to allow skylights abutting the round-ended service staircase. Nevada glass tiles (later replaced with sheet glass) provide natural lighting over the entrance hall.

Innumerable changes of detail followed, but the plans were agreed on in June 1930, with construction beginning on 5 June. Pierre's estimate, which lacked many of the tenders, came out at 591,250 francs (30 June), but was rejected by de Beistegui, who calculated that at least another 100,000 francs would be required to complete the job. Although he demanded that the tenders be reduced by 100,000 francs accordingly, nothing seems to have been agreed, and the work proceeded on the basis of repeated submissions of extras by all the entrepreneurs. The final cost, by 15 April 1933, estimated at 1,325,300 francs and led to a long dispute in July for the payment of the architect's fees, in which Le Corbusier finished up threatening legal action.

One of the causes of the extra cost was the provision of immensely costly changes caused by the piercing of the concrete slabs in order to fit the revolving periscope with its tall chimney-like protruberance (April–July 1932). Furthermore, part of the spiral staircase had to be demolished and rebuilt, due to failure in the construction. Numerous leaks were diagnosed and repaired at the same time. Even the provision of a sound-proof cinema projection booth in the space under the external staircase proved immensely complex, with automatically deployed metal screen and a system of pulleys to withdraw the chandelier from the projection beam (FLC 17668, 5 May 1931). Furthermore, the very celebration of the roofscape of Paris, with the Arc de Triomphe and Eiffel Tower forming the key landmarks, which had begun by 'natural' solution (the viewing platform over the staircase housing in the 14 November scheme) ended up in the realms of artifice. The banks of hedges could be slid away by electric power on the roof terrace, while on the top terrace, a deliberately high wall laid the basis of the Surrealist sensations on which de Beistegui built. As completed, this open room, with its lawn carpet and mock fireplace, mocked the simple pleasures of the early schemes.

De Beistegui was, despite his continual peregrinations around Europe, an attentive and fastidious client who chafed at the casual methods of the Corbusier atelier in supervising his construction. A letter of 31 January 1931 is full of accurate details cataloguing the errors of his architects:

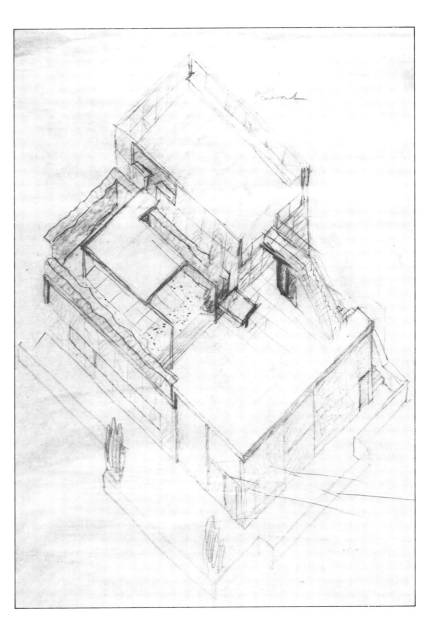

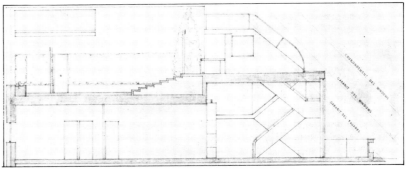

184. Beistegui apartment, Champs Elysée. Above: redrawn axonometric, based on Le Corbusier's designs, c. May 1930

185. Below: redrawn plan of upper level, based on Le Corbusier's designs, c. May 1930

You are too busy: literature, broadcasting your ideas round the world, huge urban planning projects, University City, Moscow, etc.... With this kind of schedule, I imagine that it is impossible to supervise carefully the design of a door or trellis work... I understand you very well and, furthermore, would have no doubt done the same in your place.[2]

This must stand as one epitaph for the villas of the 1920s. But we must set alongside it Le Corbusier's own:

My view is that you have created, with us, something quite exceptional. Everyone agrees. You are proud of your work, so are we... We have overcome formidable technical difficulties. To do it we have dedicated work, time and effort far above the normal.[3]

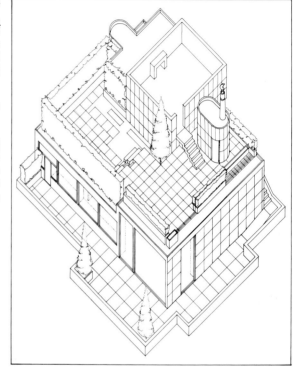

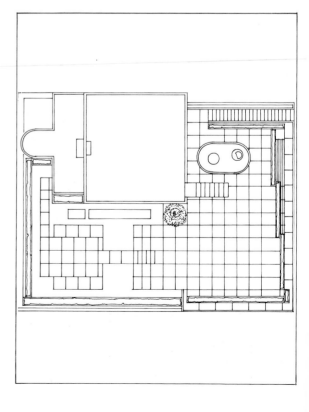

2. Dossier Beistegui, H1 (14), Doc. 1, 31 January 1931.
3. Dossier Beistegui, H1 (15), IV, Doc. 208, 12 July 1933.

186. Beistegui
apartment, Champs
Elysée. Roof terrace
with Arc de Triomphe.
The steps on the right
lead up to the enclosed
open air living room
with its furniture,
fireplace and grass
carpet

187. Salon

188. Beistegui apartment, Champs Elysée. Roof terrace showing the periscope fitting of the camera obscura on the right

APPENDICES

VILLA BERQUE, Auteil

Client: Monsieur Berque, 10 rue Poussin, Paris, 16ᵉ.
Projects:
  A. Autumn 1921:
    1) Redecoration of house (furniture, curtains, repainting of partition walls, new fireplace).
    2) Extension with salon-music room built on.
    3) Enlargement of terrace.
    4) Reordering of garden and terrace (unexecuted)?
Completion: July 1922.
Cost: c. 93,500 francs.
Architect's fees: apparently calculated on basis of 7% (first 50,000) 6% subsequently: about 6,110 francs (cf. FLC 9337, where a calculation based on 60,000 francs on this basis gave the erroneous total of 3,100 francs).
Projects:
  B. 8 September 1926: for a new garage at the end of the garden (unexecuted).
  C. Date unknown, c. 1925–6(?): four or five dwelling *lotissement* on the site, various versions.

VILLA KER-KA-RE, Vaucresson

Site: Route de Vaucresson.
Client: Georges Besnus, 1, rue Cassini, Paris 14ᵉ.
Project A: January to April 1923.
  Estimates for first project: Client stipulated a total of 70,000 francs, including cost of site.
  Brief: 29 January 1923.
  Tenders: 12–14 April (Vié: 72,000 francs; Guillard: 70,500 francs; Summer: 64,000 francs)
Project B: Contracts 23 April 1923, an inclusive contract with Summer for 64,000 francs. Architect's fees at 7%.
Contract drawings: FLC 9214–5.
  Construction drawings: May–June 1923, details followed.
  Estimate for enclosing the property, in addition to the original contract: 2 October 1923, 4,509 francs, by Summer.
  House inhabited December 1923
  Total cost: 82,595 francs, including the site, an extra strip of land, the enclosure earthworks and gate, but less garden, gas and electricity.

ATELIER OZENFANT, square Montsouris

Site: corner of avenue de Reille and square du Montsouris.
Client: Amédée Ozenfant, 35 rue Godot de Mauroy, Paris IX.
Entrepreneur: Pierre Vié, 106 rue de la Tour, Paris XVI, tender 10 April 1923, contract with Vié for 65,000 francs (excepting the garden), to complete by 31 August, with penalty clause of 50 francs per day. The contract was an inclusive one. The architects' fees were at 7%.
First designs: January–February, 1923.
Contract drawings: April, 1923.
Contracts signed: May, 1923.

Altered designs (external spiral staircase): June, 1923.
Gros oeuvre completed: autumn 1923.
House inhabited: spring 1924.

VILLAS LA ROCHE AND JEANNERET, Auteuil

Site: Private road, square du Docteur Blanche, in a property flanked by the rue du Docteur Blanche, rue Raffet, rue Jasmin and rue Henri Heine, Auteuil.
First projects: various proposals for separate houses for a number of clients (but not La Roche), March 1923–May 1923.
First scheme of four houses: May 1923 (Jeanneret-Raaf, Marcel, Motte and one other).
Second scheme for four houses: c. July 1923 (La Roche, Jeanneret-Raaf, Marcel, 'Boul')
First tenders for Jeanneret house: July 1923 (about 104,740 francs)
Revised scheme for three houses (La Roche, 'aunt', Jeanneret-Raaf), August 1923
Modifications: (two houses) September 1923 to February–March 1924
Revised plans and estimates, Jeanneret-Raaf house: submitted 20 March 1924 (140,000 francs).
Revised plans and estimates La Roche house: 19 February 1924, about 200,000 francs.
Construction began on both houses: February 1924.
Gros oeuvre completed: autumn 1924
Jeanneret-Raaf house inhabited: 18 February 1925.
La Roche house inhabited: 13 March 1925 (finishing continued into summer).
Total cost: Jeanneret-Raaf house: about 180,000 francs (plus extras for furnishings = about 222,013 francs) honoraires paid: 13,096 francs.
La Roche house: about 280,028 francs, honoraires paid: 19,630 francs.
In both cases, extra sums were spent in each year after 1925, which make it difficult to compute the precise sums relating to the original construction.
La Roche gallery redesign:
  Estimate: February 1928 (32,900 francs).
  Construction completed by November 1928.
  Total cost: 50,986 francs (by November); honoraires 5,093 francs.

HOUSE PROJECTS FOR MARCEL, CASA FUERTE AND MONGERMON, Auteuil

Site: 5.45 metre strip adjacent to Lotti Raaf's, sold by Lemasson to Sigismond Marcel (c. November 1923), to which it was hoped to add a two metre strip belonging to Mlle Stern.
Project for speculative client: February–August 1924 (5.45 metre plot).
Project for M. Casa Fuerte: January 1925.
Project for Mongermon: March–April 1925.
Marcel's plot sold to Soule: May 1925.
Architects' fees: 9,000 francs paid by Soule in compensation for loss of earnings over the Mongermon project.

LIPCHITZ–MIESTCHANINOFF STUDIOS, Boulogne-sur-Seine

Site: Three plots on the corner of allée des Pins and rue des Arts, Boulogne-sur-Seine.
First contacts: May 1923: Lipchitz and Miestchaninoff contract with architect; c. November 1923. Canale bound to buy the third site from the other two.
First projects: (three houses) January–February 1924.
First tenders: 23 January 1923 (Summer) and, shortly after, Kuntz and Pigeard.
Second project: (two houses) March 1924.
Second tenders: (masonry only: summer 65,000 francs (7 March), Kuntz and Pigeard: first 71,600 francs (13 March) then 65,000 francs (15 March).
Revised plans and estimates: submitted to clients 25 April, 1924; 100,900 francs (Lipchitz), 105,600 francs (Miestchaninoff). The fees were to be fixed at the 'friendly' rate of 7% for the first 50,000 francs, 6½% for the next 50,000 francs, and 6% for subsequent expenses. In effect, 7% seems to have been charged. Construction began: 6 May 1924.
Modifications to plans: June–July 1924.
Gros oeuvre completed: c. October 1924.
New extra work: March–May 1925.
Houses inhabited: Spring 1925.
Total cost: Lipchitz: 122,745 francs (plus 8,592 francs honoraires).
  Miestchaninoff: about 150,000 francs (plus about 10,500 francs honoraires).
Estimate and plans for the Canale house submitted in August 1924 (without consequences).
New plans prepared in May–June 1927 for Canale (again, without result).

TERNISIEN HOUSE, Boulogne-sur-Seine

Clients: Paul and Mme Ternisien.
Site: Corner rue Denfert, Rochereau and allée des Pins, Boulogne-sur-Seine.
First contacts: 1923.
First projects: 1924–25.
Contracts: June 1925 (estimates about 83,000 francs).
Construction: June 1925 onwards.
Gros oeuvre finished: c. December 1925.
Presentation drawings: December 1925–March 1926.
House inhabited: summer 1926(?)
Final cost: about 105,000 francs (by December 1927).
First projects for extension of the house; November–December 1926.
Further schemes for extension: December 1927–28.

VILLA CHURCH, Ville-d'Avray

Clients: Henry and Barbara Church, 1 avenue Haplphen, Ville-d'Avray.
Site: Two adjoining properties owned by the Société 'La Maraysienne' (Capital 2,500,000 francs), administrator R. Moreau-Lalande, rented by Henry Church.
First contacts with client: Before 11 April 1927.

Three Projects:
  A. Bâtiment du Haut: rebuilding the old stable block to the west of the main house.
  B. Bâtiment du bas: partial reconstruction of a summer-house on the adjoining property to the north-east.
  C. Redecoration and extension of the main house on the upper property, in which the Churches lived.
Chronology:
  A. First projects: April 1927 (April estimates 245,000 francs).
     Tenders: May–June 1927.
     Contracts: 17–23 June 1927 (about 422,800 francs).
     Plans revised: June and September 1927.
     Nearly complete: July 1928.
     Total cost: 502,985 francs.
  B. First project: July 1927.
     First tenders: July 1927.
     Revised projects: 'Large' (15 September, 267,600 francs); 'Small' (17 September, 202,200 francs).
     Final revisions and details: September–December 1927.
     Construction begins: October 1927.
     Nearly finished: March 1929.
     Total cost: c. 536,315 francs.
  C. First projects: before December 1928(?).
     First presentation project: 11 March 1929 (estimate 450,000 francs).
     Revisions: July–August 1929 (320,000 francs).
     Total cost: not known (over 320,000 francs).
     Total fees received for three buildings by winter 1929: 160,390 francs.
All three buildings have been destroyed.

VILLAS MEYER AND OCAMPO, Neuilly-sur-Seine

Villa Meyer

Client: Pierre Meyer, his wife and mother-in-law Mme Hirtz.
Site: avenue de Madrid, Neuilly.
First contracts: April 1925.
First project: April–May 1925(?).
Second project: October 1925.
Third project: April 1926.
Fourth project: May–June 1926.
Scheme abandoned December 1926.

Villa Ocampo

Contact with Comtesse de Vera, friend of Mme Ocampo, 27 August 1928.
Presentation drawings: 18 September 1928.

PLANEIX HOUSE, Paris

Location: 10 boulevard Masséna, Paris 13ᵉ.
Client: Antoine Planeix, 4 passage Morel, Grand Montrouge (Seine) and La Garandie, near Aydat, Puy-de-Dôme.
First contracts: November 1924(?) or summer 1925.
First estimates: Tenders in June and August 1925, summarised on 6 November 1925: 123,700 francs.
Final estimates: summary for the client 9 June 1926: 155,100 francs.
Contracts: July–August 1926.
Global estimate (for purposes of loan), 4

September 1926: 229,820 francs (including cost of land, party walls, architects' fees).
Construction begins: End July 1926, carcase finished in October.
Annexe: Duplex mezzanine apartments proposed by client in December 1926.
Estimates: February–April 1927: 100,500 francs.
Construction of annexe: July–October 1927.
Finishing continued into the summer, 1928.
Total cost: c. 345,843 francs (fees: 32,000 francs).

VILLA COOK, Boulogne-sur-Seine

First recorded contact with client: 28 April 1926.
Site: 6, rue Denfert Rochereau, Boulogne-sur-Seine.
Client: William E. Cook (and his French wife Jeanne) 2, rue d'Anjou, Versailles, S et O (moved during summer 1926 to 23 boulevard Bessières, Paris XVII).
Tenders: 8–15 June 1926 (summer, Selmersheim and Monteil, Celio, Pasquier, Guillaumeau, etc.).
Contracts: 17 June 1926 (summer), rest follow shortly. Estimates add to about 200,000 francs, honoraires at 10 per cent (20,000 francs).
September–December 1926, negotiations over payments over party wall to Mme Colinot, neighbour (house designed 1926 by Mallet-Stevens).
Main carcase up by September 1926.
House inhabited March 1927.
Work continued through 1927 on miscellaneous details.
Accounts drawn up December 1927: about 265,067 francs spent by then.
Closure of accounts March 24, 1928.
September–October 1928, negotiations on sum due for party wall by Raymond Fischer, architect of other neighbouring house.

Maids' Room Back Extension

Estimates: May 1929.
Completion: October 1929.
Total cost: about 27,000 francs (22,500 francs used as basis of honoraires at 10 per cent, i.e. 2,250 francs).

VILLA 'LES TERRASSES' (STEIN-DE MONZIE), Vaucresson

Clients: Gabrielle de Monzie, 59 rue de la Tour (from March 1928, reassumes her maiden name Mme Colaco Osorio). Michael and Sarah Stein, 58 rue Madame.
First contacts: 7 May 1926 (brief).
First dated project: 20 July 1926.
Contract with Gabrielle de Monzie: 10 November 1926 (honoraires 22 November).
Variant projects: October 1926 to March 1927.
Tenders: 29 March–13 May 1927.
Construction begins: 12 April 1927.
Estimates: April 1927, 779,000 francs.
Carcase finished June–July 1927 (mason's work not finished till March 1928).
Inhabited: October 1928–January 1929.
Accounts drawn up: September 1928: 1,263,448 francs estimated; January 1929, accounts: 1,270,783. I estimate total cost at around 1,497,606 francs, 127,078 francs honoraires paid.

VILLA SAVOYE, Poissy

Client: M and Mme Pierre Savoye, and their son Roger.
Site: 'Parc de Villiers', Poissy (693 HA).
First contracts with client: Uncertain, probably September, 1928.
First project: Presentation drawings 6–14 October, 1928 (LC 1096–2008, 2011).
Estimates for first project: calculated on 5 November. (785,000 francs).
Second project: include drawings dated 6 and 7 November, 1928.
Estimate for second project: approx. 350,583 francs.
Third project: Presentation drawings, 26 and 27 November, 1928. (LC 2030–3).
Estimate for third project: approx. 464,269 francs.
Fourth project: presentation drawings 17 December, 1928 (LC 2054–8).
Estimates for fourth project:
  a) December 1928: 387,000 francs.
  b) 15 February 1929: 558,690 francs.
Fifth project: presentation drawings, from 12 April, 1929 (LC 2104–5) onwards, until June 1929.
Lodge:
  a) First dated project 27 April (double house).
  b) Second dated project 6 May (double house) (LC 2124–5).
  c) Third dated project 5 June, 1929 (double house) (LC 2160).
  d) Fourth dated project 9 June, 1929 (FLC 18273) (double house).
  e) Fifth dated project 7 July, 1929 (LC 2189) (single house).
Work on the site:
  a) begins April 1929.
  b) reaches first floor level, June 1929.
  c) masonry largely finished, December 1929.
  d) interiors, electric installations, general finishing, continued throughout 1930 and early 1931.
  e) house inhabited spring 1931 (painting still in progress in July).
  f) repairs every autumn until 1927 to house and lodge.
Total cost: about 815,000 francs.

DE BEISTEGUI APARTMENT, Avenue des Champs Elysées

Site: 136 avenue des Champs Elysées, 6th and 7th floors, rented by Charles de Beistegui from France-Monde, on 15 July, 1929.
First design: 3–4 June 1929.
  Estimate: 190,500 francs.
Second design: 14 November 1929.
  Estimates: 300,000–400,000 francs.
  Mason's tender: 120,000 francs, associated with this design.
Fourth design: 8 January 1930.
Fifth design: 24 January 1920.
Definitive plans: 14 February onwards.
  Estimate: 30 June 1930 (591,250 francs, incomplete; rejected by client).
  Contracts: June 1930 onwards.
Gros oeuvre finished: winter 1930 (but work continued due to design changes).
Periscope added: April–July 1931.
Repairs and partial reconstruction of staircase: summer 1931.
Inhabited: autumn or winter 1931 (cinema screen still not finished in November).
Final cost: 1,325,300 francs.
Honoraires (disputed): 129,879 francs (15 April 1933).

SYNOPTIC TABLE OF VILLA PROJECTS

	1922	1923	1924	1925	1926	1927	1928	1929	1930	1931
Ker-Ka-Ré		BD C G I								
Ozenfant		B D C G	I (?)							
Jeanneret		BD D	C	G	I					
La Roche		B D	C	G	I		BDC I			
Lipchitz–Miestchaninoff		H	D C G (?)	I (?)						
Casa Fuerte/Mongermon			B	D B D						
Meyer				B	D					
Ternisien			B	DC	I					
Cook					BDC G	I		BDCGI		
Planeix			B	D	DC G B	DC G	I			
Stein-de Monzie					B	DC	G	I		
Church A							BDC G	I		
B							B D C	G	I	
C								B	D C	I
Savoye							BC	DC	G	I
de Beistegui									B D	C G to (1933)

B: Brief; D: Tenders (Devis); C: Contracts; G: *Gros oeuvre* completed; I: Inhabited.

TABLE OF CRAFTSMEN AND BUILDERS

Houses	Masons	Carpenter/Joiners	Glass/Painters	Metalwork	C. heating/hot water	Electricity	Garden	Misc.
La Roche/Jeanneret	SU	LO, RO, SM	CE	GU, DO	PA, ZA	BA, PR	CR	PT, DS, TH
Lipchitz-Miestchaninoff	KP	LO, RO	BL	GU	PA, ZA	PR	(?)	TH
Ternisien	KP (SU)	SM	BL (CE)	(?)	PA	(?)	(?)	
Cook	SU	LO, SM (RI, 1929)	CE	GU (DU, 1929)	PA (FE, 1929)	BA (PR, 1929)	CR	
Planeix	Su, BA	LO	CE (glass) RL (paint)	GU	PA	BA	CR	
Stein-de Monzie	SU	LO	CE	GU	PA, FE	BA	CR	BU, DS, SG
Church	SU	LO	CE	GU, DU	PA, FE	BA	CR	EC, KN, SI
Savoye	CO	LO, RI	CE	GU, DU	PA, FE	BA	CR	KN, BW, SI
de Beistegui	GT, SU, DB	RI, PL, JM	RL, CE	GB, DU, DO	BS	CA	TO	GM, SI

AL: Auguste Lachapelle, Fabrique de Parquets, 34 route Militaire, Mortsel-les Anvers.
BA: Barth, Electricité Moderne, Installations D'Art, 20 rue Franklin, Paris, 16e.
BE: G. Bertrand (Fils de A. Charpentier).
BL: Lucien Bled, Peinture, Miroiterie, 68, rue du Rocher, et 204 boulevard Jean Jaurès, Boulogne-sur-Seine.
BR: Camille Barbier (mason), 20 avenue d'Ivry.
BS: Brosse.
BU: Stores Baumann (roller blinds), rue Abel.
BW: Boucquey et Winckelman (ceramic tiles).
CA: Cassat & Fils, 57 bis rue de Tocqueville, Paris, 17e.
CE: A. Celio, Entreprise Générale de Peinture (Miroiterie, etc. même maison), 218, rue St. Jacques.
CO: E. Cormier, Entreprise générale de Constructions, 12, rue de L'Isly, Paris, 8e.
CR: Lucien Crépin, Horticulteur paysagiste, 2, rue Erlanger, 16e, (culture: 2, rue George Sand).
DB: Dunet Fils et Bompar.
DO: Dousse, 20 rue Voltaire, Alfortville.
DS: Daudergnies et Sauvage, Sculpture & Gran de Décoration, 20 and 26 passage St. Bernard, Paris, 11e.
DU: G. Duflon, Serrurerie d'art, 67, boulevard Voltaire.

EC: Electro-cable, 62, avenue d'Iéna, Paris, 16e.
EH: E. Henry, puisard.
FE: Maurice Ferrari, Fumisterie, chauffage central, etc., 68 rue de la Tour, Paris, 16e.
GB: G. Barriaux, La Construction Metallique, 91 boulevard National, La Garenne.
GM: G. Massiot (successeur, Radiguet et Massiot), Instruments pour les sciences, 13 and 15 boulevard des Filles du Calvaire, Courbevoie.
GT: Société des Grands Travaux en Beton Armé, 25 rue de Courcelles, Paris, 8e.
GU: R. Guillaumeau, (metalwork), 14–16 rue de la Coubevoie.
JM: Jacquemet et Mesnet.
KN: Compagnie Générale d'Assèchement et d'Aération, 'Procédé Knapen', 57, rue Pigalle, Paris, 9e (and Brussels).
KP: Kuntz et Pigeard, (masons).
LO: Raphael Louis, Entreprise Générale de Menuiserie, 14, rue de la Corvée, Courbevoie (atelier, 18, rue Edouard-Nieuport, suresnes).
MP: Société Marbrière de Paris, 3 place des Vosges, Paris, 4e.
PA: Pasquier frères, Entreprise Générale de Chauffage, 109, rue de Tocqueville, Paris 17e.
PL: Plomba, hangars et constructions economi-

ques bois et fer, 20 avenue de la Porte de Clichy, Paris 18e.
PR: Primard, Travaux d'electricité, 18, rue du Dragon.
PT: Grands Magasins du Printemps.
RI: Riou, (joiner), 22 rue Vincent, Paris, 19e.
RL: Ruhlmann et Laurent, peintures d'interieure, etc., 10, rue Maleville.
RO: Roneo, 27, boulevard des Italiens.
SC: Schmittheissler, (joiner).
SG: St. Gobain.
SI: Sirandré, Miroart, 134, rue Saint-Maur, Paris, 11e.
SM: Selmersheim et Monteil, Meubles, decorations, bronze et Installations Générales Menuiseries, 62, boulevard St. Marcel, Paris, 5e.
SP: *Société Perfecla.*
SU: G. Summer, *Ingenieur constructeur Entreprise Générale*, 38, avenue Junot, Paris 18e.
TO: Toutin et Roussel, *parcs et jardins*, 26 et 34 rue Washington, Paris 8e.
VI: P. Vié, *Ciment Armé, Entreprise Générale*, 106, rue de la Tour, Paris 16e.
TH: Thonet Frères, 137, rue du Mont-Cenis, Parix, 18e.
ZA: Zanotti, plomberie.

TABLE OF FEES

Year	Berque	Kar-Ka-Ré	Ozenfant	Jeanneret	La Roche	Lipchitz Miestchaninoff	Ternisien	Cook	Mongermon	Planeix	Stein de Monzie	Church	Savoye	de Beistegui	Totals
1922	6,110														6.110
1923		2,000	1,000	2,000		3,092									8,092
1924			2,000	5,000	1,000	5,000									13,000
1925			1,500	5,000	7,000	11,000	2,171		9,000						35,721
1926		2,000		1,096	11,630		2,328	13,334		5,667	20,000				56,055
1927		795						10,046		5,667	32,000	20,000			68,508
1928				5,093						5,667	34,666	65,000			110,426
1929										15,000	40,352	42,390	37,246	2,000	139,238
1930												20,000	13,550	28,000	61,500
1931												25,000	23,688	33,334	82,022
Totals	6,110	4,795	4,550	13,096	24,723	16,000	4,500	25,629	9,000	32,000	127,018	172,390	74,484	128,492*	580,722

* The total 128,492 includes estimates for 1932 (16,666) and 1933 (48,492)

CATALOGUE OF DRAWINGS

The numbers given below are those of drawings in the collection of the Fondation Le Corbusier, Paris. They can be referred to in the 32 volumes of *The Le Corbusier Archive*, Garland Publishing New York and London, 1982. The author would like to thank those who have drawn attention to errors in the first edition of this book. A complete catalogue raisonné of these and other drawings is in preparation.

This list of drawings represents a compromise between criteria of precision and concision. It is intended to enable those interested in studying the drawings to begin with a reasonable order. The drawings are grouped into 'projects' (A, B, C) whose limits are clearly distinct. Normally, a 'project' is defined as a sequence of designs leading up to a formal submission to the client. I have also used the project groupings to distinguish different buildings (e.g. the three Church buildings, or the various lodges) and for identifying distinct undertakings (e.g. remodelling the La Roche gallery). Within these groupings, I have indicated sub-groups (A1, A2) which correspond to stages in the design. Within these subgroups, plans, elevations, sections and perspectives are broadly consistent. Sometimes these sub-groups correspond to a particular category of drawings, such as those of an entrepreneur (see Besnus, A4). The intention has been to present the drawings in an order which makes sense in terms of the documentation.

Berque

A1. (1921, 25 September) Dated set and associated drawings.
9313, 9314, 9315, 9316, 9339, 9352.
A2. (1921, 1922) Construction drawings for terrace and salon.
9312, 9318, 9319, 9320, 9321, 9322, 9323, 9336, 9340, 9341, 19331, 19333, 19334, 19336, 19341.
A3. (1921, 1922) Interior decoration old house.
9327, 9328, 9329, 9330, 9331, 9332, 9333, 9334, 9343, 9344, 9345, 9346, 9348, 9349, 9351.
A4. (1921, 1922) Garden and pergola.
9324, 9335, 19337.
C1. (1925, 1926) *Lotissement* of site.
19338, 19344, 19345, 19346, 19347.

Besnus (Ker-Ka-Ré)

A1. (1923, 4–5 April) L-shaped scheme.
9208, 9234, 9235, 9236, 9241, 9248.
A2. (1923, 23–28 April) Signed set.
9214, 9215.
A3. (1923, ? May–June) Lettered set.
9212, 9213, 9216, 9218, 9219, 9220, 9221, 9222.
A4. (1923, ? May) Summer plans.
229

A5. (1923, ? May–June) Details of construction.
9207, 9209, 9210, 9211, 9228, 9231, 9237.
A6. (1923, ? August) *Cloture*.
9217, 9223, 9230.
A7. (1923, May (or October)) *Lotissement*.
9205, 9224.

Church

A1. (1924, December) Plans by Falconer, Baker, Campbell.
8109, 8110, 8111.
A2. (1927, ? April) Building A: *Pavillon des Amis*, preliminary sketches.
8080, 8083.
A3. (1927, 5–11 April) Building A: *Pavillon des Amis*, presentation set.
8067, 8082, 8186.
A4. (1927, 12 May) Building A: *Pavillon des Amis*, interim project (some numbered and dated).
8081, 8144, 8183, 8195, 8198, 8199.
A5. (1927, 19–20 May) Building A: *Pavillon des Amis*, modified version of A4 (some numbered and dated).
8114, 8117, 8196, 8197, 8200, 8202, 8203, 8204, 8217.
A6. (1927, June) Building A: *Pavillon des Amis*, contract drawings.
8076, 8086, 8099, 8105, 8122, 8123, 8143, 8182, 8193, 8205, 8206, 8207, 8208, 8209.
A7. (1927, 16–20 September) Building A: *Pavillon des Amis*, revised set.
8087, 8118, 8119, 8121, 8164, 8220, 8221, 8222.
A8. (1927, November to January 1928, ?) Building A: *Pavillon des Amis*, Details, including kitchen.
8070, 8093, 8104, 8116, 8163, 8171, 8187, 8192, 8227, 8228, 8229, 8230, 8231, 8232.
B1. (1927, ? July) Building B: *Pavillon de Musique* first scheme (some numbered).
8017, 8161, 8168, 8189, 8210, 8211, 8212.
B2. (1927, ? July–September) Building B: *Pavillon de Musique*, variant with *passerelle* to E.
8115, 8177.
B3. (1927, 8 September) Building B: *Pavillon de Musique, Grand Projet*.
8074, 8075, 8091, 8214, 8215, 8216.
B4. (1927, 17 September) Building B: *Pavillon de Musique, petit projet*.
8158, 8159.
B5. (1927, September–November). Building B: *Pavillon de Musique*, definitive set (some numbered).
8069, 8072, 8085, 8094, 8097, 8100, 8160, 8162, 8167, 8169, 8170, 8180, 8191, 8218, 8219, 8223, 8224, 8225, 8226.
B6. (1927, 19 December, ?) Building B: *Pavillon de Musique*, staircase details.
8068, 8173.

B7. (1928) Building B: *Pavillon de Musique*, definitive floor plans
8233.
B8. (1928, ?) Building B: *Pavillon de Musique*, interior plans, elevations and details.
8089, 8092, 8095, 8101, 8102, 8103, 8106, 8112, 8113, 8152, 8155, 8178, 8185, 8190, 8194, 8234, 31415, 31417, 31429, 31463, 31464, 31465.
B9. (1928) Building B: *Pavillon de Musique*, site and garden, with *passerelle*.
8078, 8090, 8096, 8108, 8120, 8142, 8151, 8153, 8165, 8166, 8179.
C1. (1928–1929) Building C: *Restoration of old house*, plan of old house (later modified).
31416.
C2. (1929 or late 1928) Building C: *Restoration of old house*, sketch of major re-build.
8098.
C3. (1929, March) Building C: *Restoration of old house*, first project according to brief.
8145, 8147, 8148, 8149, 8150, 8156, 8181.
C4. (1929, ? March) Building C: *Restoration of old house*, reworked project before C5.
31423, 31424, 31428, 31431.
C5. (1929, 11 March) Building C: *Restoration of old house*, numberd set.
8137, 8139, 8239, 8240, 8241.
C5. (1929, 11 March) Building C: *Restoration of old house*, numbered set.
31419, 31420, 31421, 31422, 31425, 31426, 31427, 31430.
C6. (1929, March) Building C: *Restoration of old house*, survey sketch of B for bar.
8140.
C7. (1929, March, April, ?) Building C: *Restoration of old house*, variant of C5.
8133, 8136, 8253.
C8. (1929, April–July) Building C: *Restoration of old house*, studies of service staircase.
8128, 8129, 8130, 8131, 8132, 29845.
C9. (1929 July to September 1930) Building C: *Restoration of old house*, modified version of C5.
8071, 8124, 8126, 8127, 8135, 8138, 8235, 8236, 8237, 8238, 8242, 8243, 8244, 8245, 8247, 8248, 8249, 8250, 8251, 8252, 8286.
D1. (1929?) Unidentified details and perspectives.
8084, 8088, 8146, 8174, 8175, 8188, 31418.

Cook

A1. (1926) Mallet-Stevens, elevations of neighbouring house.
8374, 8375.
A2. (1926, 1 May) Rough sketches, (four on a sheet).
8588.
A3. (1926, May–June) Preliminary variant of elevation (cf A4 or A5).
8329.
A4. (1926, May) Short version of plans.

8322, 8324, 8325, 8348.
A5. (1926, May) Long plan, charcoal version.
8323, 8326, 8327, 8347, 8349.
A6. (1926, May) Corrected elevation, curved top.
8330.
A7. (1926, 1 June) Numbered set.
8292, 8293, 8350.
A8. (1926, 1–22 June) Modified version of A7.
8294.
A9. (1926, June) Details, before A10.
8328, 8331, 8334, 8336, 8342, 8343, 8344, 8345, 8358, 8359, 8384.
A10. (1926, June) Definitive plans (numbered).
8288, 8289, 8290, 8291, 8295, 8296, 8297, 8298, 8299, 8300, 8301, 8302, 8303, 8304, 8305, 8337, 29842.
A11. (1926, 29 June) Summer set (Dossier 390).
8353, 8354, 8355, 8356, 8357.
A12. (1926, July–October) Axonometrics and details (some numbered).
8306, 8307, 8308, 8309, 8310, 8311, 8312, 8313, 8314, 8315, 8316, 8317, 8318, 8319, 8320, 8321, 8332, 8333, 8335, 8346, 8352, 8360, 8373, 8387.
B1. (1929, May–June) Rear extension, maid's room.
8361, 8363, 8364, 8365, 8366, 8367, 8368, 8369, 8370, 8371, 8372, 8376, 8377, 8379, 8380, 8381, 8382, 8383, 8385, 8386.

La Roche-Jeanneret

A1. (1922–1923) Site plans.
15126, 15131, 15132.
A2. (1923, March–April) House for Sarmiento.
15123, 15124, 15135, 15146.
A3. (1923, April) Houses to NE.
15102, 15199, 15201, 30957.
A4. (1923, 24–26 April) Houses at end.
15108, 15121.
B1. (1923, 7–10 May) Three houses.
15099, 15100, 15111, 15119, 15120.
B2. (1923, 15–16 May) Four houses.
15107, 15115, 15116, 15117, 15282, 30238, 15113.
B3. (1923, July) Jeanneret-Raaf house, titled and numbered.
15122, 15147, 15148, 15149, 15151, 15153, 15154, 15181.
B4. (1923, ? July) Second four house scheme.
15101, 15103, 15104, 15223, 15254.
B5. (1923, August) Corrected blueprints of Jeanneret-Raaf house.
15150, 15152.
B6. (1923, September) two or three houses, post Le Masson sale.
15105, 15106, 15112, 15114, 15127, 15190, 15225, 15292.
C1. (1923, 22 September) Two house scheme, first variant.
15118, 15166, 15169, 15193, 15197, 15198, 15263, 15273, 15274, 15275, 15276, 15277, 15291.
C2. (1923, October) Wooden model variant.
15109, 15110, 15195, 15216.
C3. (1923, October) Variant.
15129, 15133, 15185.
C4. (1923, October–November) La Roche house, measured plans (variant).
15189, 15205, 15206, 15207, 15285.
C5. (1924, 30, January, ?) Summer plans.
15163, 15180.
C6. (1924, February) Jeanneret-Raaf house, titled and numbered (second set).
15139, 15140, 15141, 15142, 15143, 15145, 15155, 15171, 15173, 15174, 15175, 15183, 18186, 15208, 15209, 15232, 30852, 31923.
C7. (1924 February or winter 1923), Correction to La Roche staircase.
15224.
D1. (1924, February) Summer construction drawings (Jeanneret-Raaf house).

15162, 15164.
D2. (1924, February–March) Summer construction drawings (L.R.).
15214, 15215, 15217, 15218, 15219, 15220, 15221, 15222, 15256, 15293.
D3. (1924, April–June) later drawings (*mitoyennete*, etc.)
15134, 15182.
D4. (1924, October) La Roche, Jeanneret and Marcel house.
15130.
D5. (1924, August) Interior details, Jeanneret-Raaf house.
15156, 15157, 15158, 15160, 15161.
D6. (1924–1925) Miscellaneous details, windows and doors.
15125, 15128, 15184, 15191, 15192, 15194, 15211.
D7. (1924, ? September) Details, La Roche house.
15172, 15178, 15210, 15212, 15213, 15227, 15229, 15230, 15231, 15234, 15236, 15255.
D8. (1925, April) Details, La Roche house.
15167, 15176, 15243, 15271, 15294, 15295.
L1. (1925, April) Lodge at mouth of private road.
15144, 15237.
L2. (1925, ? December) Lodge as built (?)
15136, 15137, 15138.
M1. (1974 ?) FLC alterations to La Roche bedroom for archive.
15298, 29892.
R1. (1928, ? January) Divan-table-bookshelf designs.
15188, 15200, 15226, 15240, 15244, 15245, 15261, 15267, 15286.
R2. (1928, April ?) Fitment under ramp.
15168, 15170, 15187, 15228, 15235, 15238, 15239, 15247, 15248, 15249, 15250, 15251, 15252, 15253, 15258, 15259, 15260, 15262, 15264, 15268, 15270, 15272, 15279, 15280, 15283, 15284, 15287, 15288, 15290, 15296, 15297, 19363.
R3. (1928, February) Dated and numbered set.
15202, 15203, 15204, 24059.
R5. (1928, June ?) Fitment under ramp as built.
15242, 15265, 15266, 15269, 15278, 15281, 15289.
R6. (1930 ?) Unidentified furniture (Bossu?).
15159.

Lipchitz, Miestchaninoff, Canale

A1. (1924, January) Numbered set (1–8), for Lipchitz, Miestchaninoff, Canale.
8051, 8052, 8053, 8054, 8059, 8060, 8061, 8062.
A2. (1924, January) Second numbered set (9–17), for Lipchitz, Miestchaninoff, Canale.
7986, 7987, 7988, 7989, 8055, 8056, 8063, 8064, 8065, 8066.
B1. (1924, March) Variant for Lipchitz atelier, with external staircase.
8014, 8015, 8016, 8057.
B2. (1924, March) Variant for Miestchaninoff atelier.
7880, 8029, 8030, 8031.
C1. (1924, 15–19 March) Titled set ('LM') and associated drawings (Lipchitz and Miestchaninoff only).
7876, 7878, 7879, 8048, 8049, 8050.
C2. (1924, April) Titled set for Lipchitz atelier and associated drawings.
7881, 7882, 7969, 7970, 7971, 7972, 7973, 7974, 7975, 7976, 7977, 7978, 8012, 8013, 8018.
C3. (1924, April) Titled set for Miestchaninoff atelier and associated drawings.
8022, 8023, 8024, 8043.
C4. (1924, ? June) Variant drawings for Miestchaninoff.
7877, 7885, 8027, 8035, 8042, 8058.
C5. (1924, May–June) Drawings by Kuntz and

Pigeard (or become connected with them).
7984, 7985, 7992, 7993.
C6. (1924, May) Miscellaneous details and alterations.
7990, 7991, 8021, 8026, 8028, 8032, 8033, 8034, 8036, 8037, 8038, 8039, 8040, 8041, 8044, 8046, 8047, 30236.
C7. (1924–1925) Plan of gardens.
8045.
D1. (1926, 12 July) Alternative site for Canale.
8019.
D2. (1926) Page of notes of brief for Canale house.
7952.
D3. (1926?) Alternative proposition for a house for Canale, or an extension, between Lipchitz and Miestchaninoff.
7883.
D4. (1926–1927) Set of preliminary sketch plans for Canale house.
7954, 7955, 7956.
D5. (1926–1927) Alternative project for Canale house.
8172.
D6. (1927, May) Set of titled and numbered plans and elevations for Canale house.
7867, 7868, 7869, 7870, 7871, 7872, 7873, 7874, 7875, 8020.

Marcel, Casa Fuerte, Mongermon

A1. (1923, November to February, 1924) Elevations of house next to Jeanneret-Raaf; for Marcel (?).
30857.
A2. (1924, February–August) Set of plans of house on 5.45 metre plot; for Marcel (?).
23041, 23049, 30979, 30990, 30992.
B1. (1924, August–December) Set of plans and elevations for house on 7.47 metre frontage; for Casa Fuerte (?).
23021, 23022, 23023, 23029, 23031.
B2. (1924, December) Interior elevations, Casa Fuerte.
23037, 23038.
B3. (1924, December) Studies of kitchen and pantry (labelled 'Casa Fuerte'), inconsistent with B4 Casa Fuerte.
23025, 23032, 23033, 23036.
B4. (1925, January) Titled set for Case Fuerte and associated drawings.
23011, 23013, 23015, 23016, 23017, 23018, 23019, 23020, 23030, 23034, 23035, 23039, 23042, 23043, 23050, 23051.
B5. (1925, 25 January) Summer set (Dossier 295), following B4.
23014, 23024, 23026, 23027.
B6. (1925, January) Blueprints of drawings from B4 (Casa Fuerte) with alterations added, pointing to C1.
23052, 23053, 23054.
C1. (1925, March) First adaptation of B6 and B4 for Mongermon.
30980, 30987, 30994, 30996.
C2. (1925, March) Intermediary variant for Mongermon.
30982, 30995.
C3. (1925, April) Final variant, with stairs instead of ramp, not fully worked-out; Mongermon.
30981, 30984, 30988, 30989, 30993, 30997.

Meyer

A1. (1925, April–May) First project (?) Site seems to fit.
8338, 10401, 10402, 10403, 32000.
B1. (1925, October) Second project, (as in O.C.).
8339, 29843, 31525.
C1. (1926, April) First variant, third project.
10395, 10397, 10398, 10399.
C2. (1926, 10 April) Second variant, dated.

10377, 10388, 10389, 10391, 10392, 10393.
C3. (1926, 21 April) Final variant, third project.
10370, 10371, 10373, 10379, 10380, 10394, 10400, 29844, 31514, 31538, 31539.
D1. (1926, 20 May) First variant, fourth project.
10404.
D2. (1926, 26 May, ?) Second variant, fourth project.
10381, 10382, 10386.
D3. (1926, May–June) Third variant, fourth project.
10383, 10384, 10387, 10390.
D4. (1926, 11–13 June) definitive version, fourth project.
10374, 10375, 10378.

Ocampo

A1. (1928, 27 August) Mme Ocampo's sketch plan (with brief).
31043.
A2. (1928, September) Preliminary sketches.
31046.
A3. (1928, 18 September) Numbered set.
24231, 24232, 24233, 24234, 24235.

Ozenfant

A1. (1922, December or March 1923), Site plans.
7815, 29932, 29933.
A2. (1923, March) Site plans.
7821, 7822.
A3. (1923, March–April) Signed Set.
7825.
A4. (1923, April) Titled and numbered set.
7816, 7817, 7818, 7819, 7820, 7824, 7832, 7848, 7849.
A5. (1923, April) Interior details (lettered).
7833, 7834, 7835, 7836, 7837, 7838.
A6. (1923, May–June) Modified set (spiral exterior stair).
7826, 7839, 7841, 7846, 7847, 31370.
A7. (1923, June) Later details.
7823, 7827, 7828, 7850, 29931.
A8. (1923, June–August) Hautemulle window details.
7829, 7830, 7831.
B1. Project to adapt interior.
7840, 7842, 7843, 7844, 7845.
M1. Miscellaneous, to identify.
17178, 31810.
M2. Missing (1983).
10873.

Planeix

A1. (1924, 1 May) Site plan.
8934.
A2. (1924, 1925) Preliminary sketches by Planeix.
8947, 8948, 8977.
A3. (early 1925) Le Corbusier sketches, atelier in middle.
8964, 8972.
A4. (early 1925) Atelier to north.
8908, 8931, 8944.
A5. (1925, June) Preliminary to A6.
8941, 8943, 8945, 8962, 8971.
A6. (1925, 20 July) Dated project, with variants.
8905, 8096, 8907, 8911, 8935, 8950, 8963, 31454.
A7. (1925, July–October) Modified version of A6.
8904, 8915, 8920, 8925, 8927, 8932, 8936, 8940.
B1. (1926, March) Scheme modified by Planeix.
8909, 8910, 8913, 8914, 8917, 8918, 8919, 8937, 8938, 8942, 8949, 8951, 8953, 8965, 31545.
B2. (1926, 25 May) Titled and numbered plan and axonometric.
8902, 8939.
B3. (1926, ? June) Details of window mouldings
8926, 8958.

B4. (1926, 29 June ?) Revised scheme, G clear.
8924, 8967.
B5. (1926, July) Detail.
8923.
B6. (1926, August) Elevation (refusal of building permission?).
8921.
B7. (1926, 24 October) Detail of bay window.
8912.
B8. (1926, 24 November) Revised top floor plan.
8922.
B9. (1926, 18 December) Planeix sketches.
8966, 8969, 8970, 8973, 8979.
C1. (1926, 21 December) Planeix plans.
8928, 8946.
C2. (1927, January) *Ier projet*, response to C1.
8959.
C3. (1927, January) Planeix sketches with amendments.
8975.
C4. (1927, 7 February) Revised scheme, numbered.
8930.
C5. (1927, 16 February, ?) Planeix perspective.
8968.
C6. (1927, 28 March) Revised scheme, numbered.
8882, 8901.
C7. (1927, July–August, ?) Variants of garden (some by Planeix).
8954, 8955, 8956, 8978.
C8. (1927, 28 July) Summer plans of drains.
8903.
C9. (1927, 28 July) Details of 'annexes', numbered.
8929.
C10. (1927) Planeix page of notes.
8976.

Stein-de Monzie

A1. (1926, 7 May ?) Sketches of site and first outline plans and elevations.
10501, 31047, 31051, 31052.
A2. (1926, May–July) Symmetrical plan variants (ABABA grid).
10580, 10581, 10583, 31048, 31049.
A3. (1926, July ?) Bird's-eye view sketches, prelim to A4.
10584, 10587.
A4. (1926, 20 July) LC numbered and dated project, and associated drawings.
10406, 10407, 10409, 10509, 10511, 10512, 10513, 10514, 10586, 31480.
B1. (1926, 7 October) Condensed project, first variant.
10410, 10508.
B2. (1926, 13 November ?) Variant with triangular balcony.
10411, 10506, 10510, 10541, 10582, 10588.
B3. (1926, 16–17 December) Variant with cantilever to north.
10412, 10413, 10414, 10415, 10533, 10568, 10573, 10574, 30858.
B4. (1927, 8 January) Modified version of B3.
10416, 10417, 10489, 10490.
B5. (1927, January–March) Preliminary sketches for B6 (cantilever north and south).
10498, 10505, 10516, 10517, 10518, 10565, 10569.
B6. (1927, 1–14, March) Project as tendered for by contractors.
10418, 10419, 10420, 10421, 10422, 10472, 10519, 10534.
B7. (1927, April–May) Contract plans.
10423, 10424, 10425, 10436, 10437, 10438, 10439, 10440, 10441, 10442, 10443, 10444, 10459, 10461, 10462, 10463, 10470, 10471, 10487, 10488, 10493, 10502, 10543, 10552, 10555, 10572, 10576, 10579, 30235, 31053, 31513.

B8. (1929, May–July) Drawings showing cess pool.
10499, 10551.
B9. (1927, May) Central heating plans.
10535, 10536, 10537, 10556.
B10. (1927, 29 March) Summer's plans, (Dossier 423).
10548, 10560, 10561, 10563.
B11. (1927, June) Revised Summer plans.
10515, 10546, 10547, 10549, 10562, 10575.
B12. (1927, June–November) Modified plans, some numbered.
10426, 10427, 10428, 10429, 10430, 10431, 10432, 10433, 10434, 10446, 10448, 10456, 10466, 10468, 10477, 10481, 10482, 10483, 10484, 10485, 10486, 10497, 10503, 10527, 10554, 10557, 10566, 10567.
B14. (1928, March–September) Publication plans and elevations.
10451, 10452, 10453, 10454, 10491, 10492.
B15. (1927, March–June) Interior details (bookshelves, etc.).
10450, 10474, 10475, 10476, 10504.
C1. (December 1935 to April 1936), Redesign of marble fireplace in salon.
10457, 10460, 10464, 10465, 10507, 31050, 31054, 31462.
C2. (1936, March) Scheme for new furniture in salon.
10494, 10495, 10496.
C3. (1936, March) Project to face façades in marble (Steen?).
10529, 10530.
L2. (1926, November–December) Variant preliminary design for lodge.
10478.
L3. (1927, January–May) Variant of Lodge with car port.
10544.
L5. (1927, May–July) Variant of Lodge (small).
10473, 10538.
L6. (1927, May–September) Variant of long loge, with external staircase.
10523, 10539, 10545.
L7. (1927, July) Transitional variant (L6–L8).
10469, 10480, 10532.
L8. (1927, September) Project with *abri* to west.
10435, 10447, 10479, 10520, 10521, 10524, 10525, 10526, 10540.
L9. (1927, September) Summer plan for lodge.
10564.
L10. (1927, 8, November) Definitive plan, numbered.
10449.
L11. (1927, November) Details of entrance gates.
10458, 10500, 10528, 10542, 10550, 10553, 10558, 10570.
L12. (1936, March) Project for marble facing of lodge (cf. C3).
10531.

Savoye

A0. Possible references for Villa Savoye, 1928 (?).
25044, 8522.
A1. Site plans. 1928.
29928, 19544, 19545, 19718.
A2. Related designs to first project, March–September 1928.
24985, 24983, 8507, 31044.
A3. Group of sections and perspectives marginally different to A4, September 1928.
19515, 19677, 19575, 19638, 19679, 19681, 19647, 19517.
A4. First developed variant of First Project, September 1928.
19583, 19634, 19682, 19576, 19639, 19514, 19516.
A5. Intermediary variant between A4 and A6,

223

September 1928.
19645, 19668, 19644.
A6. Preliminary drawings for A7, September 1928.
19683, 19653, 19713, 19648, 19704, 19652.
A7. Numbered set of first project and associated drawings, 6–10 October 1928.
19670, 19649, 19671, 19676, 19672, 19412, 19673, 19413, 19646, 19667, 19414, 19415, 19678, 19680, 19577, 19417, 19675, 19669, 19650, 19651, 19418, 19578, 19419, 19582, 19420, 19421, 19422, 19423, 19424, 31522, 19640, 19425, 19426, 19506, 19511, 19512, 19518, 19525, 19527, 19590, 19589, 19510, 19524, 19513, 19519, 19591, 19509, 19508.
B0. Charcoal sketch plans exploring reduced area, 5–6 November 1928.
25036, 25043, 25039.
B1. Variant of B2, c. 6 November 1928.
19659, 19699, 19698.
B2. Variant dated 6 November 1928.
19660, 19635, 19636.
B3. Variant dated 7 November 1928.
19663, 19662, 19714, 19523, 19661.
C1. Preliminary to C2, 7–27 November 1928.
19700.
C2. Variant of C3, c. 7–26 November 1928.
19491, 19484, 19522, 19485, 19493, 19548, 19606, 19552, 19521, 19482, 19494, 19502, 19488 19549, 19550, 19536, 19703, 19495.
C3. Numbered project of 26–7 November 1928.
19537, 29747, 19427, 19553, 19490, 19694, 19483, 19428, 19551, 19492, 19429, 20753, 19605, 25037, 19430, 19702, 19486, 19710.
D1. Preliminary plans for D2, 27 November–early December 1928.
19709, 19701, 19558.
D2. Variant with service staircase oriented differently, early December 1928.
19560, 19559, 19555.
D3. Preliminary drawings for D4, early December 1928.
19557, 19712, 19708, 19561.
D4. Set of plans studying structure, early December 1928.
19556, 19568, 19711, 19528.
D5. Numbered set, 17 December 1928.
19707, 19697, 19431, 19567, 19565, 19566, 19564, 19705, 19695, 19696, 19432, 19543.
D6. Plans and details working up D5 for contractors' tenders, December 1928–February 1929.

19563, 19572, 19574, 19573, 19570, 19569, 19433, 19687, 19434, 19688, 19435, 19505, 19478, 19664, 19665, 19655, 19654, 19593, 19659, 19656, 19657, 19623, 19616, 19614, 19615, 19619, 19618, 19617, 19620, 19622, 19621, 19632, 19633, 19626, 19627, 19628, 19629, 19630, 19631, 19625, 19624, 19584, 19586, 19585, 19587, 19588.
D7. Details of salon window, c. 21 February–2 March 1929.
19500, 19686, 19502, 19535, 19437, 19534, 19637, 19532, 19438.
E1. Preliminary drawings for definitive scheme, 21 February–March 1929.
19436, 19685, 19529, 19530, 19581, 19580, 19579, 19554, 19684.
E2. Definitive drawings, 12 April–June 1929.
19439, 19441, 19504, 10501, 19571, 19533, 19440, 19562, 19442, 19503, 19443, 19444, 19541, 19445, 19446, 19706, 19693, 19447, 19448, 19498, 19489, 19487, 19531, 19451, 19452, 19453, 19454, 19455, 19456, 19458, 19459, 19460, 19666, 19461, 19462, 19463, 19464, 19465, 19466, 19467, 19468, 19469.
E3. Details of altered windows, 24 August 1929.
19507.
E4. Site plans with alternative arrangement of garden, and detail of gates, 13–20 January 1930.
19674, 19539, 19477.
E5. Cupboard detail, master bedroom, 15 February 1930.
19526.
F1. Detail of long window; August 1962.
19480.
L1. Early references to lodge in site plans, etc., October 1928.
19544, 19545, 19718, 23276, 19648, 19556.
L2. Preliminary ideas for a lodge (internal stairs), January–April 1929.
19720, 19612.
L3. Preliminary drawings for L4 and L5, c. April 1929.
19642, 19641.
L4. Variant of double lodge, c. 27 April 1929.
19609, 19608, 19715, 19611, 19610.
L5. Variant intermediary between L4 and L6, c. 7 May 1929.
19602, 19595, 19597, 19596, 19598, 19599, 19613, 19603, 19449, 19450.
L6. Final variant of double lodge, c. 5 June 1929.
19594, 19457.

L7. Variant of single lodge, for chauffeur (?), June 1929.
19717, 19604.
L8. Preliminary variant for L9, June 1929.
19719, 18312, 19607.
L9. Definitive drawings for lodge, 7 July 1929.
8618, 19716, 19470, 19471.
L10. References to E4 site plans, 13–20 January 1930.
19674, 19539.
L11. Planting and dog kennel next to lodge, January–24 February 1930.
19538, 19547, 19643, 19601, 19600, 19481, 29930, 19546.
L12. Repairs to lodge, 30 September 1937.
29929.

Ternisien

A1. (1925 ?) Site plan.
7887.
A2. (1924 ?) Project for five apartment-studios.
7947, 7948, 7949.
B1. (1925, ? January) Small project.
7939.
B3. (1925, January) Second titled set.
7903, 7904, 7940.
C1. (1925, January) Preliminary to final version.
7912.
C2. (1925, January) Penultimate set.
7921, 7936, 7938.
C3. (1925, ? April–May) Definitive set.
7913, 7916, 7917, 7918, 7919, 7923, 7925, 7927, 7928, 7929, 7931, 7932, 7933, 7934, 7935, 7942, 7943, 7944, 8340, 8341.
C4. (1925, June) Details.
7898, 7922, 7926.
C5. (1925, December to March 1926) Numbered plans, elevations and perspectives for publication.
7891, 7892, 7893, 7894, 7895, 7896, 7897.
D1. (1926–1927) Plans for extension over atelier and *salle*.
7909, 7911.
D2. (1926, November–December) Plans for extension, over *salle*.
7888, 7910, 7941.
D3. (1926–1928) Plans for extension; maid's room next to atelier.
7908, 7930.
D4. (1926–1928) Plans for extension next to atelier, details.
7889, 7890, 7900, 7901, 7902, 7905, 7924.